The Many Faces of DYSLEXIA

32° Masonic Learning Centers for Children, Inc. Bangor, Maine

The Many Faces of DYSLEXIA

by
MARGARET BYRD RAWSON

Introduction by
WILLIAM ELLIS

THE INTERNATIONAL DYSLEXIA ASSOCIATION

The International Dyslexia Association
8600 LaSalle Road
Chester Building/Suite 382
Towson, Maryland 21286-2044

©The International Dyslexia Association

First Printing 1988
Second Printing 1992
Third Printing 1996
Fourth Printing 2000

Printed in the United States of America

Cover design: Joseph M. Dieter, Jr.
Compositor: Brushwood Graphics, Inc.
Printer: BookCrafters

ISBN 0-89214-005-4

Contents

FOREWORD

The Orton Dyslexia Society is honored to present this selection of Margaret Byrd Rawson's writings. Acknowledged as a pioneer in the field of dyslexia, Mrs. Rawson has inspired several generations of professionals, parents, and students through her lectures, papers, and teacher-training sessions dealing with language and its meaning in our lives.

Mrs. Rawson possesses a thorough understanding of the structure of our language and a gift for making it come to life, as this collection amply demonstrates. Further, she takes joy in mastering research findings and examining new theories and concepts which bear on the workings of the mind.

Selecting from her prolific writings papers to represent the scope and depth of Margaret Rawson's work has challenged the author and the editor. The papers, written over several decades, are here arranged topically, rather than chronologically. Readers interested in the history of the field should note the years in which the papers were written; often these dates underscore how far advanced Mrs. Rawson's thinking about dyslexia has been.

The volume includes a number of previously unpublished works. Those which have appeared elsewhere are presented as originally written, with such editing and abridgement as required to limit duplications and to reflect current information and style. "Developmental Dyslexia: Educational Treatment and Results," contains two figures (Figures 2 and 3) which are referred to in several other papers. For the reader's convenience, these figures are reproduced on page 249 as an Appendix.

A list of Margaret Rawson's works, including papers published in numerous journals and books, as well as the publication data for previously unpublished papers which appear in this volume is found starting on p. 251.

For The Orton Dyslexia Society, I am delighted to offer to all who care about language and learning the opportunity to share in the wisdom and the wit of Margaret Byrd Rawson.

Rosemary F. Bowler, *Editor*

PREFACE TO SECOND EDITION

The favorable reception accorded this volume has prompted a second edition to keep the work in print. Not only have individual readers expressed interest in the collection as a whole and in its papers, the book has proved useful in university and other courses of study. The volume has had the distinction of bringing to its author the 1991 Margot Marek Book Award of the New York Branch of The Orton Dyslexia Society. For all of this, I am most appreciative and, consequently, I am pleased to concur with the plan for publishing a second edition.

The contents of the volume remain substantially unchanged, save a few changes of format, the corrections of errata, and some updating. The bibliography contains two papers published since 1988 and lists one, a 50-year followup study of the Rose Valley students, which I hope to see in print in the near future.

In the four years since the first edition appeared, we have seen growing public interest in the causes of and educational treatments for dyslexia and a greater appreciation for the contributions to community, workplace, and human relationships of those who have what I call "the dyslexic cast of mind." I hope that this work will foster that interest and appreciation with a new group of readers.

In preparing the work for the new edition, I have been ably assited by Valerie Beatts who spent many hours sharing with me her thoughtful insights. And, again, I acknowledge the special contributors of Charlotte Chamberlain and Rosemary Bowler to the initial edition as well as to this one. To these and to all who have commented on the book, I am deeply grateful.

Margaret B. Rawson
Foxes Spy
Frederick, Maryland
October 1992

PREFACE TO FIRST EDITION

The title of a book is like any other label. It can but point to the entity it names, with at best some indication of the nature of the object or idea it symbolizes. The complexity of the issue addressed in this volume defies brevity. As you read the papers and comments selected for inclusion here perhaps the different styles, dates, and settings of the chapters will suggest to your imagination, as they have to mine in retrospect, the varied situations in which they were first used and the wide range of people to whom they were, and still might be, addressed. I hope you will share some measure of my enjoyment in reliving them.

Dyslexia, or ineptitude in acquisition of one's native tongue, shows itself in many ways. As it presents us with problems to be solved they lead outward to the study of language as a whole and for everyone, whatever his level of talent. There comes to mind the analogy of a tree whose crown grows higher and wider in search of light even as its roots spread and penetrate deeper into the soil from which it draws nourishment. It becomes thus not only language difficulties that concern us, but the entire symbolic aspect of life. We find ourselves in deep; it is the human mind and the brain that is its developing organ that we find ourselves trying to understand and, if we can, do something about.

However this book is primarily about dyslexia as we relate to it through science, education, and social and emotional realities. It is a hopeful book. It aims to clear the scene by showing how well, often superbly, people who address life with what I like to call "the dyslexic cast of mind" can and do make their way in the world, right along with their fellows. I have chosen papers about *faces* (of individuals), *facets* (of the problem with which they contend), and *interfaces* (of cultural and professional relevance to their needs and interests). The topics divide rather easily into five groups.

Part I is largely descriptive and analytical of the population that especially concerns us. It speaks to professional colleagues in research and practice, to novices and laymen unfamiliar with the field, and to dyslexics themselves as their interests and insights direct, all with "The Bright Future" as a realistic goal.

With the belief that in dealing with dyslexia, "the treatment is educational," the papers in Part II follow its theme-paper by considering "the essence of education," its principles and practices, and their results, especially where language learning gives particular difficulty. As a practical example there is consideration of the structure of the language our children must learn, accompanied by a step-by-step sample of pedagogical procedure found helpful in meeting this kind of need.

Clio, the Muse of History, co-edited Part III, "The Orton Trail." My enlightening and helpful early contacts with Dr. Samuel T. Orton and my later professional associations and personal friendship with June Lyday Orton and with Anna Gillingham led me to feel that these strong trail-blazers should be known and appreciated by their successors. Part III, therefore, both biographically appreciates them and their associates and reports the course and consequences of their work, including a summary review of the foundation and growth of that specialized professional organization, The Orton Dyslexia Society, whose affairs have so deeply interested and involved me since its beginning.

In Part IV we turn more specifically to the real, multidimensional children and older dyslexic students whose needs are the primary focus of all our effort and concern. We look at representative, generally positive, aspects of their clinical appraisal, their real-life schooling, and the adulthoods some of them have achieved. A few case vignettes used in illustration of theory and in bits of relevant life history barely touch upon the human richness that gives warmth and zest to participation in this field and to its personal memories.

Part V, in answer to some requests, includes a bit of autobiography of the professional segment of my life. It gives opportunity to look at a few of dyslexia's many dimensional interfaces, and to engage in the pleasure of some philosophical reflections and conclusions.

Although it comes out over one name, this is by no means a single-author book. In the very nature of the endeavor, I am indebted to many and diverse friends and associates, as well as less personally known authorities. I cannot begin to name them nor point out the many ways they have influenced my life as it comes to expression here. My benefactors, you mostly know who you are, but whether you do or not, please accept my enthusiastic and heartfelt thanks!

Without The Orton Dyslexia Society's encouragement the presentation of these papers as a collection would not have occurred. Moreover, the Society as a whole, several of its Branches, and generous friends whose number happily surprises me, have given practical support to the venture that has made the publication possible this year. I can barely even begin to express my gratitude for the personal happiness and sense of fulfillment all this brings about.

If I had the genius of a Milton, I would, in addition, compose an ode to secretaries, who bear patiently with the endless tasks of manuscript assembly and preparation, and editors whose tactful blue pencils and inexorable time-clocks bring to bear on an author-editor the standards she has elsewhere long held up to others. This ode to Charlotte Chamberlain and Rosemary Bowler would still fall far short of fully expressing my loving appreciation.

Margaret Byrd Rawson
July 30, 1988

INTRODUCTION

Margaret Byrd Rawson once took on the task of describing for others her concept of the essence of education. In so doing she might not have realized that she has become a living representation of that essence. Hers is a magnificent life of scholarship, finding the roots of an idea and nurturing the plant; exploring the waters, and bravely searching the depths; capturing the goodness of an expression and putting the chaff in its place. Margaret Rawson knows that education is more than a regurgitation. It is a profound series of happenings built on a firm base. It is not surprising that she should devote her life to the exploration of the dyslexic mind. She knows that the greater the educational opportunity, the better the possibility for coming close to the center of it all, that force from which we all derive our strength and through which we are inextricably bound to each other. Language is the key. The dyslexic, so often denied that access in Margaret's lifetime, has, in her, a wonderful champion and friend. As she has used her talent as a scholar to search out the centrality, so she beckons the dyslexic to use his talent to make the search. Education continues for her, even as she approaches the peak of life. This book celebrates, for all of us who ponder the magnificence of dyslexia, the uniqueness which endows us all. In its pages you will meet a superb human being.

The special blend of creative thinking and humane acuity so evident in Margaret's life and work owes much to its Quaker genesis. The Society of Friends rests on the concept of the inner light, present in all of us. The discovery of it in ourselves leads to its discovery in others producing a unification of understanding. Quakers are not afraid of discovery and consequently they are often helpers. It was into the fields of social work, psychology, and education that Margaret Rawson entered. Educated at George School and Swarthmore College and finally at the University of Pennsylvania, she learned from the beginning that ideas are to be explored, mulled over, cherished, dismissed very sparingly, and always respected. The concept of dyslexia was not, through much of her working life, generally explored or cherished and was very easily dismissed.

Such a daunting reality might have had no interest for her had she not allowed herself to become intrigued, during the 1930s, by the

plight of a student at The School in Rose Valley, PA, who had great difficulty in learning to read. The pursuit of the resolution of that problem
became a lifelong vocation. It was the start of a unique thirty-year longitudinal study of dyslexic boys reported in *Developmental Language
Disability: Adult Accomplishments of Dyslexic Boys*. The love of fellow
man inherent in such an endeavor, to follow fifty-six boys through
thirty years of their and her lives is a truly imaginative occurrence. It
takes persistence, patience, and a love for the search to do it. The advancement in our understanding which the study continues to produce is profound. It is that same pioneering spirit and concern which
led her to persuade Hood College, where she held the post of Assistant
Professor of Sociology in the late 1950s, to offer a credit course for
teachers of dyslexic students. As far as is known, this was the first such
course in the United States.

Born in 1899 in Rome, Georgia, Margaret Byrd Rawson's life is full,
dedicated, inquisitive, and adventurous. A pilot until recent years, the
driver of intrepid George—her faithful Cadillac—a world traveler and
participant in current activity in her field, Margaret's contribution is
enormous. She continues to serve as an advisor or consultant to many
schools and institutions throughout the United States. She has served
on innumerable committees and commissions including the White
House Conference on Children and Youth (1970), the White House
Conference on Handicapped Persons (1977). She was Chairman of the
Task Force on Learning Failure and Unused Learning Potential for the
President's Commission on Mental Health 1977–78. She is a much
sought after lecturer, retains her interest in research, and continues to
write.

Perhaps the most compelling of all professional activities for her
has been her association with and leadership of The Orton Dyslexia
Society. She was introduced to the work of Dr. Samuel Torrey Orton in
her days of lively activity at Rose Valley. She recognized as did others
that Dr. Orton's work would have ever-growing influence on the lives
of the special young people she came to know in those early years. She
remains an indomitable supporter and retains the puckish gleam of
youth when recalling the defense of Orton against the nonbeliever or
when checking off the continuous revelations which support Orton's
various contentions. She contributed mightily to the development of
the Society which bears his name and continues to serve on its Board of
Directors and as the Society's Editor.

Margaret Byrd Rawson is a central figure in the lives of countless
dyslexics and professionals in the field of dyslexia. She continues to
educate, and no conversation with her is left without an understanding
or new way of looking at something. She taps into that inner light in all
of us and is surely to be credited with raising continuously the human
dignity associated with dyslexia. In writing about her it is tempting to

check off in minute detail all of her enormous accomplishments and activities. There is, however, only one which seems to be of importance and it is her consummate loyalty to the notion of the dignity of mankind in its pursuit of truth. A significant segment of the population has Margaret Rawson, among others, to thank for considerable improvement in attitude towards dyslexics in recent years. As a scholar she has never forgotten the immense potential of a once forgotten or largely ignored group. There is nobody who has ever been with Margaret Rawson who can forget the brightness of the encounter. In bringing her work together in this volume, The Orton Dyslexia Society offers to innumerable individuals the opportunity to spend some valuable time with Margaret. It is an encounter which will not easily be forgotten.

William Ellis
Clearwater, FL
July 1988

Part I
The Many Faces of Dyslexia

1
The Many Faces of Dyslexia

Dyslexia: a theme in individual and social life, whether dominating or subtly pervasive, needs periodic reexamination. Its outward and inward expression in individuals is seen to be more varied and complex even as we learn to understand it better and live with it more productively. We want to give special attention today to the connections between the overt behaviors we know so well and shall review briefly first, and the newer research findings represented by Dr. Galaburda as he joins us. We should be aware, also, of work of other scientists and educators whom you may meet here and in the conference corridors.

Let's concentrate on just a few of the many *current* "faces of dyslexia" and their significance. As proper scholastic representatives of our culture, we have been grounded in respect for the demand: "First of all, define your terms. What is dyslexia?" If it is true, however, that we see things as we do because of the way we talk about them, we can hope that all those years we have spent in the search for definitions have sharpened our sense of who we are and what we are working on—and also how to say it in public. As time goes on though, I am becoming more and more convinced that the usual route of definition is not the most productive one.

Such a word as dyslexia does make a useful noun in a typical English subject-predicate sentence. With it, someone can say to you, the would-be learner, "You—have—dyslexia!" You may be relieved or you may be devastated, but "that doctor" says you have *got something!* It sort of swallows you up and it may be saying to you that you are "somehow not all right." But it seems to me that dyslexia is not that kind of a noun. It is not a *thing* that you have or get, but rather a one-word summary of the way some people's minds (good minds, too) are built to work.

Dyslexia is not a disease entity; it is a name for a range of variable ability for language acquisition. (See, e.g., Orton 1925, 1937.)

Reprinted with permission from The Orton Dyslexia Society from *Annals of Dyslexia* 36:179–195 1986.

If you look at it that way, you begin to see how many faces it has. Just when you might think you have it pinned down, along comes something else, with a difference in kind or degree. Then, like the Very Old Man in Wanda Gag's (1928) nursery tale, with his "millions and billions and trillions of cats," you "just have to take in that one more kitten, too." Now we are so far from a succinct and conclusive definition that the Carping Critic says, "See, you don't even know what you are talking about. Away with you!"

But there is a way out. "The English language" is a noun-phrase, a Something, to be dealt with as a *fact*. On the other hand, "learning and using language" has the sense of a verb, of something going on; we *do* it, and in all sorts of ways. We can now shift our thinking to terms of a variable *process*, rather than an entity, and process entails, even requires, permutations, degrees, flexibility. We can say that the person's processing has "gone awry," or "failed to go right." In fact, it's still not going right for *this* person.

Now we are dealing with a major dimension of human life, on which there is room for us to live in a complicated variety of ways. We can call it the *language* (or "lexic") *dimension*.

We can think of its "eulexic" pole at one end, where everything we are considering in the language process is going "*eu*," or very well indeed. (That's the prefix *eu*, as in *eu*phoria, *eu*genics, and so forth.) People who function here are often called linguistically gifted or talented. Next comes the large, conglomerate middle part of the range called normal in both common speech and statistical usage. At the farthest section of the other end is the dyslexia pole. There the going is "*dys*," that is, from difficult to really rough.

We might calibrate the whole, after a fashion, to provide a "language learning facility scale." What factors are taken into account, who is included at any given point, and where dividing lines are drawn along the whole way depends on so many considerations that the combinations involved are almost infinitite. Absolutes and panaceas find no place in such a climate.

We are often asked to identify dyslexic subtypes. Properly done, this has its uses, but if we try to subtype the people who are said to have dyslexia we find that an unmanageably large percentage of them just won't fit into, or stay confined in, the categorical pigeon-holes we arrange for them. Instead, it may make better theoretical and practical sense to look carefully at the phenomena that go into language learning and processing.

Why not, in short, subtype the manifestations of dyslexia, rather than the people who very complexly exhibit them? That leaves us still in position to make the "diagnoses" which seem to be demanded at the present time if we are to get funds and treatment provisions for our clients.

It is, as John Money pointed out in 1962, not by any single symptom that we can determine the presence (or absence) of dyslexia as a recognizable entity, for its uniqueness is rather in the pattern of signs that appear with each other, signs that can also be found elsewhere, in other connections or lesser degrees.

Now let me remind you of The Orton Dyslexia Society's four-way analysis of the language problem in which it specializes. We say:

1. The differences are personal.
2. The diagnosis is clinical.
3. The treatment is educational.
4. The understanding is scientific.

The Orton Dyslexia Society serves the united whole.

(MBR, after RES, ca. 1982)

I don't suppose I really need to say much about the specifics of the first one. You have read countless descriptions, ranging from Klasen's (1972) medical-sounding "Syndrome of Specific Dyslexia" to the most recent popular press (Lytle 1985). You know we have come a long way, yet have far to go to reach general public understanding. How will the following do as a summary of that first, or personal, postulate?

The many, many people who fit the broad general designation of dyslexia are notable, first of all, for their seeming likeness to everybody else. Their ranges in age, IQ, and social and other circumstances are just as wide, and, in every sense of the word, normal. Their learning and skill problems are specific to language.

They do have many reading, writing, math, and especially spelling problems of varying degrees and etiologies. These are apparently more of subtle, constitutional, persistent, neurologic origin than from emotional or environmental causes, although the several kinds of conditions may coexist, and there are important emotional and social consequences of dyslexia to consider. Rote memory, laterality, and sequencing seem frequently involved, but cognitive and rational capacities are generally good, often very superior. Those younger children who lag in language and development in preschool and nursery years seem particularly vulnerable to later academic insufficiencies. Even up to very advanced levels, dyslexia may be reflected in trouble with "symbolic formulation and expression" (Head 1926). There are plenty of problem-clusters for us to subtype, if subtype one must.

In general, people who process language in dyslexic ways are predominantly male (about 4:1), more often left-handed or nonright-handed than one would expect, prone to more than their fair share of allergies and other immune disorders, and often under stress as a result of their dyslexia problems. On the other hand, or in the other brain hemisphere, perhaps, they frequently have spatial, mechanical, athletic, and other talents which are, be it noted, inherent gifts, not just compensatory abilities. They generally have families who share their gifts and shortcomings, one way or another. These component characteristics apparently don't cause one another, but may be related, further back, to a common cause (or causes) that we shall discuss later.

That's Point 1: "The differences are personal."

About Point 2: "The diagnosis is clinical," there is a large body of literature, so here we need only a brief statement. Looking systematically and closely at the features of dyslexia (call them symptoms if you will) requires the knowledge and skill of an expert clinician—psychologist, physician, educator, or other. Clinical diagnostic expertise contributes precision and depth to our understanding of what is, and isn't, going on in the life of the individual client or patient. Such diagnosis enables the practicing educator to help the developmental processes go better. It also tells the neuroscientist something of what he may find and how and where he might profitably look, in his quest for deeper-rooted understanding of that brain which we say is the organ of the mind.

Now for Points 3 and 4: what to do in educational practice and how to understand its justification in theory. Inquiry in the dyslexia field is currently taking these two directions in research. One interest is education, both in the special practices that seem appropriate to the needs of dyslexic persons and in the results of such practices, past, current, or projected. The other interest is in science, especially in the neurobiological structure and functions of the brain. Current studies have to do with microscopic and other laboratory examination of the human brain and limited experimentation with suitable animals.

What are we looking at, and what are we finding?

The Dyslexia Field

One of the facets of the language dimension in the lives of people is the age range of those who meet the problems of dyslexia. When Orton and his immediate predecessors first became engaged with such patients, it was predominantly young people of secondary and elementary school age who came to their attention. However, in New York, Dr. and Mrs. Orton soon found themselves seeing preschool and still younger children as well as postsecondary and adult patients. As one would expect, Orton's subsequent papers expressed recognition of the essential continuity of the ages of his patients with language problems (J. L. Orton 1966a).

From the start, to be sure, Orton thought of the language difficulty as a neurophysiological, developmental variation rather than as evidence of defect, disease, or abnormality. Still, to most teachers, school administrators, and clinicians, it was a troublesome deviation from what was expected, something "wrong with the student" and so it has remained in many settings. (But the winds of change are blowing.)

The field covered, as well as the age range, has now been broadened to include most aspects of the "language continuum"—heard, spoken, written, mathematical, organizational, and abstract, where each is pertinent. Many cordial relationships exist among the professional specialists engaged in these fields. Furthermore, dyslexia has, though more slowly, become an increasingly recognized specialty in educational circles despite remaining skepticism at all levels. There are, we are all too often reminded, many still unrecognized and mismanaged cases.

But, to me, it is especially the coming together of the scientific research and the educational rationale behind The Orton Dyslexia Society's efforts and their successes that is a real cause for intellectual excitement which I feel privileged to have lived to experience.

In 1962, over twenty years ago, Norman Geschwind urged that always we should " . . . keep in mind . . . the interweaving of our functional with our anatomical knowledge." In October 1984, after several interchanges about how to do so, and what Orton—and he, himself—had said on both subjects, Geschwind wrote me this, alas final, message:

> I think the dyslexic can function well in two ways. On the one hand the anomalies that you have described correctly in the language areas [of the brain] lead to an enlargement of certain other areas and very specifically produce superior talents in certain areas. On the other hand [the dyslexic] can usually make the best of his residual talents in the ways you have described so well. And I could not agree with you more about Orton! As you recall the last word in my description of him at the library dedication [Columbia University, 1980] was 'teacher of the teachers'! I think that *you* should say it, because . . . [i]t is necessary *for someone who has worked directly with the dyslexic* to say it, loud and clear. (Geschwind 1984).

So, in a sense, I shall try to speak for both of us as I go on, first in the educational and later with my layman's understanding of the neurological views that Dr. Galaburda is here to correct and supplement.

Education

Geschwind (1982b) gave thirteen reasons "Why Orton Was Right." In 1983 I proposed a fourteenth, summarizing Orton's educational recommendations (part of what Geschwind was referring to in the letter just quoted). Orton's general treatment philosophy and its specific applications are substantially contained in The Orton Dyslexia Society statement "What is Dyslexia?" (1982).

Over the years, several people have published versions of that scientifically sound, pragmatically successful approach. Suited to a variety of uses and users, their methods are mutually consistent in following Orton's advice to reduce the language to its elements—its 44 sounds and the 26 letters with which they can be written, and to teach these components thoroughly, through all the senses coordinatedly. "Structured, systematic, sequential, cumulative, thorough, multisensory, individualized, cognitive, and therapeutically-oriented" are terms that apply to both the materials and the recommended manner of their use. This sums up an educational way that seemed to Geschwind, as it had to Orton, to be well-designed to help the dyslexic use all his needed language talents.

It is hardly surprising that the successes experienced under such a regime are real, liberating, lasting, and sometimes dramatic, though they are difficult to report quantitatively. There have been a few studies published in the scientific modes, and there will be more. I have found it personally rewarding, during the past half-century, to have watched so many dyslexic people grow up successfully, to know some of their children, and to have watched carefully some fine prevention experiments among the "at risk" juniors, particularly as beginners get off to a favorable start.

So, though we have much to learn, we think we, and our colleagues, know quite a lot about how to meet the needs of dyslexia-prone school-age children, older students, and adults, and about helping with language development among preschoolers.

One of the most challenging interfaces today seems to me to be between the people who work with the very young preverbal infants and the other people who explore human embryology and the prenatal brain and nervous system. Is there a chance, with what is currently being learned in both camps, that we shall be able to apply the "ounce of prevention" right at the start with babies whose heredity and neonatal status suggest risk? It seems to me, and some experts have thought it not too far-fetched, that something of the sort is a thing to try. The literature indicates great sophistication in much that is already being done.

There is reason to believe that a large degree of natural "lexic" aptitude is present at birth. Bickley Simpson, in a recent paper (1985), suggests that the newborn infant with what I call a "dyslexic cast of mind" may be less sensitive than his age-mates to the acoustic cues that allow most very young infants to recognize differences in voicing and in basic phonemic sounds. Adults don't notice this degree of fine-tuning because during all his first years the youngster is busy sorting out, among all the human sounds he can make his vocal apparatus produce, just which ones are coin of his cultural realm. Acute observers incline to think that he is communicating, perhaps even symbolically, well before he has mastered the verbal code that makes sense to us adults, who then recognize that he is, we say, "talking in words."

We observe that the infant tries to say, and continues to say by preference, what he hears. If he really is by nature dyslexic, say through inheritance, perhaps this is the period for intervention. We could, for instance, try deliberately to provide, in our hypothetical newborn child's risky linguistic life, at least one adult who can model for him some crisp, clear English speech (or French or Czech, or whatever). Is this too Utopian? It just might provide him, we could say by prescription, with some neuronal experiences he will need to marshal as he lays down patterns for speech. It seems like a properly early starting point for the implementation of our Point 3: "The treatment is educational."

Now what can we say about Point 4: "The understanding is scientific"? I'll try to put a bit of it in layman's words, and then call on our in-house scientist.

Neuroscience

Any subject of great concern looms very large in the life of a specialist in that area, whether as participant or student. We need, accordingly, to keep in mind that even when the dyslexia factor is center-front in consciousness, it represents only a corner in the life and a small part of the brain of the whole person who does the living. Whatever our involvements, we should keep reminding ourselves of how our orbits of interest do, and do not, overlap.

As I understand it from those of Galaburda's papers that I have read (1978, 1985, 1986), the part of the neurological development of the individual that is pertinent to our subject right now begins at about the sixteenth week of a child's life in utero. In the core area of what is to be the central nervous system, the place known as the germinal zone, neurons are being formed. During approximately the next eight weeks, in sequences that we don't need to go into now, the process will continue, with each neuron being, as it were, dispatched to its appropriate destination according to what we may think of as the individual's genetic blueprint.

If everything goes according to plan, neurons of appropriately programed variety (or varieties) will find themselves arrayed in neat columns, closely ordered like troops on parade, perpendicular to the surface of the correct sections of the cortex of the individual's growing

brain, ready to be called on when needed during his further development. All the neurons that are supposed to get there will do so, but
they will stop migrating just before they get to the outer layer of the
cortex.

For the present, we are looking at a section of the brain in what is
called Wernicke's area, specifically the subsection under the planum
temporale, where it seems that an important part of this newcomer's
language processing will go on. We can expect, in most people, that
this area will have substantially more surface and volume in one brain
hemisphere than the other, usually the left, whence spoken language
is eventually to come; this is one mark of the language-dominant or
language-specialized hemisphere of the human brain.

For knowledge of the asymmetrical structure of the brain we have
Geschwind particularly to thank, with due appreciation for his colleagues and scientific progenitors. For appreciation of the brain's functional asymmetry and its relation to language learning we go back
much further, especially to Samuel T. Orton (who also had his historic
sources, see 1925, 1937 and J. L. Orton 1966a), and the insights that
came to his "prepared mind," beginning in 1925. We are all the fortunate heirs of these two pioneers and, of course, the many other men
and women of what I think we are justified in calling "the scientific
world of dyslexia."

With technology now available, it is possible to see some of the
anatomical basis for the difficulties arising in the area where, as Geschwind has said, Orton correctly located the problem though he envisioned it as only functional. Although we are told that in his years as a
neuropathologist Orton had dissected more human brains than any of
his contemporaries, he shared the then current view that the brain
hemispheres were symmetrical.

It is just here that it is appropriate for the Society that bears Orton's
name to be helping support the kind of innovative research of which he
could only dream. This is in pursuit of our fourth objective, "the understanding is scientific." When, in the scenario of fetal development I
have outlined, something "goes wrong," or "fails to go right," or "goes
a different way," what can the neuroscientist tell us about it?

If I have read aright the reports of Geschwind, Galaburda, and
their co-workers, the electron microscopic studies show that in the
brains they have thus far examined of people who in life were known
to have been dyslexic, two conditions have appeared in the language
areas. They have been found so consistently as to be well beyond the
normal range of chance or coincidence. We can quite safely say that
these results are both statistically significant and scientifically important. They seem to confirm some of the theories on which we have been
working and to necessitate revision in others.

First, in each brain studied, the results of the neuronal migration in the critical prenatal period have not gone entirely as expected. There seem to be plenty of neurons, but they are not all where or as they should be. Some seem to have lagged behind, not reaching their prescribed cortical destinations. Others have overshot the mark and come to rest, out of bounds, in the outermost layer of the cortex or projecting themselves as "warts" in that surface. Those neurons that are in the right place are, however, as one might say, "lolling about in some disarray, instead of being properly lined up for duty." These lesions as they have been found in brains of dyslexics are not pervasive. They are few and small and not identical from person to person, but are still found more often than is common in unselected brains.

When we have this much substantial physical evidence, perhaps we are justified in thinking that we are coming a stage closer to seeing the roots of language difficulty. As examples, we might mention a few of them, such as: (1) basic difficulty with spoken language going back to early infancy; or (2) later-than-usual achievement of literacy; or (3) all the way on through adulthood, inadequacies in certain more abstract skills needed for academic success. Still these items expose only the tips of the iceberg of language learning. Some of the problems of life-organization that often beset dyslexic persons could, perhaps, be traced to this same source. At least, what with these findings and those of the newer scanning techniques (CAT, PET, BEAM, NMR and the rest), we begin to feel that we are once again on our way toward better understanding of what is going on "in there," in the brain.

The other new observation that I find especially interesting has to do with hemispheric symmetry. The studies of unselected brains show the plana temporale smaller in the right hemisphere in some 65 percent of cases and in the left in about 11 percent, with the remaining quite considerable 24 percent of equal size (Geschwind and Levitsky 1968; Wada 1969). Yet, surprisingly, in the dyslexic brains examined (Galaburda 1985) *every one is in the equal size category!* Not only this, but the hemispheres are equally large, and, as I read the diagrams, the presumably nonlanguage right area may have fewer neuronal anomaly sites than the left, probably language, area. Is it so wild an oversimplification to think that there may be here some connection with the more than expected bilateral language activity Geschwind and others have noted in special populations over the years?

It might even be that we are on the trail of a fifteenth reason "why Orton was right." Perhaps the would-be language masters in the two hemispheres really are fighting for the crown. Which one is to control the dyslexic person's language processes—the speaking left, with its anomalously arranged neurons, or the supposedly silent right? Perhaps that usually right-brain contender is more ably active and less inhibited than it should be for linguistic sureness. Perhaps it does, as Orton thought, from 1925 on (J. L. Orton 1966a), keep interfering, forcing its perhaps oppositely oriented input into the consciousness of the person concerned, thus confusing him. Something of this sort might help explain the Delos Smiths (Pollack and Branden 1982), the "Louise Bakers"[1] (Rawson 1982) and many less extreme phenomena, observed by and since Orton. It could reinforce his theory of the dominance-confusion motif in the etiology of specific language disability, providing another validating point to the Geschwind-Orton Dyslexia Society list.

There is also the whole range of associated phenomena (Geschwind 1983) of negative value (like autoimmune conditions), neutral (like nonrighthandedness), and positive (like very important superior talents apparently lodged in the nonlanguage brain sections). The relation of all these, as well as dyslexia, to the sex hormone testosterone in fetal life is a research interface where Drs. Galaburda and Behan are working, sparked, as so many others have been, by the late Dr. Norman Geschwind.

Our understanding has been increased importantly by these and other observations from the current revolution in the neurosciences. Although the clear evidence that "there is something there" in the actual structure of the brain has made some of us alter long-accepted views and statements, we find this, in the spirit of science, a positive experience. It takes us a convincing step further toward explanation of many puzzling observations. The neuronal anomalies and the strong relationship between the equal, and large, sizes of the planum temporale regions could point to two pieces of the puzzle. Also, the relationships, noted in many quarters, between dyslexia and maleness, higher than expected abilities based elsewhere in the brain, and a number of other qualities of life open up challenging vistas.

We are glad to find ourselves receptive to what seem to be sound new ideas. What we see around and ahead looks like corroboration of most of the diagnostic and educational theory and practices that have seemed for years to be empirically justified by results in services rendered to children and older dyslexics, with considerable benefit to the quality of their lives. I like to put it that, while dyslexia, of whatever form, presents *real reasons* for individuals being as they are, there is in this fact *no excuse* for the patient-client-student failing to do what he is at any given time able to do, nor for society failing to provide him, or her, with the opportunity and support necessary for achieving up to his ability.

We can take the dyslexic person as he comes, without thought of

---

[1]I get letters from Delos Smith in mirror writing. He was diagnosed in childhood by Orton and taught by Katrina de Hirsch, so he can go either way with ease, but prefers the looking-glass world. Louise, when tired, sometimes slips unconsciously into the mirrored form for a whole second page of her letter, without realizing she has done so. She seems to be putting on paper an alternate, exactly "anti-tropic," image from somewhere in her brain—the other hemisphere?

altering his genetic structure, for we believe we know what can and should be done to set him free. **The challenge is to get it done— keeping our minds open all the way!**

Response to "The Many Faces of Dyslexia" by Albert M. Galaburda, M.D.

It is a great honor for me to comment on Dr. Rawson's paper. Let me stress, however, that my doing so gives only the illusion of a peer relationship between us. In reality I, as most of you I am sure, am awed by what she has to say and view her as the teacher she really is for all of us. But what makes her a great teacher, I am convinced, is that she is herself a perpetual student. It is clear that she has thought a great deal and for a long time about many facets of dyslexia, and therefore, it is not surprising that she can arrive at what I believe to be profound conclusions. However, I know for a fact that she could not have thought about the anatomical findings for very long; after all, the earliest observations date back to only 1979. I must conclude, therefore, that Margaret has remained the attentive student, and you can rest assured that what she has told us in her present lecture includes reflections that are undeniably au courant.

Why do I say that I believe Margaret Rawson's conclusions are profound? Simply, it is because they agree with my own. But wait, it is not what it sounds like. We have both come to similar conclusions, approaching the analysis from broadly different perspectives. This is, in fact, the aim of science: to reach the same conclusions using widely different methods. But, in addition, she did it first.* Furthermore, she

---

From the Rawson notebook: PS to Al Galaburda

I have long thought (recorded in 1967) that this power (from the "too symmetrical cortex") might be a cultural (eventually evolutionary) step beyond the specialization represented by cerebral dominance. One experiment reported simultaneous bihemispheric activity in the brain of the "speaking" dolphins. One might speculate (but never know) that Leonardo could have been drawing with one hand and with the other simultaneously mirror-writing his often misspelled notes. Who knows where what Geschwind would later call "the pathology of superiority" might lead?

It also may account for the advantage some people seem to have in recovering from aphasias after destruction of actual tissue in the dominant hemisphere in the language subserving regions. In these cases the structure of the language is often retrieved as the life-history memories that constitute so large a part of the individual's personal identity. It is as if, with the dominant hemisphere structure nonfunctional, or even completely gone, the learned habits of inhibition in the nondominant regions can be released. This takes time,—hours, days, or months perhaps—but is of a very different order from relearning the whole from the start. It is the congenital dyslexics, often nonrighthanders, who are often at advantage in this respect.

Orton surmised from what he thought to be the symmetry of the hemispheres that both had developed through simultaneous irradiation, as they apparently do in the sensory receptive and perceptual areas. The "talent for language learning" was essentially a talent for giving selective attention in consciousness to the activity, in the

did it first without the help of the modern tools of neuroanatomy that have helped me reach my conclusions. Let me take the next few minutes to underscore what I think are some of her most important messages.

Dr. Rawson first tells us that she is becoming more and more convinced that the definition of dyslexia is not very positive or productive. It somehow does not ring right with her that dyslexia is something you have, or get. It is depressing, is it not, that after my colleagues and I have made gargantuan efforts to describe what is different about the brains of dyslexics, which, if nothing else, says that dyslexics have got something, Dr. Rawson has doubts about dyslexia being something people have, or get? But if you think about it, what she says makes sense after all. Let me borrow an example from medicine to illustrate the fact that what my colleagues and I find in the brain and what Margaret says are not at all at odds with one another.

You have all heard of a medical condition known as coronary artery disease (CAD). You have also heard about angina. People with CAD are susceptible to having angina. But what is it that one has? Is it angina, or is it CAD? Clearly, not every one with CAD experiences angina, and for those who do, the angina of one need not be identical to the angina of another. Moreover, not everyone with CAD who does experience angina does so unremittingly. In fact, patients with CAD often find ways of avoiding the angina, and when they run out of ideas, their doctors can usually add this or that to abolish it altogether. So what is it that the patient has? To me, it seems inescapable to conclude that the patient has CAD, which simply makes him susceptible to angina, but nothing more.

The distinction between CAD and angina is far from trivial, since, considering only practical issues, it is much easier to treat the latter than the former. After all, most angina can be controlled by simple, if not trivial, environmental modifications. Thus, for instance, if you get angina when you climb two flights of stairs, climb only one at a time, or take the elevator. In some cases, of course, pharmacological intervention is needed.

Do social factors affect angina? In addition to diet and smoking, some of the social effects may be quite fantastic: in Houston and in Boston, one complains of angina and the next thing one gets is a triple

---

association areas only, of the hemisphere which thus became dominant. Attention to the other (hence nondominant) hemisphere was simultaneously inhibited. If selectivity is learned well and almost effortlessly by the eulexic, well enough and with reasonable effort by most people, less and less well despite more and more effort by dyslexic persons, the degree of impairment might measure the severity of the dyslexia. For Orton this theory accommodated, under a single rubric, his observations of his various patients' behavior.

bypass, which clearly affects reporting statistics. Do social factors affect CAD? To some extent they do, but genetic and other biological effects are more important. Therefore, angina is more malleable than CAD, but is CAD itself a big problem? Let me mention an additional surprising fact: the study that followed the Korean war on the incidence of CAD among American soldiers, which included people (mostly men) in their early twenties, disclosed that significant coronary pathology was highly prevalent. Few, remarkably few, however, had angina. So there is a large number of people with coronary artery disease who have no angina. Obviously, it is partly a function of the severity of the CAD, but we also know that it is possible for one to have only moderate disease and severe angina because of obesity, untreated hypertension, and chain-smoking, while his neighbor, whose coronary arteries are worse off, but who is lean, exercises moderately, and does not smoke, suffers no angina.

You may agree now, after considering only a few illustrations, that coronary artery disease, which is something one can have, is, however, relatively hidden and fixed, whereas angina, which is much more functional and ethereal, is out in the open, acting like a flag. So it is no great surprise that most people come to believe angina itself to be the problem, rather than the hidden coronary disease.

Now, is dyslexia like CAD which, as we saw, is something one can have; or is it more like angina, which, like the flag, can be displayed or not? Margaret, I believe, thinks the latter, and I agree. Thus, the findings in the brains of the dyslexics we have studied are in a certain sense like CAD; thus, they can make a person prone to displaying dyslexia. But it is the dyslexia, and not the brain findings, that is variable among individuals, that is modifiable by social factors, and that is eminently treatable. It may not be proper, therefore, to say "I am dyslexic." Instead, the sentence "Under the proper circumstances, I can be quite dyslexic" may be more applicable. The implicit positivity of this message is that, as with angina, dyslexia is modifiable and manageable.

I do not mean for a second to imply that the brain findings in dyslexics are unimportant or uninteresting. However, it should be clear that their importance and interest lie in a different sphere. Thus, the understanding of the nature and origin of the brain changes are apt to teach us much about medicine. We may learn, for instance, how the vulnerability comes about and how to predict it in order to insure early treatment. It may tell us, and it already has, what other vulnerabilities may coexist. We may also learn more about that ever elusive relationship between structure and function, brain and language, or the modern version of the mind-body problem that has haunted us for thousands of years.

Now, let me turn briefly to some of the other points. There is much more variability in the manifestation of angina than of CAD. Thus, two patients with identical obstruction in their coronary blood vessels may experience markedly different types of angina, depending on the pain fiber innervation of their hearts, for instance. It is clear that the understanding of angina subtypes depends in part on knowledge about the coronary circulation, but also on several aspects of the rest of the system. Until the organic substrate is better understood, therefore, it makes sense to separate out in as formal a way as possible the different components of angina which can be later related to specific underlying organic substrates. In this sense, I agree with Margaret that subtyping dyslexics is less useful than dissecting out the components of dyslexia.

Now, it may not be fair to compare the findings in the brain of dyslexics to a disease like CAD without further explanation. This is especially true in view of Margaret's statement that the underlying substrate of dyslexia represents a case of developmental variation rather than a defect. However, this is a case where the boundary between defect or pathology and variability becomes blurred. Norman Geschwind called an aspect of this the pathology of superiority. I tend to lean to the side of pathology also, albeit with a special meaning for the word pathology. My reason is simple: all of the brains I have examined disclose unarguably pathological findings, which means that under any other circumstances a neuropathologist would have no problems with calling the differences pathological. What is not nearly as well understood is whether all of the consequences of these pathological changes are in themselves pathological. Going back to the example of coronary artery disease, it is irrefutable that arteriosclerotic plaques in the inner walls of the coronary arteries are pathological. However, in some patients this leads to the enlargement of collateral blood vessels and better protection of the heart muscle, which is beneficial. When the compensation is incomplete, the patient may still experience symptoms from the effects on the occluded vessel, but will remain less vulnerable to symptoms arising from the region supplied by the enlarged collateral vessels. Likewise, the brain findings may be pathological, but their consequences on language and other behavior may not.

One last word about "genetic blueprint," which Margaret uses to describe some aspects of brain development. It is important to understand that genetic effects can be modified. There are so many ordinary examples of this principle that it still surprises me how much in awe people are of genes. It is as if once something is in the genes, the ball game is over. The most basic way by which genes are modified in their expression is by the actions of the other genes. Thus, for instance, if one is born with the y-chromosome, but one also has a gene that will make tissues insensitive to the effects of male sex hormones, one will not look like a male. Environmental factors, both chemical and psychosocial, can also modify the expression of the genes. The importance of this realization is that it is then possible to alter gene reactions and particularly to modify pathological gene effects. In the case of dyslexia, however, I wholeheartedly agree with Dr. Rawson that there is no need for "monkeying around with the genes."

2

The Nature of the Dyslexic Learner

One of our central objectives in the preparation of teachers is to help them learn how to teach their subject as it is to their students as they are. This, of course, means that teachers need to become increasingly adept in the science and the arts of pedagogy, to know well the subject they are teaching, and to understand as much as possible about the ways people learn, both as human beings and as individuals with unique capacities and needs.

Much of what we need to know applies to any good teaching in any good school, but this symposium* is especially concerned with helping teachers to add to their professional competence in ways that meet the needs of a particular set of students. From the veriest beginner to the administrator, or at the very top of the pedagogic chain, the teacher of teachers, professional educators may well be concerned with a backdrop that paints in something of "the nature of the dyslexic learner" who is being increasingly recognized as common among us.

When the word dyslexia is used, people are apt to think first either specifically of "childhood reading disability," or of "learning disabilities" in general, especially as met with in school-age children. These are two gateways to a field that most people think of as at least "atypicality," if not outright deficiency. However, I want to talk about concepts and persons to be met in a specially bounded area that is at once broader than reading and more specific than the umbrella term "learning disabilities."

Samuel T. Orton made it clear in his first public statement in 1925 that he was concerned not just with reading, but with the whole of the human language function. As a neuropathologist and a psychiatrist, he looked at the structure of the brain that is the organ of the mind, where behavior must have its roots and learning its seat. The best sci-

Reprinted with permission from The Orton Dyslexia Society from *Intimacy with Language*: 10–14 1987.
*Dyslexia and Evolving Educational Patterns, Airlie House VA 1987.

ence of his day, still true in our own, pointed beyond the reading of print to the wholeness of language as we know it and use it. Listening, speaking, reading, writing, verbal formulation, and their interweaving are all mediated by what happens in the human cortex—the gray-matter of the brain. It has long been known that these processes can be interrupted or destroyed by damage to particular parts of that cortex—especially those called the "association areas in the language dominant hemisphere." Such results have been seen in study of the aphasias.

Reasoning from this neurological knowledge, it was logical for Orton and his successors to speculate that language learning problems came from some kind of built-in developmental anomaly in those same brain areas. To some people this meant constitutional deficiency, but as Orton looked at the structure and functioning of the developing Central Nervous System, he thought that the evidence pointed to a physiologically functional cause. He called the condition a "specific developmental language disability", and he descriptively named it "strephosymbolia," for the "twisted symbols" so frequent in his patients' reading and writing. He did not use the term "reading disability" alone because it seemed both too general—since it might refer to *any* kind of reading failure—and, at the same time, too narrow—if one meant *only reading*. Orton deliberately avoided the term "dyslexia." He was steering clear of definitional argument about Dr. James Hinshelwood's 1917 usage of it. It was the differences in their concepts that were important to Orton (see The Orton Trail, pp. 136–148).

A case can be made for holding that Specific Developmental Dyslexia, by whatever name, is a *describable* entity, however hard it is to *define* unequivocally. Considerable knowledge about it has developed since 1925 (not 1963 as is often stated), and that knowledge is presently in a period of rapid expansion. Dyslexia commonly puts roadblocks in the way of learning. Whether it is itself one form of learning *disability* depends on the nature of the roadblocks in given cases and how they are dealt with. We shall come back to this matter later.

Reading may be the subject to engage us first, since it is such a basic and complex skill of both early schooling and lifelong importance. This initial interest is understandable; yet, on further examination, starting here may seem like coming into the theater in the middle of Act II.

Reading is based on spoken language. Early language is dyslexia's Act I, Scene 1. But even before the play—or behind the scenes—comes this preliminary overture: Man, it seems, has innate wiring for spoken language, established through evolutionary eons. It is ready at birth for further biological growth and cultural "triggering" and teaching. We know much, and yet so very little, of what has happened in the long history of the universe, of life itself, of the human race, and even during the gestational period of separate individual persons. Language, we know, is the most recent, still unfinished, stage of human evolution. We know something but there is still a lot we need to find out about the nature of those who acquire language, whether they do so with ease or with difficulty.

Let us begin not with reading but where each human newborn starts. It is his senses that connect him with his world. Through them, using his mind, he must learn for himself all he needs to know. He experiences the world's physical realities, its language and its culture, but no matter how wise are his elders nor how concentrated into his embryology is the summary of the millennia stretching from the Olduvai Gorge to the world of 1987, it is he himself, through his own senses, language, and mind, that must embody, literally incorporate, his world. It is the individual who performs the miracle of the learning.

This is how a poet friend of mine has summed up what is also my point of view:

We know the world
by finding what's beneath
and using it
to make a life that's rooted
in the order of the universe.
                                        (Stone 1986)
. . . part discovery, part invention,
interweaving, whole . . . (Rawson 1987)

My task is to explore the nature of the dyslexic learner. To get started we might go first to an allegorical picnic and meet some imagined, but far from unfamiliar, kinds of people. That should be pleasant, and maybe just as pertinent as a description in more academic prose. Dozens of appropriate case stories kept coming to mind as I addressed the metaphorical invitations. Agatha Christie's Miss Marple would reminisce with them, but I'll spare you, I promise!

We might imagine ourselves coming upon a "representative" gathering of people who are, just for the purpose of this exercise, somehow "known to be from moderately to severely dyslexic." We might set up a "Dyslexia Day in Community Park" in the town of your imagination's choice. Imagination is wonderful! Not only can we see at a glance what the celebrants look like. We can give ourselves temporary clairvoyance, strictly confidential of course, so we can know more about what has entitled the attenders to tickets to this party than could any single one of their clinical advisors.

Our first impression is of a generally alert, healthy, good-looking crowd, of varying ages—like anybody's attractive brothers and sisters, but with a large preponderance of brothers. For the most part, at least today, they look happy, energetic, and competent. Yet, perhaps more often than is really comfortable, we sense psychological stress, worry, and, in some cases, almost palpable discouragement, and we wonder about the differences. We know that if there is underlying stress, people will, by their very natures, react to it in different ways. Some of these dyslexics, for instance, show depression, a sense of defeat or a lack of self-esteem (and that hurts worst). Some are tense, with a kind of drivenness; or perhaps with high-hearted courage they are determined to make it through to the end. The socially desperate and deviant ones we know about, too, but they are incognito, hiding even from us, or have decided it isn't their kind of party; they may turn up later to vent their anger with the world by trying to break up the show; "It's a way to have fun," they may say.

There is one thing in common among the crowd, a definitional requirement for "joining the club." Each one has had some problem, or cluster of problems, in mastering his mother-tongue language. Here it is American English but "it would look the same the whole world over," say students of comparative dyslexia.

Yet within the party's unity, there is wide diversity. In this picnic group each person is like some of his fellows in some ways, but he is as unique in his mind as in his thumb-prints. Moreover, there seems to be little or no correlation with other factors. These people "range the range" in each attribute, being quite often highly intelligent, affluent, musical, good-looking or athletic, or else *not* gifted in these ways—like everybody else. We recognize an Olympic diver as a qualifying guest of a local decathlon winner. We note several varsity T-shirts, and also spot some clumsy "klutzes" (who may be called dyspraxic in their physicians' files). We see several obvious southpaws in the ball game, and know of many more in the gathering who are at least to some extent nonrighthanded. In their occupations, there seem to be more artists, mechanics, engineers, architects, all-purpose handy-men, and the like than you would expect. One girl is a map-maker, one a lawyer, and one a reporter. A gourmet chef and a pastry cook from the ranks have volunteered to sustain their reputations at this evening's banquet.

A lot of people here laugh, or groan or sweat, about poor or undependable spelling, or recall having had a very hard time with beginning reading and writing. If they have not had effective help some are still illiterate and can't write words, even as adults. Remembering how a word looks or sounds, dialing a phone number correctly, or managing even simple math computations can still be problems for some of the brightest of the teen-agers. Some of them might qualify for advanced sections in their school or technical courses—if only they could keep up the expected pace! Their thinking may be superior.

Many have difficulty keeping track of homework, organizing possessions or appointments, coming home with everything on the grocery list, knowing left and right securely, and not losing their way or leaving the lunch bag on the bus again—each can be hard for some of *these* dyslexics, and the list goes on and on as they reminisce and learn to laugh at themselves a bit.

Orton's and other early case files, like those of today, include many otherwise promising college students. Our varsity T-shirters are worried about meeting reading requirements, learning foreign languages or calculus, passing organic chemistry, getting satisfactory term papers in on time. If they do make it in college, they may find some related crises in graduate school, and adult life poses others— but they have a much better chance of having developed coping skills along the way than did their parents' generation. In some places they can get good help now, if they can bear to admit their need for it.

If this is your town, you recognize quite a few close and distant relatives among those present today. On family trees our omniscience has revealed many others to have had language problems in some form or other.

The records tell us that these folks seem always to have been the kind of persons they now are. They may change in their behavior and coping abilities, yet all their lives they seem to stay basically the same in the ways they tackle life. Perhaps this is true of all of us, but in teaching as in all the helping professions, understanding the personal equation is especially relevant.

At today's party, as on any occasion when congenial people with several similar interests get together, we see our Dyslexia Day friends moving about and forming new small groups to compare notes with a few others on special things that they have in common. This sort of grouping and realignment may be a delight to a hostess, but it confuses the infiltrating diagnostician on the prowl for "subtypes of dyslexia." He might do better to take notes on what each temporary group is discussing. Then the would-be categorizer could organize just the notes, leaving the people free to shift around. That, to my mind, would fit more closely to the way life really works.

You notice that I have left until last comments on the little guys in the park, the preschoolers and toddlers. That was not just because they were afternoon napping. Historically, only few of the professional pioneers considered these youngsters and their speech development and problems as being in the same language continuum with the all too obvious school difficulties. (see Johnson 1968). This interdisciplinary gap is not entirely closed, but is less of a problem in the dyslexia world than it used to be.

It is not surprising to see a lot of little youngsters in our group. We can surmise that if they are here it is because they have been slow at mastering some of the scheduled sequences of spoken language. Perhaps they have been slow to talk, or to talk distinctly, or they may be hard for adults to reach and hold with verbal messages. Sometimes they exhibit dysfluency—stuttering, or cluttering (which is quite different)—and difficulty calling up the right word for expression of meaning. These speech problems may begin and end in early childhood, but they may persist for many years or for life.

Experience tells us that trouble at this early stage may well indicate vulnerability to school-age dyslexia. Here as elsewhere, "Forewarned is forearmed," since we do have some appropriate measures to take. On the other hand, some truly dyslexic youngsters do well with spoken language, only to be baffled by the demands of the next level of abstraction, the written code. "He was fine," we hear, "till he went to school."

More and more, however, we have come to the realization of the crucial importance of the language developments of very early childhood and the desirability of the earliest feasible intervention when things are not going well. For instance, the younger infants were left out of our observed sample, yet they are most important. It often looks as though we see dyslexia precursors less sharply as we look backward from around the first birthday, near the beginning of easily recognizable verbal language. If we want to explore what it is that is inherently different about the dyslexic learner we should continue our behavioral explorations into the language responses of the first year. Much work has been done, but I am not aware of its having very often been longitudinally connected with dyslexia. It needs to be, in terms of both premonitory symptoms and possible preventive intervention. It was Katrina de Hirsch who said, emphatically, "Eighteen months is already too late!"—at least to begin. How about the birth-cry as a starting point?

But it is time for us to go back to Airlie House. As we walk away from the park, perhaps a quick summary of our observations is in order:

This noticeably masculine crowd looks, otherwise, like any other group of men, women, and children, though there are some signs of personal stress among them. They have in common enough of the characteristics of Specific Language Learning Ineptitude to make trouble for them and to make professional help desirable, if, indeed, they have not already had what they need. Their range of IQs and other characteristics and circumstances is remarkable only in being so normal. The so-called right-hemisphere talents, together with more than usual left-handedness and ambidexterity are of special interest to biological research, as is the striking familial incidence of various manifestations of the cluster of problems we sometimes call "the syndrome of developmental dyslexia."

Our picnickers have had many reading, writing, math, and especially spelling, problems of varying degrees and etiologies. Apparently the difficulties are more of subtle constitutional, persistent, neurologic origin than of emotional causation. Rote memory and sequencing seem frequently involved, but cognitive and rational capacities are generally good and useful for understanding and helping. Those who lag in language development in preschool years seem particularly vulnerable to later academic insufficiencies. This list is barely suggestive of the field's complexity, and there is plenty left to wonder about even on the reasonably accessible, behavioral level.

Another route into understanding the nature of categorical and individual differences that is especially available to us in this conference is through the neurosciences. It was here that Orton's background, research, and practice led him to hypotheses many of which we still use. Over sixty years later his professional heirs are still on leading edges of neuroscience. A current research project on Biological Foundations of Dyslexia under the aegis of The Orton Dyslexia Society was launched just ten years ago at a conference of neurologists and other specialists—*here at Airlie House.*

It is from The Orton Dyslexia Society-sponsored research that I have taken most of the next paragraphs. Here, as I understand them, are some of the findings:

The language cortex structures, examined post-mortem in the brains of an as yet small number of men known to have been dyslexic in life, appear to differ consistently in two, or perhaps many, ways from the brains not so selected. The evidence from female brains in this study, so far, is scanty and inconsistent. In life, females show a range of both similarities and differences when compared with males.

Among the males, it has been found, that *some*—by no means all —of the neurons in the language-subserving cortical regions are arranged atypically in location or organization, not according to the neurologically specified template.

Second, the language sections of each man's two brain hemispheres are unexpectedly symmetrical in size—and both are *large,* instead of one having been reduced, perhaps by dendritic pruning, at the usual development time. There is, as yet, no way of knowing what these findings meant in the particular men's life histories. It is not known whether the difference in assymetry, if it continues to appear similarly in later cases, should properly be considered pathological in the usual sense, or what Geschwind called "a pathology of superiority," with balancing advantages elsewhere, or simply a part of the normal variability inherent, and potentially very useful, in the human species.

In the end it might turn out that extra power in the right hemisphere, developed but kept under learned control, can be turned to advantage. It might, for example, provide a reserve for use in case of injury, or even fatigue, as some accident victims, or craftsmen, or surgeons even now use in their ambidextrous skills.

Between brain structure and the language behavior of the people we call dyslexic is a large gap marked as in other incomplete maps terra incognita. Yet the signs do point to some real differences, not necessarily deleterious but of the long-predicted constitutional origin. From embryology we know that the forms that researchers like Galaburda are finding were laid down early in fetal life. No doubt there are important clues here that we shall someday be able to read. I used to think nothing was likely to be found that would be anatomically distinctive about dyslexic brains, their only differences being in the ways they have learned to function. However, "interweaving functional with anatomical knowledge," as Geschwind advised, I, for one, am glad to find myself able to accept what looks like sound new evidence. It will not be the first time theory has accommodated itself to fact.

It does still seem to be true, and important, that what I have called the dyslexic cast of mind is a persistent factor in individual lives. It appears to be determined by both heredity and prenatal events. This is, so to speak, the permanent ground plan, always affecting the nature of the developing person and his ways of learning. At the same time, what goes on within his personal structure, and what issues from it, is constantly being modified by learning. Words of invariance, such as all, always, and never, seldom fit the realities of nature. Under reasonably favorable circumstances, experience has shown that as near optimum results can be achieved by the dyslexic as by the nondyslexic person with otherwise equivalent powers.

It is an important task of society's elders to lend each neophyte their expertise to substitute for his immaturities and innate ineptitudes, whatever they may be, until he has achieved for himself those ways of maturity that each must learn. The opportunities and pitfalls of humanity's long and useful childhood fill the elders' lives, too, with challenges.

If, for example, the term dyslexia applies to the young person's kind of mind, we want to know how to help him to see that fact as a liberating explanation for certain of his shortcomings, not an excuse for their continuance. Appropriately taught, he can use it as a condition to be met and a source of growing strength.

A sketch of the fully developed person with a dyslexic cast of mind will show him like any other person, as a whole, multidimensional being of almost infinite variety and true uniqueness. He will not be diminished, but rather strengthened by the knowledge and use of his powers, the conquest of his difficulties, and a proud and satisfying appreciation of continued growth. His well-developed sense of his own accepted self will inform his sensitivity to the differences of others and their right to such differences. Further he will know the beauties of fellowship and mutual helpfulness with each particular person in his life, and also with small and larger groups in terms of varied interests and common humanity.

Knowing that he has a good mind, whatever its complex constitution, and more potentialities than a single lifespan will give him time to develop, he should be moving toward a sense of fulfilment because he is in a continuing state of growth [which is my definition of a State of Grace].

But, you say, all these qualities and experiences could be ascribed to *anyone*. In my view, that is just the point. Whatever his position with regard to language mastery, the individual at the center of our discussion is capable of becoming such a person. As you and I consider together the education of his teachers what could be more appropriate than that we should have given primary attention to the *nature* of the *dyslexic learner?*

3

Language Learning Differences in Plain English

Language learning differences are coming to seem very real to many people, and so it should be possible to discuss them in that plain English which seems closest to where we really live.

Often, we explore the nature of man and his world in fields of science where plain English is not much spoken. But if we construct a verbal map of these territories with geographical features and place-names consistent with our familiar body of experience, we feel more at home and, at the same time, more ready to see well-known landscapes in a new light. It is a truism that one's own backyard, freshly studied, is a good starting-point for examining and enlarging—even reordering—one's world outlook.

A Boy's-Eye View

One of the inhabitants of my own imaginary backyard is the 10-year-old who said of his language problem, "What's *wrong* is my *words*. I forget them!" I have always liked that Anglo-Saxon simplicity. It may be worth our while to examine the problems of language learning which some people call dyslexia in company with this fictionalized lad who has come to be a real character in my world under the appropriately Old English name of Alfred. Let Al do the speaking:

What's wrong is my words. It always has been. It makes me mad, because I can understand and I can think. It's just the words. When I was very little they said I didn't seem to hear folks talk, although I heard the bell ring and the dog bark—but I soon caught on. I knew what Mom and Dad were saying, but I got my own sounds tangled up and couldn't say what I wanted to. Sometimes I couldn't think of the right words. Sometimes I still can't,

Reprinted with permission from *Academic Therapy* 7(4):411–419 1972 and from The Orton Dyslexia Society, Reprint No. 40.

but now I can think of others, and after a while the right ones sometimes pop up.

About the biggest trouble with me is that I forget the words I want to read. Either I just can't learn them, or I work very hard and do learn them, only I forget them right away, or some I know so I mostly get them right but without warning they get away. Then the other kids say I'm dumb, and I know the teacher and my folks think so, too, whatever they say. I guess I am, because I know I work hard, even though the grown-ups say I'm lazy. You should hear my teacher. She gets mad when I forget. She says, "You know that word. You knew it yesterday. You could read it if you'd only try!" But I can't help it. I do try, but I forget, even if only some of the time.

I have a hard time with writing and spelling, too. I can't seem to make the words look right. That is harder than reading them, because I have to think them up in my own mind and make them just right, no guessing. Make one letter wrong and you're done! I know why they say, "Mind your p's and q's." I'm always getting them backwards; b's and d's, too, and lots of others, and when I mean to write *saw* it's just as likely to come out *was*, or *left* may get to be *felt*. Lots of times they don't even look like real words, they are so twisted up.

Then there is the trouble with what I write—nobody else can read it. I can't read it myself, to tell the truth. It doesn't look the way I mean it to, and my hand gets all tightened up and tired. It's slow, too. People are always saying, "Do hurry up! You're keeping us all waiting." I feel like a dummy. I get so fed up I have to go to my shop and make something—and then do I catch it for not doing homework!

My big brother used to have trouble, too, but he can read now. He still can't spell, though, and he gets bad marks on his high-school work because of that. My older sister stutters like nobody's business. Dad says my little brother is "all thumbs and has two left feet!" My baby sister (she's four)—well, just try to understand her! But to hear them talk about my other two sisters, well, they just whizzed through school and college, and everybody asks, "Why can't you be bright like that?"

My dad says to cheer up, though, because he was dumb in school and hated it—but look at him now. Maybe he can't tell left from right, but he has a good job with high pay, and he says I'll probably be able to make a living, too. Actually, we have a lot of mixed-up lefties in our family, like my mom and Uncle Jim, but I can use one hand about as well as the other, one for some things and the other for others. I tell you, we're a crazy, mixed-up family, all right!

They gave me some tests the other day and the man says I'm bright but that I've got real problems. He can say that again! I heard the man who gave the tests tell Mom it was "a bad case of dyslexia"* or something like that. It sounded so awful Mom cried. He said we could do something about it if we just get the right teacher, one who can teach me the way I can learn. All I have to say is let's hurry, because this word business is driving me crazy. I'm either going off my head or I'm going to get mad and smash things up.

Say It in "Plain English"

Now Alfred is so understandably bothered by his inability to read and spell that his overriding concern is, "Let's get busy and do something about it, *but* quick. I don't care much about *why*. Just help me get out of this mess!" I have made up a composite, intelligent Alfred. Although not all children nor all families with language learning difficulties have all the problems he describes (their variety seems almost infinite), still the patterns go together.

Perhaps we can carry the linguistic exercise one step further and put the whole subject more nearly in Al's language than is usually done. It may help those of us who work in the field when we try to explain to our students and some of their elders what it is all about. Furthermore, the very act of translation may help us clarify and sharpen our own thoughts. Besides, what's wrong with sometimes talking in plain English even just among ourselves?

Here, then, is an attempt to state as simply as is possible some background knowledge of how we all learn human language, and an outline of our aims and methods in helping children to master this all-important tool of thought and communication.

First a child has to know how to understand the talk he hears and how to talk so that other people can understand him. He has to be able to listen and speak the way people around him do, and that means to think in words and be able to find in his head the words with which to say what he means.

Most children of five or six, anywhere in the world, can do this very well. They use their mother tongue skillfully. If they can't do so, it is the grown-ups' job to help them learn whatever they lack. After that, the growing person goes on all his life learning more and more about using words for speaking and thinking. To help him with this is the job of all of his schooling, and of his family, and of the world in which he lives. But maybe he gets most of it from the learning he does for him-

---

*Note that *all* the rest of Al's words have common English roots.

self because he wants to do it and because he can do it as a human being, and not just a bright beast.

All American children have seen a lot of words in print by the time they get to kindergarten and first grade. Most of them know, or are ready to learn, that words in print or writing are spoken words stored up. You don't have to speak to someone, or hear him, to get meaning across from one to the other. With 26 letters in English, you can write down signs for all the English language sounds you make; then the reader can turn them back into the words you were thinking. You think it in your mind, write it down in the order in which the sounds come in speech, using the letters the other person expects. Then he can read what you have said, either out loud or to himself in his mind. This is handy, because you don't have to worry about being with him or making yourself heard. Besides, what you say will keep forever this way. You can read it yourself tomorrow, in case you might forget, and your great-grandchildren can read it many years from now, if they should happen to want to.

That is how you find out what's been written on the page; but the meaning behind the words is what you are really after. Otherwise, who would bother to write or read? If this point is clear in your mind, you will be able to understand what you read at least as well as you can understand the spoken words. It will seem worth the work of learning how the language plan goes for reading and, if you want to, for writing so that other people can read what you have to say when you are not with them. Everybody knows that reading is not just calling out words. Why would anyone bother to do that, unless maybe to read aloud to a blind friend about something he could understand but you couldn't? That might be useful, but not very often! Reading for yourself is something you can do any time and all your life, to find out things and for fun.

But you are not born knowing how to read and write; you have to learn how. For some lucky people this is so easy they don't seem to think much about it. They just do it. Most people have to work at it for a while but it is fun, like learning how to work out a puzzle. For some people this learning is harder, sometimes very hard indeed; but we feel sure, because we have seen it happen so often, that just about all the people, even those who have the hardest time, can learn to read as well as they can think. Writing may be harder, and spelling almost always is; but most people can learn them at least well enough to make themselves understood.

When a person thinks well, we say he is bright. But how bright he is and how easily he learns the skills of reading and writing seem often not to go together. Some not very bright people can read fairly smoothly. Which is all right if people don't ask them to do thinking-work which is beyond them. On the other hand, some very bright people have a very hard time learning to read and find writing even harder because of spelling. This puts a real block in their road in school, but the worst thing it does is to make grownups think that the children who have trouble are dumb and lazy. Worst of all, sooner or later the children come to think this way about themselves. Then everybody gives up. A child may stop trying, or he may strike back by acting silly or naughty or doing something he knows is bad.

Things don't have to be this way. Not all children have the same ways of learning. Often (but not always) we can tell which children will be likely to find it hard to learn to read and spell and in what ways. If we find out early, as we mostly can, we can teach each child in the way that is best for him. Many such children learn so well that they don't know they might have had trouble if they had been started wrong— that is, using ways which were wrong for them even if these ways worked well for many other children.

This does not mean each child has to be taught all by himself, unless he has been on the wrong track for years, or has bumped along only halfway on the track that is right for him, before someone finds out what is wrong.

Two things we can count on—what human beings are like, in general, and what our own language is like.

How We Learn English

Human bodies and minds and senses work, by and large, in the same ways. But this is only "by and large." There are many paths by which a person's growth and learning can lead him to the goals he needs to reach as a human being. He learns about the world through his senses as he lives in the world and learns habits of dealing with it, *but when he learns how to learn, his mind is the master of his learning.* If he learns with all his senses they check and help each other to tell his mind about the world so he can see how it goes together, plan what he wants to do, and carry out his plans.

Nobody knows *exactly* how the brain works. One thing we do know, though, is that the part of brain-work that has to do with words —listening and speaking, reading and writing, understanding and thinking in words—is done in the left half of the brain in almost all people. We are not born that way. The right half of the brain can be just as good a boss as the left, and in a few people it is. To have one side running things, for language, seems to get them done most quickly and with least mix-up, both when we are learning language and when we are using it. If all our senses and our word thinking have strong habits of working the same ways and together with each other, then we are skilled masters of language.

Not all people reach this goal easily. Some seem to do it largely by themselves, without thinking about how it happens. Others seem to need lots of help and practice every step of the way. Most of us are in between, with hard spots and easy places mixed and needing to be sorted out so we can make our learning pay off.

We can't say, "Left brain, do this; you are the boss," the way we say, "Right foot, kick the ball." We have to get the left-brain habits worked out by as much practice as we need, wherever we need it. We have to practice, but we don't have to learn every small part of the whole, or even each single skill, like reading or spelling, by itself. Because we can think and plan and reason, we can learn how to learn. This leads to shortcuts and to becoming our own teachers.

This knowing how to learn also helps us feel sure of ourselves for two reasons. First, we have the know-how, and we know it. Second, when we forget something we know we can work it out again. Mostly we will have learned to do it without always thinking about how. That means the person is really free to put his mind on the meaning—what someone else has said and written down and also what he himself wants to say and to write down for someone else to read. Still, it is good not to have to be scared about forgetting, which can still happen any time without warning. There is safety in being able to think your way out. Besides, when you are not worried about forgetting you are not so likely to forget, so it seems.

This is how human beings learn language. We are not exactly alike, but we are enough alike to have the same goal and to be able to reach it by learning with our bodies, senses, and brains.

The Language We Learn

There is a second big field to think about along with the way we learn language, and that is the language itself. Every people in the world, no matter how simple their lives may seem to us, has a well-worked-out language, with words and a plan for putting them together—a grammar. Not all of these languages have been written down, and those that are written do not all use the same ways of writing. Each has a plan for speaking which all its speakers use and, if it has a written form, a plan for writing. Without these patterns people could not understand each other. Nobody is born knowing any of these things, but just about every person is the world is born able to learn them. His elders teach him the language they use, and he grows up speaking Chinese or Eskimo or English—or whatever he hears.

In the English language, as in all others, the spoken words are not things or happenings or feelings or thoughts—they only stand for them, and you have to know English to know what is in the speaker's mind or to let him know what is in yours.

In English, and the many other languages which use the alphabetic, or letter-sound plan, a sign on paper stands for a sound. When the signs are written (or printed) in the order and groupings in which the sounds are spoken, a person who knows the language can put the written signs back into sounds blended into spoken words and get at the meanings they stand for. In English, 26 letters are all the signs we need (instead of, for instance, the many thousands of Chinese). The rules and the plan for putting these signs together to stand for the language we speak are not simple, but they can be learned by any person who can think, if we teach him by the ways in which he can learn. Besides, this is the way our language is put together, and it makes sense to learn it as it is so we can make it work the way we want it to, and not just let it happen to us. This is part of being human.

Some children seem able to pick up the language plan and use the rules just from what they hear and see around them, without thinking much about it. They can use shortcuts right from the start. Many other children need to have the sign-sound plan shown to them and to have some help at the beginning. After that they can stand pretty much on their own feet. More children than most people think need even longer and more careful help with these first steps. If they get it in class early enough, thoroughly enough, and through all the learning pathways together (seeing, hearing, speaking, moving, touching), they may never have much trouble. A few children may need a great deal of help, right from the start. Older children who had a bad start need to go back to the beginning and learn how language goes together. They generally find it helps to learn by the *thinking* way, rather than the "try again and see if you get it *this* time" way. Each will need his own teacher who knows as much as she can about how English is put together and how it works and just what kind of things are easy and hard for this student, so that they can work well together.

Of course, if a child already knows how to do something and can do it, he should not have to spend time on it. There is plenty else for him to do. But he should have all the help he needs, not only to keep him out of schooling trouble but to keep him learning at his best. He may not want to know as much as his elders do about his language, and he won't want to have it forced on him. Still, many children find that the way we think, and how we let each other know our thoughts through language, are as much something they want to know about as anything else about themselves and their lives. Why not give them all they want and give it to them straight, in words they can understand, but without talking down to them?

If each child is getting what he most needs and wants to know, he will learn a lot more and have more fun and zest in school and in life.

A Summary in Technical Terms

It takes much longer to say it in plain words, than it does to put a similar message in more technical terms. Each form may have its uses. Technical terms are useful shortcuts when everyone involved agrees on their definition. However little interest Al and some of elders may have in such a statement, his teachers and their professional colleagues may find value in a concise, precisely worded formulation of these ideas for review and reference, such as the one which follows.

The goal in language teaching and learning is the rapid, smooth, automatic mastery of the communicative process for the reception and transmission of symbolic language, built generally on consciously acquired and retrievable systematized structure. Such mastery should lead to a sense of competence and enjoyment in linguistic activity in thought, in spoken language, and with the printed word.

The acquisition of competence in human language is dependent upon the anatomical status and the physiological development of the sensory and cortical components underlying the language function. These, in turn, depend upon constitutionally, probably genetically, determined primary equipment, influenced by physical, sociocultural, intellectual, emotional, and educational factors. There are large and small individual differences, based on wide variations in these components and their dynamic interaction. Specific to the language function itself there appears to be a continuum of degrees of natural aptitude. This aptitude seems much less causally related to intelligence or environmental factors than is often assumed on the basis of their frequently significant mutual interaction.

Whatever the nature and status of language-learning aptitude, language functioning seems to be modifiable, not only by adverse circumstances, but positively, by appropriate educational intervention for the prevention and correction of disabilities. When the language is English, such education should take full account and advantage of its linguistic structure and its alphabetic-phonetic writing system (both of them complicated but largely predictable), as well as of both the generalized and the idiosyncratic neuropsychological nature of the individual learner. Appropriate educational procedures need to be carried on in an emotionally therapeutic climate and with flexibility in adapting to individual needs and interests. At the same time, they ought to be rational, structured, systematic, cumulative, and thorough, and seem most effectively taught through the simultaneous and integrated training of the visual, auditory, and kinesthetic (tactile-proprioceptive) modalities, with heavy reliance on conscious, thoughtful, cognitive learning to promote independent competence and ongoing heuristic development.

Speaking the Language of the Host Country

There are many linguistic modes between the Anglo-Saxon and Old French derivatives of Alfred's manner of speech and the heavy reliance on words of Latin and Greek origin in the technical summary of the same ideas. Effective communication and common courtesy both dictate that we should first take the trouble to find out how the other people in any conversation think and talk, and then use the same language. On the varied uses of words, no one has put it better than Humpty Dumpty: "The question is, which is to be master [you or the words] that's all." He's right, whether one's purpose is to talk with specialists in the council house, or to walk through the woods in the same kind of moccasins as some other fellow-traveler, as we move toward a common destination of understanding and helpfulness.

4

A Physician's Primer on Dyslexia

Layman and professional alike, we all tend to fit any strange phenomenon into our familiar frames of reference. Life is such a complicated affair that it is rare that any patient will not have at least some symptoms or circumstances to which one could attribute school failure. If, however, further inquiry reveals learning problems, even though the child "seems bright" and there are no physical findings to account for his failure, it is quite possible that his is a case of dyslexia.

This condition, since its first published descriptions, has been called by 40 or more names, some emphasizing symptomatology, some etiology, some social or educational problems, some indications for treatment, and some a mixture of these and other elements. First it was called congenital word-blindness by Drs. Hinshelwood, Morgan, and Kerr, working independently in England in 1895 and 1896. While Hinshelwood later thought of these cases as probably more numerous in fact than on record, it remained for the American neuropathologist and psychiatrist, Dr. Samuel T. Orton, and his associates to demonstrate the prevalence of specific language disability or strephosymbolia (the twisted symbols of which the patient may be complaining). A now commonly used term is dyslexia, or, more accurately, developmental dyslexia. In 1968, nineteen members of the World Federation of Neurology's Research Group on Developmental Dyslexia were drawn together from four continents to discuss this world-wide problem. In a rare instance of international and professional unanimity, they came up with this definition of dyslexia: "A disorder in children, who, despite conventional classroom experience, fail to attain the language skills of reading, [writing and spelling] commensurate with their intellectual abilities." Having ruled out the things it was *not*, they agreed that this disorder " . . . is dependent upon fundamental cognitive disabilities which are frequently of constitutional origin."

We may look upon these children as being at the ineptitude end of

Adapted from "I can think, but what's wrong is my words." *Medical Insight* 2(12):27–39 1970.

the continuum of a capacity for learning human verbal language, which is the last skill acquired in human evolution—one requiring a most complex integration of cortical functions. Recent evidence from the laboratories of neurophysiology and neuropsychology tends to substantiate Orton's hypothesis. However, since many man-hours have been spent on the question of definition without universal agreement, perhaps it is better left at the level of the patient's self-diagnosis, for it is here that we may be able to do something immediately helpful. "What's wrong is my words. I forget them—the look, sound and feel of them—even though the grown-ups say I am bright and have nothing else wrong with me, and I've had schooling that worked all right for the other kids."

How many of these children are there? Figures vary widely because of differences in definition and standards of case selection. This is only part (but a very significant part) of the nation's admittedly serious reading problem. The dyslexia component of the problem is estimated to be 10 percent of the otherwise normal population. These persons have sufficient disability to prevent them from attaining functional competence in school; another estimated 10 percent is unable to achieve at or near their intellectual potential. Many of these young people are unrecognized or inadequately treated. But once the physician is aware of the syndrome, he is likely to find quite a few of them among his patients. There are at least four boys to each girl. Dyslexia occurs among the middle-class and well-to-do families as well as among those of lower socioeconomic status, although the complications of poverty seem to exacerbate any condition. My own experience suggests that in our current justifiable concern for the disadvantaged, we may be overlooking the needs of the non-poor children, condemning them to failure or underachievement, with personal and social consequences which are wasteful at best, and often disastrous.

These results may be devastating for any child, in terms of frustration and loss of a sense of self-worth, especially during the school years, when achieving competence is the main business of psychosocial development. We see this in the disruption of school, home, and neighborhood life, and in the high rate of school failure, dropout, delinquency, unemployability, and neurotic disturbance among unhappy and frustrated nonreaders. It is particulary striking in the relatively unproductive lives of those who "just get by," functioning far below the levels of their potentialities.

Children may, and often do, have more than one handicap, be it physical, neurological, emotional, socioeconomic, or educational. But when a child is presenting problems of behavior or physical symptomatology, it is helpful to include the language learning dimension in assessment of cause and in planning of desirable treatment. The doctor will be alerted by findings or history of:

Early incomprehension of speech, delay in learning to talk, persistence of misarticulation, distortion of sound-sequence in speech, difficulty in word-finding and self-expression, marked and persistent stuttering or cluttering;

After school entrance, inadequate or erratic memory for printed words, reversal of orientation or sequencing in spatial patterns, with consequent misreading of words, lack of development of adequate word-attack skills in spite of some instruction (which, to be sure, is by no means universally to be counted upon);

Spelling which ranges from the frequently unconventional to the bizarre, and is generally below the level of reading competence (which, in turn, is likely to be below achievement in arithmetic and other subjects insofar as they are not dependent on reading);

Penmanship which may (or may not) be slow, poor in form, irregular in slant and general appearance and often not as the writer intends it to come out;

A kind of nonspecific clumsiness or perhaps motor difficulty shown only in the writing of letters and numbers while large and small muscle skills often permit excellence in sports and in fine handwork such as model-building;

Late choice of handedness and continued confusion or uncertainty about left and right, geographical directions and, in extreme cases, other dimensions, such as time and up-down, and the like;

Familial incidence of any of the above symptoms, in variable patterns.

Emotional disturbance, whatever its manifestations, may be either concurrent or consequent upon the language problems, but is, our experience suggests, seldom specifically causal. When present, as it usually is, it serves to tangle the evidence and sometimes to complicate the treatment, although success in learning often obviates the necessity for specific treatment of the emotional problems.

A few simple tests in his office will take the examining physician a long way toward a tentative diagnosis of dyslexia and suggest further referrals to colleagues with special fields of competence in this respect. In this quick series of screening tests one might ask the child to do the following tasks: write his name; tell the date of his birthday; name the days of the week and tell which comes before Wednesday and after Thursday; point to his own left ear with his right hand and tell which is the left hand of the examiner who sits facing him; read a short paragraph which seems to the examiner "probably too easy" and then one or two progressively harder ones; write in his own spelling, "I am a big boy," and "This is my very best writing." If he is older, he might write a few sentences or a short paragraph to dictation and read a paragraph from a newspaper. Let him draw a bicycle and hop across the room on one foot and back on the other. It is surprising how much the physician can thus find out about his young patient's language-related development in a very short time.

If dyslexia seems the likely verdict, a refinement of diagnosis is highly desirable before treatment is begun. Ideally, one refers the child to a language disorder clinic, but these are regrettably scarce. A clinical psychologist should be consulted if possible. The results of group psychological tests, such as those given in schools, are unreliable for these children, since they rely on the use of verbal, often reading, skills and on clerical facility which are just the handicaps in question and which therefore intervene between the child's true intelligence and its demonstration. An assortment of other exploratory tests of visual, auditory, and motor skills and achievements can be drawn on as the experienced clinician thinks appropriate. Thus the specialist will substantiate and amplify the diagnosis and be able to advise the parents, either directly or through the physician, as to the appropriate educational treatment.

While there are more uncertainties and fewer justifiable pronouncements in this field than most, one can say with assurance that, "However the diagnosis is arrived at, the effective treatment of dyslexia depends on education." Appropriate remedial training administered individually, in a therapeutic climate by a skilled teacher with relevant special education and experience in this field, is the optimum answer. Some good work in early preventive programs with properly screened classes is now being done. Treatment of older children can sometimes be carried out satisfactorily in very small groups. However, students differ so widely that the efficiency of the instruction is likely to be less than in the situation in which teaching can be individually tailored to the initial and developing needs of the child.

The absolutely necessary condition for this sort of program, however, is the careful, continuous supervision by a highly qualified specialist-teacher. The remedial education of a dyslexic child is not a job for an amateur, no matter how kindly, well-meaning, or even skilled in some other form of teaching or helping. The chances of failure are too great, and *this* child cannot afford another failure or the time which would be largely wasted en route to such failure!

During the past 65 years, educational procedures have been refined which do make the successful education of most dyslexics possible. The best of these are closely tied to understanding of the neurophysiological and neuropsychological development of the human being, the structure of the language to be taught, and the individual patterns of strengths and relative weaknesses of each diagnosed individual. "Teach the language as it is to the child as he is," is the maxim often used. But the actual process is by no means simple. The underlying principles were formerly held to be uniquely appropriate to children with language disabilities, but are now beginning to be accepted as desirable in general curricula; for dyslexic children they are quite essential.

Since whole words are configurations too large and complicated for these youngsters to master and retain as units, they are broken down into their coded elements, the sounds of speech and the letters used to represent them. The objective is to make the components of language automatically useful in reception, formulation, and expression of thought; but at the same time to build in a set of rescue-techniques, to be used in moments of unpredictable breakdown to which the dyslexic individual will always be more or less prone. These constitute a store of back-up knowledge, by the conscious use of which the dyslexic can think his way out of an impasse.

What is the outlook for these children? Can they be helped to "make it" in an America built on a foundation of literacy? We have described, of course, a fictitious composite of the many boys and girls known to diagnosticians and teachers of dyslexic youngsters. However, given recognition of their problems and support in solving them, dyslexics need not fail, nor even lower their academic and vocational sights.

On a case basis there are many hundreds, even thousands, of young people who, over nearly 65 years, have been helped back into the academic mainstream, or, identified early, have been so taught that they never left it. Unfortunately, not many of their stories have been published, either biographically or as contributions to statistical studies, but they do exist. Under even reasonably favorable circumstances, experience encourages us to say that a dyslexic student of any age, child or adult, can learn to read up to the level of his intelligence, to write legibly though perhaps not beautifully, and to spell well enough to hold his own until his wife, his secretary, or his computer can take over.

Biographies of such illustrious men as Edison, Hans Christian Andersen, Harvey Cushing, Albert Einstein, Auguste Rodin, A. Lawrence Lowell, and many others, including perhaps the greatest of them all, Leonardo da Vinci, give evidence that their subjects struggled with some of the same problems which plague today's dyslexics. Like many lesser folk they made some adaptations and went on with their careers. Many others, less able to cope with their difficulties, have joined the ranks of the quietly, or unquietly, desperate.

We cannot, in the present state of knowledge, prevent dyslexia, any more than we can prevent tone deafness or make tolerable musicians of everyone, but enough is known so that we can prevent many of the consequent problems. If we identify these individuals with variant learning patterns as early as we can, and often this is the physician's opportunity, and give them the right kinds of educational help, we can make a large contribution toward the solution of the problems of school failure, illiteracy, underachievement, and the waste of one of our most valuable national resources—human potentiality.

5

Social Implications of Dyslexia

Effects of Dyslexia on Others

In many of the papers in this volume we are looking at social relations from the inside, but what about the outside view? How does the rest of the world look at the person, especially the dyslexic person, and how does it treat him? Of course, there are many factors in each ordinary social situation, but we are focusing on one often troublesome aspect of life where it is possible, even with present knowledge, to alleviate discomfort and liberate large numbers of individual persons to manage a more satisfying life. If we start where we know we can do something constructive, who knows but that this will open the way to improvement in other areas and the solution of other problems which now seem overwhelming.

Family life seems a good place to begin considering the outward social implications of dyslexia. We can consider the inter- and intrapersonal effects of the dyslexic child on the parents and siblings, and all of this on the quality of family life. Fear, guilt, resentment, tensions of misunderstandings, blame, jealousy, and other negative feelings are rife. Until understanding and help are obtained there is little room or energy for compassion, helpfulness, comradeship, respect, and appreciation—ingredients of love—but they, too, *can* flourish in families beset by dyslexia. Grandparents and other relatives, family friends and neighbors are important, as are associates in church and other social connections of the family.

When the dyslexic person grows up he is still his complicated dyslexic self, as illustrated in Eileen Simpson's moving autobiography (1979). No matter how well he has learned to cope, as this author has done, the results of the battle with dyslexia are part of how he (or she)

Reprinted with permission from *Dilemmas of Dyslexia*. Proceedings of a Conference at University of Virginia 1979.

relates to the new family of adulthood as husband and father, or wife and mother, as citizen.

Family stability and viability are too complicated as a set of inter-relationships for us to say it is dyslexia which *causes* domestic dissension, divorce, dependency, desertion, or other specific ills; but it is certain that the language problem does not help in any of these situations. On the other hand, its resolution often does have a very beneficial effect on the troubled climate of family life and its unfortunate consequences.

There is no magic, however it may sometimes seem. The student feels that he is understood, sees that improvement has already begun, that hope is realistic. He can drop some of the old burdens and begin to forge ahead. This, we know, is just a start. We have to make sure, as far as is humanly possible, that the reality continues to be favorable and that he realizes that someone is there to sustain him in hard places and discouraging plateaus, and that he, like his predecessors, can "make it." This is a joint venture of family, school, and treatment agent.

The relationships of the dyslexic child in the standard school are complicated and many-faceted, too. In the classroom he impinges upon his peers, sometimes disrupting, sometimes being the clown or the butt of their derision, which is bad for him and the deriders. This behavior sometimes interferes with his classmates' education and often his teacher's mental and physical health when she is unable to cope with him. In his general school life he's often in trouble for going "up the down staircase," being truant or belligerent or strange. Either in fact or in somebody's anticipation he may live in the "rotten apple syndrome" of being (or associating with) "bad company," the ringleader in school mischief, or a bad influence. He costs the school and resentful taxpayers money by having to repeat grades or requiring special educational facilities (expensive, however inadequate they may be). The world thinks of him as a nuisance; he thinks of himself that way. The self-fulfilling prophecy gets in its work and things may go from bad to worse. Of course, they don't have to. Answers are available, and they are cost-effective in the long run. The word is getting around, but it is still hardly a full chorus in crescendo.

In community life, the kid who "can't do"—especially if he doesn't excel in sports or has what his peers think of as maverick tastes, doesn't know the words of current songs and the like—is unlikely to bring out the best in others. Think of what happens in the neighborhood, church, playground, ball club, corner store, everywhere. Many adults see him as undesirable, a neighborhood contaminator, and so he comes to see himself. The adult attitudes of guilt, wish-fulfillment, and so on could stand some looking into, but it is still the dyslexic youngster who too often bears the brunt, added to the already heavy realistic burden he must bear in language learning without appropriate help. All this costs society dearly, both in money and in the quality of life for all concerned.

What the sociologists are wont to call the social pathologies are generally mixed together into multifaceted problems which seem to defy solution. I don't think of dyslexia itself as a social pathology (and this I would emphasize), but because of society's ineptitude in dealing with it, it often gets entangled with such identifiable conditions as economic disorders, physical and mental ill-health, antisocial behavior of both youngsters and adults, suicide, and general human wastage.

In the economic world there are many reasons for unemployment and unemployability: real mental subnormality, the circular effects of impoverished home and neighborhood background, psychological and emotional conflict at home or within the individual, bias and prejudice of bosses, disease, malnutrition, and a host of other factors. In the presence of these unfortunate conditions some people do still succeed in coping with life. A few investigators have undertaken to find out why so many do not, but again, the causes seem to be multiple. One thing is sure, however; the illiterate or ill-schooled person is at a severe disadvantage in most economic situations. He may be where he is for a variety of reasons, but dyslexia is often a major contributing factor, and it is one which we can do something about. I, for example, recall a Job Corps Center in Texas and a program for "unemployables" in California where the sorting out of dyslexics (about one-third of the illiterate or educationally inadequate clients) and their appropriate teaching achieved excellent results. During the Depression physicists sold apples on street corners, but most breadlines and unemployment offices today are largely peopled by functionally illiterate job- or relief-seekers.

The costs at this extreme level are obvious, but the often hidden costs of unfulfilled potential to both society and the marginal or incomplete persons themselves are no less real for being less visible. Despite vast effort and printer's ink expended, one cannot be sure in any given case whether such situations as dependency, illegitimacy, and the like are cause, consequence, or simply complicating concomitance with learning difficulties of one sort or another. In any case, being unable to compete in a literate technological world has nothing to be said for it, especially when the conditions could be alleviated.

Results of Unremediated Dyslexia

The toll taken by physical and mental ill-health has been noted many times in individual cases. People who are looking for causes tend to find them in the fields they know best. Still, there are some items of case evidence and a few studies which should give one pause to think.

Emotional Disorders

Years ago, beginning in 1934, Lauretta Bender observed that at least 50 percent of the children treated for behavioral and psychiatric disorders at Bellevue Hospital in New York had severe reading problems and that many of them responded well to appropriate tutoring. Kline and associates (1968) reported on the treatment of 50 cases of behavior disorders associated with school failure at a community mental health center. Instead of beginning with the customary psychotherapy program, the children were assigned to tutors qualified to teach by a structured, multisensory approach. For most of these youngsters, successful work on their language problems appeared to eliminate the emotional disorders or alleviated them to such an extent that they readily became manageable at home and in school. One child needed psychiatric help along with tutoring, and only one had to be treated first by the psychiatrist. For most of the students, this was truly a case of *Tutoring as Therapy* (Arthur 1946).

Then there is an, alas, not unique boy I know named Mickey who was rescued, literally, in the nick of time after five years of school failure which had driven him to the brink of emotional disintegration and hospitalization. A well-known clinic had diagnosed him as severely dyslexic at six, and, on each yearly visit thereafter, recommended placement in a special school. Each year the local authorities insisted they had a program for him, and provided what the clinic characterized as inappropriate and inadequate teaching. A more serious emotional situation developed year by year until the only placement the school could offer was one for seriously emotionally disturbed children. Fortunately for Mickey, that facility was filled when he finally went out of control. Although its children are not in that category, the school originally recommended was persuaded to give him a trial. Apparently the clinic had been right, for Mickey now appears indistinguishable from his schoolmates unless one reads his record and knows the wounds which may take a long time to heal. (One wonders how many Mickeys there are in the facility which was too full to take him, a place where he could only have been made worse.)

Antisocial Behavior

The most obvious and perhaps best documented material on the relationship between social problems and dyslexia comes from the field of criminology, from the juvenile and adult penal systems. Among the juveniles are what are called the "statutory offenders": youngsters whose behavior gets them into trouble with the law because they are children, although it would not if they were adults. These include tru-

ants, runaways, and certain kinds of sex offenders. It is easy to see why
the statistics show approximately half of these children are school failures. A good many of them are dyslexic, though not all.

In a few schools for delinquents, reeducation has been a potent
means of improving life for the youngsters and their society. The cor-
rectional school at Gatesville, Texas, had one such program, and, I
hope, still does. My favorite story of what I like to call constructive
recidivism comes from there. A boy we'll call Tex was sent to this
school at the age of ten or eleven. It was found that he couldn't read, so
they put him in a program with a good tutor from the Scottish Rite
Hospital Language Unit in Dallas. Tex began to learn to read; he was
ecstatic. Then his time was up and he had to go back to the little town
where there were still no facilities for continuing his special help. Tex
did his best to persuade the authorities to keep him at the school until
he had really learned to read, but no, they couldn't do it. His place was
needed for some other incorrigible child. So Tex went home and did the
intelligent thing. He went downtown and broke a plate glass window
in one the stores so he would be sent back to the school to finish learning to read. Constructive recidivism!

Children don't usually start off with violent crimes, but one thing,
like a stolen car, may lead to another, to prison and graduation from
crime school. Alcohol and drug abuse and their results are other consequences. The costs are enormous both in dollars spent for apprehension and institutional care and in the loss which cannot be calculated,
except in the statistics of days *not* spent in productive labor, but which
may be thought of far into sleepless nights. As a delinquent youth, you
may be a bright guy and a good student and also become a super crimi-
nal; or you may be stupid, a tool for the bright guy, and get caught. But
if you can't cope in the business of living and making a living you are
much more vulnerable, whatever your other characteristics. The high
percentage of the ill-educated among offenders is not, I am sure, an
accident (Ramos 1978).

Suicide

At the end of the line is suicide. An alarming number of young
people each year are driven, for one reason or another, to take their
own lives. The youngster who breaks windows, breaks rules, and
breaks and enters is at least still fighting back. He makes trouble and
often gets attention—of a sort. It may make bad matters worse, but at
least somebody *may* be clever enough and concerned enough to reach
him. The suicide, however, is often a bright and law-abiding boy or
girl—although he may be filled with hatred for the adults who do not
understand his predicament. His chief hatred, though, is for himself.
Yet he may get some wry satisfaction from imagining what his final act

will do to avenge himself on his world. Chiefly, however, he is at the end of his rope—so he draws back and ties a hangman's noose in it. He is convinced that either he is hopelessly stupid or, if there is some way out, nobody knows it or will tell him about it.

Sometimes those who really care about such a youngster have spent agonizing years searching for a solution, only to be sent away time after time with the common turnoffs, put-downs, or there-now-it-will-be-all-rights. Consultants say: "See that he works harder" or "She should pay closer attention." There was Bernie's principal, who said to me, "Lower your sights; he may be one of our boys who just isn't ever going to be able to read." To another boy's mother a famous psychiatrist said: "If you don't take Nils out of school and apprentice him to a machinist, he'll soon be in a mental hospital as a schizophrenic. With his IQ of barely 100, he'll never make it through prep school." At 16, scared to death (literally, since he was thinking of suicide) by his failures and worry over his future, Nils had been almost unable to function during the tests, so one could see how the doctor came to his conclusion. The boy's mother, fortunately, was not awed but angered and searched further. Under more favorable circumstances, his IQ turned out to be 138 and his problem a long-unrecognized dyslexia. Now, a productive adult, he has a happy family life and satisfying job and is finishing his dissertation for a Ph.D. in electronics. But not all stories end so happily. Far too many young people take their own lives, as did Robin, whose story appeared in the *Bulletin of the Orton Society* (Jones 1978). The heartbreaking tragedy is that at least some of these bright and sensitive people could have been saved for satisfying and effective lives, as many others have been.

Other Attempts to Cope

Most of the dyslexic youngsters, however, do grow up, some more and some less successfully, some triumphantly, most with scars—as we have heard from Eileen Simpson (1979) and Michael Clarke (1973)—scars covering wounds which need not have been suffered. These youngsters deal with problems, as Roger Saunders says, with fright, fight, or flight. According to their specific ways of coping with life, they might be classified as the following.

1. *The Really Bad Guys.* These people had more kinds and degrees of difficulties than they knew how to handle; Lee Harvey Oswald may belong to this group (Thompson 1964). Not that all assassins are dyslexic, by any means; and most dyslexic individuals are, in spite of everything, "good guys."

2. *The Offenders.* Two in this group who still trouble my dreams are Charles of 1925 and Jim of 1952, victims of ignorance or social neglect, who may be still or again behind bars as when I last heard of

them. Another is Robert, who despite his parents' efforts and a tutor's diagnosis not heeded by the schools, is serving a life sentence for killing two policemen (Angell 1976; Rochmes 1976).

3. *The Defeated.* These are the suicides (whom Robert tried to join) and those who escape into severe mental illness.

4. *The Partial Copers.* Included in this group are those still *in* the world but not *of* it as much as they might have been. Some are secretive, like Jonathan's mother, who spent her life doing properly just what the world expected of a military officer's wife, all the while erecting anxious, elaborate barriers to anyone's knowledge of what seemed to her a shameful reality, her inability to read. Others lead lives of quiet desperation.

5. *The Recently Diagnosed.* Just knowing what the problem is, or even better having some corroborative tests, can make a lot of difference. A young woman recently said to me: "You mean I'm not stupid? This is a real thing and I *could* do something about it, whether I ever do or not?" What we sometimes call "diagnostic euphoria" can be counted on to last perhaps six weeks, during which time the possibility of progress had better be verified by initiated remediation.

6. *The Valiant Copers.* There are those who have succeeded in overcoming their handicap, thanks to their own preserverance and encouragement and help from caring parents. Among these are Thompson's (1969) "men of eminence": da Vinci, Einstein, Harvey Cushing, and many others. For each of these there are others, less well known, who have met common standards of success. Where does one draw the line of judgment?

Appropriate Remediation

The best results have time and again come from educational treatment of the right kind, administered by the right person and continued long enough. I could tell you heartening case story after story. We could go back to Samuel Orton's files, Anna Gillingham's records, and thousands of others in between. These successes, too, despite millions of persons still to be reached, are among the social implications of dyslexia. Most of the life-saving heroes are still unsung. There have been a few studies made and published, and more are now in progress. The cultural lag between formulation and practical action is beginning to be overcome.

Exactly what constitutes appropriate remediation? To promote one way of teaching rather than others might not be appropriate here. I can, however, report that the success of many cases in my files has depended to a large extent on what can be summarized as the "Orton approach." Very briefly, this involves early clinical diagnosis and educational treatment continued to the level of the student's independent competence (described elsewhere in this volume).

The result of appropriate remediation is one of the most important social implications of dyslexia. While there are at present many negative social consequences of this kind of mental makeup and developmental pattern, such consequences are not inevitable. We have evidence, I firmly believe, to show that almost every "intact" person (and even many who are less favored) can learn to read up to the level of his intellectual ability. He can generally learn to spell passably, if not always consistently, and to write at least legibly. Moreover, people starting with ineptitudes in the language learning fields often have not only high intelligence but important gifts in other areas which should be available to society. Technology, the arts, creative imagination, and holistic, spatial functioning are parts of the total heritage of *Homo sapiens*, with bihemispheric brain, which need to be fully liberated in the life of modern society.

People need not fail in school and life because of dyslexia. The costs of social and personal failure are too great for our society not to use all available knowledge, skill, and resources to press vigorously toward solutions of the problem. This we can and must do, in the interest of justice to individuals and for the positive health of society.

6

The Bright Future

It seems too obvious to need stating that, for good or ill or neutral areas of vantage, we bring to the world what the Good Book calls "gifts differing." It is well for the individual and the race that this is so, but, human life being what it is, the variety presents challenges. The good gifts we can (but don't always*) accept with rejoicing and use with profit. Those in the neutral areas are, by definition, the ones that are expected. We think of them as average, normal, unremarkable, and they are often unnoticed; they are taken for granted as needing no special attention; they are "just OK." It is one of the, shall we say, "negative gifts" or sets of traits and its concomitants which brings us here to face the problems and appreciate the rewards of the complex we may call "language learning ineptitude, type dyslexia."

As we consider the "ills that man is heir to" we observe that there are individuals, and often family lines, showing one type of vulnerability or another. We say "born that way," "runs in the family," or in current jargon, "is at-risk." Now if we can find wherein the real vulnerability lies and how it works we may be able to take countermeasures preventive of the damage to be caused by the "flowering of the vulnerable agent." For example, we know that the TB bacillus is the active agent in tuberculosis, that Isoniazid is its current prime antidote, and that active, outdoor living and good nutrition are important to prevention and cure. Patient A comes of a TB-vulnerable family. We can now be ready with the right conditions of life ahead of time for the family's young people, and at the first sign we can employ a further emphasis on a health promoting regime, including medicinal treatment if necessary. There is no longer reason for that family to fear TB as a death-sentence diagnosis as they quite properly did until about the middle of this century.

In the language area there is no active agent like a "dyslexia bacil-

Reprinted with permission from The Orton Dyslexia Society from *Annals of Dyslexia* 35:13–20 1985.
*Witness the plight of the academically-talented child in many a classroom.

lus" with which to do battle, but rather, if the neurologists are right in their recent papers and lectures (Annett 1981; Annett and Kilshaw 1984; Geschwind 1982b; Galaburda 1983; Galaburda and Kemper 1979), there are antecedents of dyslexia, real neuroanatomical antecedents, but they are not presently available to physical-chemical control. Perhaps they never will be and perhaps it is better so. At any rate, we cannot now get at the genes nor safely, considering all the possibilities, deal with the testosterone levels in utero or other possible constitutional dyslexia precursors. But we do know where to look for at-risk signs and, to some extent, how to meet them early and minimize their influence.

Some of the provisions desirable for all children in the course of ordinary nurture need to be especially emphasized at crucial points with those liable to language difficulties. If one of the critical periods for prevention is wholly or partially missed, cure must be resorted to as in the case of most of the children this paper's readership represents. In both TB and dyslexia we know effective treatments. Just physical regime is not enough, however essential, when a bacillus gets hold. Chemotherapy is necessary and effective in TB, and so is hygienic living. With dyslexia the emphasis is different, treatment is educational, not medicinal, though medical intervention may sometimes be needed supportively.

Empirically, but on a sound neuropsychological base, the needed educational treatment has been developed. Perhaps we can now see further into the reasons for believing that our educational approach is right. It works, that we know. We use it for reasons to be found in psychology and pedagogy, including the nature of man the learner and the nature of the language to be learned. We are adding scientifically derived support for what we do, speaking from the findings of the neurological specialties (Geschwind 1982b).

Now let us think of the content area of our teaching specialty— language, the language to be taught and learned. Study of language as language, in general, and of English, as the tongue we use, gives us as educators our prime cultural subject matter as well as the tool we use in teaching it. Further and deeper understanding of the brain and its processes shows how the mind learns to grasp and use language. However, for man to fulfill his purposes, play his hand well, he needs to develop the basic capacities which are the cards dealt him to begin with. One card, perhaps one whole suit, is language.

When can we say a person is well-endowed? Perhaps it is when he comes into the world with a brain that has an ample and well-structured, optimally functioning, set of neurons, served adequately by the appropriate chemicals and chemical processes. Being a human creature, and less than perfect or evolutionarily "finished" on the whole, he will not have a high, flat profile of capacities or aptitudes so he can do every human thing and do it well. But fortunately in many if not all parts of the Central Nervous System there seems to be redundancy; that is, there are lots of spare parts. There is a lot of variability in the language function, but it is not just of an odd, erratic, individual nature but as a characteristic of the human species. Language, after all, is the last physical, neurological, function to develop, both in the race and in the individual. Let us say we have just recently, through our neuroanatomical study, made a giant step in understanding the basis for this variation of the language function as found in the cortex of the brain.

Can we fit our new knowledge into the composite of already achieved observation and experience? Can we reconcile the new knowledge with the old and make the result serve either, or preferably both, of our twin goals: to *know* life better and to *make* life better? I think I see a way that satisfies me personally, at least for the present, and has relevance for our talk in this group of parents, teachers, and dyslexic students, about the "bright future" for dyslexics. I think we can tie together the brain research and the educational experience which constitute the special province of The Orton Dyslexia Society and its professional community. Given the present working state of the art and the redundancy of the brain's resources, we can talk pretty confidently about what Richard L. Masland (1976) once phrased as "the advantages of being the kind of person who may have difficulty in learning to read" —and, of course, master other languages skills.

Not only may our dyslexic (and those who share his gene pool) have extra competencies in other fields as a result of the same cause as his relative weakness in language learning, but, since none of us is perfect, he has perhaps been fortunate in the area of his imperfection. Dyslexia is, admittedly, a nuisance, perhaps a major one, but it is one we can do something about through management. It is important that we do not have to change the person drastically, surgically, chemically, but can teach him how to use to the full the capacity which needs strengthening.

His opposite number, the eulexic, who probably has an exceptionally endowed language cortex, learns to use his language largely without awareness. Most of us in the middle range master the needed skills with varying but reasonable amounts of effort. For the person whom we call dyslexic because he has a problem here, help, expert help, and often a lot of it is needed to get him on his linguistic feet, walking and striding (if not always sprinting) into his own proper future. Fortunately we do know how to give him this help. It is far easier, perhaps more possible, than to teach the verbally facile but unimaginative person to be creative.

That the dyslexic has constitutional strengths to balance his language skill discrepancies can no longer be brushed aside as mere compensation or hopefulness on the part of loving parents. Evidence is building up that this fortunate state of affairs could have its basis in the reality of relative richness of endowment in the nonlanguage parts of the brain, richness he can incorporate into his wholeness as a person. This is not to claim that every dyslexic is so endowed, but that giftedness of high order in other fields is common among dyslexic people; it should be sought out, cherished, and fostered to the benefit of us all.

When the dyslexic gets through to full literacy, as he surely can, (see, *inter alia,* Gottfredson, Finucci, and Childs 1983; Rawson 1968 and 1977) the experience of getting there may well have developed in him certain other characteristics that will stand him in good stead in any of his endeavors in life. He very often has in his arsenal: organization, cognitive power, adaptability, and the joy that comes of having tackled a hard job and seen it through to a satisfactory level. He has come to recognize his own competence and knows that he can win through again. He may well know himself better than does the chap to whom it all comes too easily. He will be in better position to appreciate others. These personal talents may be inborn, though they, too, may have needed awakening and specific guidance. He is, in short, likely to be a real, full-dimensional person, wherever he goes and whatever he undertakes.

This is reality, not just wishful thinking. The lives of successful dyslexics prove it. We point not only to the famous Einsteins and Edisons, but to the many useful, productive happy doctors, lawyers, engineers, plumbers, mechanics, and salesmen whose lives we have been privileged to share and whose histories we could talk about for many hours.

The future can be bright; dyslexics do and can succeed!

Part II
"The Treatment is Educational"

1

Education: Its Essence

To know and be part of his world is every child's birthright. To experience the sights, the sounds, the feel and the smell and the taste of it—city and country, in all seasons and weathers; to watch and feel kinship with animals and plants and their life cycles and to participate in them; to be intimately acquainted with rocks and streams, soil and sea, forest and lake—all are as important as to know his fellow man. To be aware in the present, to know of the past and how things and life came to be, to dream of the future as he may experience it and as it may be beyond his time are his predominantly human privilege. Not only to be and to grow, but to make and do, to try himself against reality, to bend it to his will or to merge himself with its forces as seems good and possible to him; to find purpose in his world and himself, stalwart courage to meet what comes; resourceful skills in coping with life's challenges; to have a basic sense of inner security which gives due realization to danger and evil, but which knows that, however biting the winds of adversity, he can deal with them with a spirit not broken but victoriously strengthened and enlarged; to relate warmly and empathetically to people, both taking and giving—sharing life positively with them in small ways and large; understanding, accepting, and welcoming diversity and coming to terms with it as constructively as lies within his powers, knowing its hazards and using well its positive potential—these he needs if he is to be a fully functioning, ever-growing human person.

These are the proper heritage of every human child. He comes into the world, we believe, with inherited potential. He is varied in strengths and qualities, but he is capable of becoming as fully human as his environment and his talents and limitations allow. It is the task and the privilege of society to provide the conditions that will permit and the stimuli that will trigger his built-in attributes and help him go forward, irrespective of the obstacles he confronts, even where inherently or environmentally the going is hard. To set the stage is society's responsibility. To help the new member learn how to play his part in his personal drama from curtain to curtain is the role of education, both as a whole and in its particular empahses as it relates to the needs and the developing purposes and values of each unique person.

2

Developmental Dyslexia:
Educational Treatment and Results

In the study, treatment, and prevention of the problems of dyslexia, one of the strengths of The Orton Dyslexia Society has been its promotion of interaction between theoretical and applied sciences, and the mutual respect of scientists, researchers and practitioners in several fields. This includes clinicians, technicians, teachers, parents, students or patients, and public. Each is uniquely important in the work of the others and essential in the whole enterprise. Their common purpose is the advancement of knowledge about the language function and facilitation of its development in human beings. In this paper we consider our common interest in providing effective treatment for those with specific needs in learning language.

Perhaps one of the most useful purposes served by collecting data for this paper has been the impetus it has given to bringing to light more material on the subject. In recent months I have searched the literature and corresponded and talked with well over 100 selected sources of information, and I am sure I have missed many more. Included have been medical and nonmedical clinics and agencies, independent schools and camps, public school systems and services, a few colleges, and many, many individuals—professionals, parents, and pupils or students. From them has come a helpful cornucopia of riches which has added greatly to the substance of this paper.

It will be of no surprise to you that I found great enthusiasm for the topic we are here considering. Everyone seems hungry to know what everyone else is doing, and with what results. There are many goldmines of unworked data in the files and minds of respondents, and some available statistics, varying from raw data in test figures and pro-

Reprinted with permission from The Orton Dyslexia Society from *Reading, Perceptions, and Language*:231–258 1975.

files to a very few sophisticated studies.* Some of the most enthralling contributions are the personal case histories of frustrated search, discovery, and full or partial success which have changed the lives of children and the people around them (McClelland 1973; Robinson 1969).

People in the helping professions, because of temperament and the pressures of their kind of work, are not very likely to design, initiate, and carry through high quality statistical studies, while those who are research-minded can usually find less amorphous or complicated and more tractable raw material elsewhere than in the domains of specialized educational treatments and their results.

Here, then, are some findings, gleaned from a lifetime of study and participant-observation in the field of language education and re-education, and a distillation of the enormous enrichment provided by recent contributions of colleagues summarizing what has happened in this specific area not only since the founding of the Orton Society, but since Orton's landmark paper of 1925.

Although Orton did not use it, in the interests of conciseness, I am going to use the term *dyslexia* in this paper with some frequency, mindful of its derivation given by Thompson (1966). If this produces semantic discomfort in any of you, please translate it into your favorite idiom representing language learning differences which sometimes give trouble. Perhaps we should have an ideographic expression, with no spoken counterpart, as in Figure 1, to flash on a screen whenever the idea comes up, but for the present paper, the *word* dyslexia will have to serve for the whole area of meaning.

For this language learning problem, educational treatment is obviously appropriate. Inevitably, treatment will have results of some kind. So we must focus on two things: first, the *educational treatment* of dyslexia, and second, the *results* of this treatment.

We are talking now specifically of *dyslexia* as just defined and not of other problems of learning, such as those related to intellectual, physical, sensory, environmental, or general educational inadequacies, which seem neither specific to language, nor causally primary. We speak of *educational* treatment, not of medical, physical, emotional, social or other approaches to alleviation. And we are considering *results* primarily in terms of *achieved competence in language skills*. This competence, in turn, provides one of the gateways to life which ought to be open to every citizen of a modern, literate society. This is by no means

---

*See for example references Atzesberger 1974; Bakker and Satz 1970; Critchley 1970; Cronin nd; East 1969; Hagin 1973; Hall 1974; Herjanic and Penick 1972; Kline et al. 1968; Kline and Kline 1975; Ley and Metteer 1974; Monroe 1932; Owen 1973; Rawson 1968; Silver and Hagin 1964, 1972; Strong 1973; Symmes 1972; Symmes and Rapoport 1972.

Figure 1.   *Ideographic representation of the idea of "dyslexia" in Chinese. Drawn for this paper by Che Kan Leong, who says the best translation is, "Reading difficulties in both read and spoken (languages)."*

to gainsay the importance of the aspects of life which we are here leaving out; they have been treated elsewhere, and as they should be.*

But language, the matrix of dyslexia, and at once the subject and the medium of this presentation, despite its richness, has severe limitations. By its nature it is time- and space-bound, for it is controlled by the utterance or representation of sounds and longer verbal forms in sequence. These determine the verbal mode of thought, of consciousness, and of communication from person to person. Words and phrases can carry both specific and connotative meaning, singly or simultaneously. But no matter how expertly we use them, they cannot represent all of life, or even all of a person's momentary life experience in all its dimensions. Still, within its limitations, verbal language is a useful and versatile tool, and a prime characteristic of man as a species. As we talk, there can and should be parallel awareness that the rest of life is still going on in dynamic interaction with linguistic thought and expression, including all those trains or fragments of thought to which we cannot simultaneously give utterance (Rawson 1971). Life is whole, though many-faceted (Rotzel 1971). It is to be divided into parts only to

---

*See references Ansara 1969; Blom and Jones 1970; Brutten, Richardson, and Mangel 1973; Hayakawa, Hamilian, and Wagner 1964; Johnson and Myklebust 1967; Kirk and Kirk 1971; Kolsun and Kaluger 1970; Money 1966; Rawson 1971; Ruchlis 1973; White 1970.

make its experience and development manageable within our human capacity to cope with its complexities. One of these complexities is the mastery by each new human being of the skills and nuances of the language of that culture into which he is born or in which he is reared —his mother tongue.

There is order and plan in every child's acquisition of verbal language (Rawson 1970a). The diagram of Figure 2 shows its fractions and their complex interactions. On the left are the audible or phonological components, the basic language of listening and speech, common in some tongue to every known culture. Spoken language is first to develop and almost inevitable in each child's life. On the right of the scheme are the visible or graphological components, reading and writing. These are taught and learned later, at what we call "school age," in literate cultures, and often they are mastered with difficulty. Cut the other way, the diagram shows, above, the receptive or input language (listening and reading) and, below, the expressive or output language (speaking and writing). All of these fractions interact continuously, as indicated by the arrows, through the mediation of the perceptual and cognitive processes of inner language, which goes on inside the brain. The diagram in Figure 3, modified from one originated in England by Agnes Wolff, shows the multisensory, intersensory linkages for learning of the language modalities. If we superimpose it upon Figure 2, it is

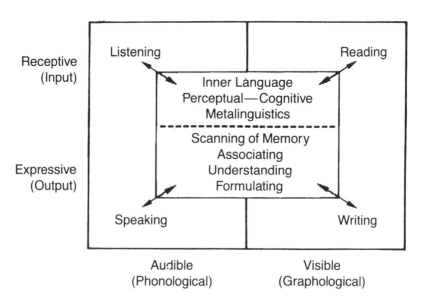

Figure 2.   Analysis of verbal language. (After Rawson 1968.)

SENSORY ASSOCIATIONS
IN LANGUAGE LEARNING

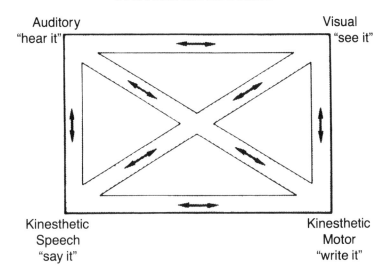

Auditory
"hear it"

Visual
"see it"

Kinesthetic
Speech
"say it"

Kinesthetic
Motor
"write it"

MBR after AGW

Figure 3.   Sensory associations in language learning. (After A.G. Wolff 1970.)

easy to see how well the two models fit each other—language, and its learning.

The rationale which we educators need to keep in mind is this: while symbolic thinking seems to be species-specific to *Homo sapiens*, its development into formulation and expression in a language must be learned from the individual's culture. This learning can be mediated only by the separate and integrated use of the sensory processes through whose gateways alone, as far as we can know consciously, man-on-the-inside is related to the-world-on-the-outside. The modalities particularly involved in language learning, as shown in Figure 3, are the auditory and kinesthetic-speech and the visual and kinesthetic-motor-tactile senses which relate, respectively, to the phonological and graphological modes of symbolic forms. The arrows suggest the mutual interaction of these senses as the learner hears while he speaks and looks while he writes, weaving a living tapestry of all the possible permutations. The keener each sense and the better it is both individually controlled and related to the others involved, the more effectively can the person function as *Homo sapiens*, the voluntary language user.

An effective educational approach will take into account the sensory aspects of language learning which all human beings have in common, and the almost infinite variations of individual capacities and their uses in learning. Our aim is to help the person develop each of the aspects of his learning, both separately and with the support and participation of the others (Childs 1968; Gillingham 1968; Gillingham and Stillman 1956, 1960; Orton 1937, 1966; Rawson 1968). The goal is a harmoniously developing, well-integrated individual; the method of choice is individualized multisensory learning, balancing cognitive direction for understanding on the one hand, with controlled practice for mastery on the other. We include, especially for the dyslexic, emphases on needed special development, judicious management of learning patterns, and use of strengths to support areas of weakness, while the latter are, themselves, being strengthened (Silver and Hagin 1972). Man is a thinker, so in this kind of learning, conscious, rational mind is the master, the coordinator of the learning processes and the ultimate reliance in the face of forgetting or uncertainty. Self-recognized success in the gradual and solid achievement of competence provides improved self-esteem and optimum motivation (Rawson 1974).

What Kind of Person is the Dyslexic?

There is considerable evidence to support the view that in the general population facility in learning the forms of language is a largely independent trait, compounded of several related aptitudes, in each of which individuals vary normally over a wide range of ability (Doehring 1968; Masland nd; Orton 1937, 1966; Rawson 1968; Roswell and Natchez 1971).

So far, what we have been saying applies to each learner of language, whatever the nature and level of his facility, but what of those for whom natural endowment has not made language learning easy? What distinguishes them, and so provides our specific educational challenge?

Many studies of specific dyslexia give evidence that a large percentage of the individuals we are concerned with is representative of the population as a whole with respect to most aptitudes. They can be found in expected proportions: throughout the full range of intelligence; with all kinds of physical, including sensory, make-up; with varying degrees of primary emotional stability; with the usual range of developmental history; and representing divergent socioeconomic conditions and varieties of educational opportunity. They differ from their fellows in one respect only: for whatever reasons, they are unable readily to master the skills of their mother-tongue language to a degree consistent with their other aptitudes, their personal and social needs, their other opportunities, and their reasonable expectancies.

Some individuals may be slower or quicker in one or more of the fractions of language learning ability. This appears most often to be a family affair, consonant with normal genetic variation (J.L. Orton 1966a; Orton 1937).

Orton's observations led him to believe that his patients were not so much deficient or defective, as his predecessors had thought, but rather that they represented "normal neurophysiologic variations" in aspects and patterns of harmonious development. Jean Symmes (1972) of the National Institutes of Health came to the same conclusions on the basis of a well-designed diagnostic study of primary dyslexia. This conviction, which most of us share for most dyslexics (Rawson 1968; Stuart 1963), has a radical influence on our educational strategies and the optimism of our outlook for the children's future.

There seem also to be a few cases of disabilities deriving from each of several specific, probably nongenetic, causes such as injuries or special deprivations, perhaps at critical life-stages. The number in each such category may be relatively small, but in the aggregate they do somewhat thicken the low end of the normal, bell-shaped curve which otherwise describes the distribution of persons on a language learning facility scale (Hermann 1959).

Because this is a complex trait which can, in each person, have variations of much or little in each of its fractions, in kind or rate of development, definitive diagnosis of the individuals and delimitation of the identity of dyslexia itself may both be difficult. From this two things follow.

First, if we find no single diagnostic sign or pattern, but only a variable group of possible indicators, how do we know that dyslexia really exists? This question admits the possibility of denial of unwelcome reality and of responsibility for doing something about it, especially in schools. But if, to quote Abelard, "By doubting we are led to inquire, and by inquiry we perceive truth," then insecurity can result in progress.

Secondly, if we admit, as I believe most of our readers would, that there *is* something there, it becomes important for treatment or education to ask the diagnostic questions. Does this child belong in this category? By what criteria? Is it just one difficulty, and how bad does that one have to be and at what point in his history? Or is it his low position—how low?—on several scales—how many, in what proportion to each other, and when? What combination of negative forces will bring defeat, and what positive ones will help him to cope? Are these factors part of his general nature, of his specific language learning aptitude, or of his life-circumstances, and in what proportions? Since there is a hardly countable variety of combinations of kind and degree, this is hardly a simple problem, nor amenable to simple solutions (Kirk and Kirk 1971; Kolson and Kaluger 1970; Money 1962; Roswell and Natchez 1971).

Still, in the process of making knowledge and understanding part of ourselves and so developing clinical judgment, perhaps we can move from the initially chaotic to the complicated to the more systematically complex. Then, perhaps, we can find organizing principles which will simplify the task. To achieve this over-arching structure, resisting the lure of fragmentary aspects and panaceas, is a valid and purposeful use of abstraction.

In our field, we are especially fortunate in those giants of past and present from whose shoulders we can focus on the children's problems and their solution. For one outstanding example, there was Lauretta Bender who observed that dyslexic children's learning, and perhaps their general behavior, is commonly characterized by too great or too long continued plasticity, defining that term as, "carrying within itself potentialities which have not yet become fixed." (Bender 1958) This very plasticity is one of the most valuable ingredients in human adaptability. Brought under control, it emerges as flexibility, a necessary condition of innovation and creativity, and is one of the several positive traits associated with the dyslexic constitution. In the extreme, however, plasticity can make it difficult to keep one's affairs and possessions organized and to learn certain language skills to the point of automatic reliability. Appropriate education needs to be directed to the adequate establishment of control of this plasticity, not into a plaster-of-Paris-like rigidity, but into a voluntarily controlled flexibility more like plasticine.

On another level, we can say that rote memory is the weakest link in the dyslexic individual's chain of mental attributes (Halacy 1970; Saunders 1962). This is not memory for events, places, and facts, or other aspects of living. These may range, as do other people's, from near-perfect to very poor. The dyslexic's particular memory inadequacy seems to be with the sequences of language symbols which in themselves have no specific meaning (Doehring 1968). He has trouble holding them in mind long enough and securely enough to process them into the language forms which do carry meaning.

The Language to be Learned

This is the kind of person the dyslexic is. Now let us turn our attention to the language he so often finds it difficult to learn, and how best to teach it to him in the light of his special needs (Markiewicz and Zakrezewska 1973; Matějček 1971; Rawson 1970).

As we look at the world's language systems we find two basic types —the ideographic (Leong 1972) and the alphabetic (Downing 1973; Smelt 1972). We recognize that each, in modern times, makes use of some features of the other, and also that many languages are written

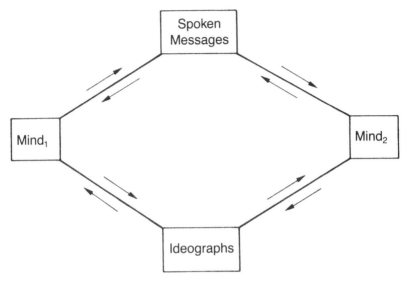

Figure 4. Transmission of thought in ideographic language systems.

syllabically. The variations are fascinatingly endless, but right now space demands that we oversimplify by looking only at the main characteristics of the *two basic* bridge systems by which ideas can traverse the gap between two human minds.

In ideographic languages, such as Chinese, the plan is shown in Figure 4, with two parallel spans from one mind to another, each span designed for two-way traffic. One route is vocal-auditory, the spoken language. The other carries meaning by a primarily visual-graphic system, whose thousands of ideographs are understood by all persons literate in the language, however mutually unintelligible their spoken dialects.

But it is with the second, or alphabetic-phonetic, languages that most of us Occidentals are familiar. Figure 5 shows this system, in basic

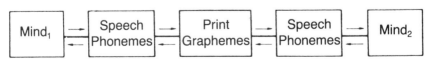

Figure 5. Transmission of thought in alphabetic language systems.

contrast. This is a linear route, by which the idea in one mind is first encoded into speech. This, analyzed into phonemic units, is then encoded a second time, into graphemic units of one or more letters of a limited alphabet clustered into words. These can then be decoded back into the speech common to the communicants, who thus read each other's messages. Of primary importance in the graphic symbols is the shape and orientation of letter elements and their sequence in written word units, which correspond in spatial arrangement to the order in time of the component sounds of the spoken words, the ultimate carriers of meaning.

In both ideographic and alphabetic systems, the language processes are common, but the intermodal connections are different. Both make multisensory and intersensory demands on learners, although the interrelationships of auditory and visual forms are different, dictating a somewhat, but not entirely, different set of educational strategies and tactics.

The speech code is inherently more complex and difficult, as modern linguistic science is demonstrating (Gough 1972; Lee 1974; McClelland 1973), but appears to be a built-in, universal human aptitude. The relatively simpler coding task of the historically much newer graphic mode surprises theoreticians by proving far harder for people generally to learn. Perhaps this is because it requires an additional level of abstraction and greater maturity.

In the alpha-phonetic languages, persons with good memory for visual symbol patterns can learn word forms as if they were ideographs. Perhaps they unconsciously generalize and subliminally realize the built-in letter-sound relationships. One mark of the dyslexic is his difficulty in doing just this (Bannatyne 1973; Doehring 1968).

We see a common core in our dyslexic group of children, and we can identify common principles in the educational treatment approach in use in many settings. Most of us know most about how this applies in English-speaking countries, but, as is often the case, parallel needs, as they have been identified elsewhere, have given rise to comparable theories and treatment procedures. One is struck with the similarities and cross-references in the large and growing professional literature of the field in many languages. Children in Prague (Matějček 1971) and Amsterdam (Bakker and Satz 1970), in Warsaw (Markiewicz and Zakrezewska 1973) and Vienna (Kowarik 1972), in New York (Clarke 1973), Vancouver (Kline and Kline 1975), and Melbourne (Smelt 1972), and in Latin America (Strong 1973) have a common look about their work, despite the babel of their vocabularies. These children are all, it seems, responsive to similar teaching approaches. And why not? The language function is common to humanity, and knows no linguistic barriers.

How, Then, Shall We Teach?

Whoever and wherever he is, the child whom we are teaching will need a regime in which all the best principles of pedagogy are practiced. If he is at the dyslexic end of the scale, he is likely to thrive if he has certain kinds of special care. Light has been shed on this need from many sources over the years, but for now, vastly oversimplifying, we may summarize them as follows.

Language is a continuum which does not begin at school entrance (Ansara 1969; de Hirsch 1970; Jansky and de Hirsch 1972; Oliphant 1972; Tower 1973; White 1970), nor even in kindergarten, so it will first be necessary to make sure that the child has developed good basic language competence, as most children have by the age of five or six. Many children who are going to develop reading and spelling problems come to school apparently well grounded in spoken language, though many others show inadequacy here. So the spoken language of the beginner or the older dyslexic should be evaluated and, where necessary, given remedial attention, in addition to the general language arts enrichment which is the province of the whole of education for all children.

Perhaps we should look at the sensory linkage diagram of Figure 3 again for at this point it provides a good working model for the teacher. Orton's first principle in teaching (J.L. Orton 1966a, 1966b), which has stood the test of time, was to reduce the language to its most basic elements, the sounds and letters—the phonemes, and the graphemes which symbolize them. These are learned well, through all the senses, singly or conjointly, with due regard for the learner's needs and his increasing capacity to handle the multisensory stimuli. He hears and says, sees and writes, in various combinations, with awareness of what he is doing and why. The sounds and letters are not presented haphazardly but in planned sequence, a few at a time, with constant review for thorough, cumulative mastery. As soon as the student has a few symbols to work with, he learns to synthesize by blending them into words, to read simple sentences, to analyze the same dependable words into their components and to write them. (Table I on page 114 shows at a glance that the most basic principles of English spelling can be outlined on a single page.)

Difficult as all this may be at the start, it does seem essential, and I have yet to meet the child of normal intelligence and reasonably intact senses who cannot learn to do it. Automatic retrievability is highly desirable and comes in time, but it is the *direct* goal only with the limited number of elements and a very few phonetically irregular but indispensible sight words.

From the beginning, the student relies primarily on the cognitive approach as he becomes adept at analyzing and synthesizing patterns, a useful skill when one is faced with new or forgotten words or with learning the essentially rational system of English spelling. By this route, as Orton thought (J.L. Orton 1966a; Orton 1937), one may establish the effectiveness of the language-dominant cerebral hemisphere of the brain, through strengthening the physiological habit of its use in attending to consistently oriented patterns of language symbols.

In summary, dyslexic students seem to come out best if we make our teaching program structured, systematic, sequential, cumulative, and thorough, responsive to individual needs and, withal, humanely and joyously therapeutic. A clear goal, clinical acumen, and pedagogic skill are all both necessary and attainable.

Instructional Materials

One master-teacher has said, "Give me pencil and paper, or even a stick and a patch of dusty ground, and I can teach any child to read." Of course she can, for the text is in her head; but even without that degree of expertise, the *essential* equipment for teaching is simple and inexpensive—writing materials, preferably including a chalkboard, and some well-chosen books. All the other teaching aids serve, often superbly and invigoratingly, the interest and delight of both child and teacher, but one *can* do without any or all of them.

The history of any science or art is filled with ideas and observations which seem unrelated until some creative person brings them together in a new arrangement and focus. Then we have a work of art, a theory, or a technical breakthrough. Such advances are likely to lead to further appreciation and knowledge and to manifold and growing applications.

Just as Orton performed such a synthesis as he worked with his associates in the theoretical areas of language and language differences, so he mobilized an equally creative group of other colleagues who began to produce clinical, scholarly and pedagogic procedures and materials (Childs 1968; Gillingham 1968; Gillingham and Stillman 1956, 1960; Monroe 1932; Orton J.L. 1966b). Reminiscences of his wife, June Orton, and others from early days in Iowa and New York point out the converging and diverging lines of development. Some of these descend directly from Orton and some through Gillingham. A few others starting independently toward solution of the same problem, joined them later. In time they developed work-plans, manuals, and other instructional materials from which we continue to learn and draw practical help. Of the publications particularly relevant to the Ortonian educational approach there come to mind those of June Orton (1964, 1966b), Childs (1973a, 1973b), Rome and Osman (1971), the Massachusetts General Hospital Group, Cox (1974), Slingerland (1971),

Hathaway (1973), Bannatyne (1973), Traub (1973), Pollack and Lane (1970), Bowen (1972), Anderson (1973), Eleanor Hall (1974), Spalding and Spalding (1972), Ansara (1972, 1973), Smelt (1972), Saunders and associates (1969, 1970, 1971), Durbrow (1968, 1973), and perhaps as many more. Many of these provide self-consistent cores around which to build a teaching plan, to be enriched by drawing on the others, which are compatible but not, usually, congruent. This is a process of enriching structure, and is a far cry from the eclecticism which puts bits and pieces together into a crazy quilt of confusion for the learner.

I know of several teachers who have in preparation their own new formulations or variations, being developed as they work with children. This is good, for there is much to be said for being in the learner's shoes oneself, while one is teaching neophytes. We are here working with an approach rather than a method, which is, as Bannatyne (1973) has pointed out, structured but not programmed, and is therefore adaptable to individual needs. It makes an invigorating contrast to the experience of the assembly-line worker who must follow the guide in the teacher's edition of a reading series.

One kind of thing we do not need for our teaching is a plethora of gadgetry, however attractive it may be to the toy-loving, button-pushing child in each of us. Trampolines and movement programs, visual aids and listening experiences are important in their own right at the appropriate times and places. They belong in the life of every child, including the dyslexic one. They can be educative in many ways, but we should not let ourselves be seduced into expecting them to teach reading and writing. To the extent that they are substituted for the direct approach, they may divert time, energy, money, and acceptance of responsibility from the proper focus. Eye-hand coordination, visual and auditory discrimination, and self-confidence can be achieved directly during the learning of critically needed language skills.

Educational Patterns in Practice

There is a sequence of growth in any specialized field which I first heard formulated by Roger Saunders: first there is recognition of a condition; then treatment; then research; and, finally, prevention. This cycle we can see repeated in the over-all development of the knowledge and treatment of language difficulties (Saunders 1971).

A historical sequence typical of what we have often observed is that, after failure and frustration a youngster comes to a clinician who can identify his problem and either start his rehabilitative education or refer him to a competent teacher-therapist. The understanding and cooperation of the child's teacher and school principal are elicited. The child makes progress, so the teacher wants to learn more, in order to help him and other children. The principal, psychologist, and others begin observing and testing all through the school. A program is set up for more thorough evaluation in the school, and some special teaching facility is developed—a resource room, class, or tutoring program. Records are kept, examined, and found impressive. Children in need of help are identified earlier, and eventually they are screened in first grade, kindergarten, and now even in nursery-age speech and language development programs. Appropriate instruction is provided for "at-risk" children and other beginners are shifted to join them if their needs warrant. Perhaps the whole school shifts to a code-emphasis method of teaching reading and spelling (Bloomfield and Barnhart 1961; Chall 1967), probably with grouping of children for language teaching to accommodate their differing needs and rates of learning (Rawson 1970). Close scrutiny of each child's growth will still bring to light those in need of special, individual care. So far I have not been aware that the later histories of these remedially or preventively taught children have been followed to see whether they may need "booster shots" at such critical periods as the beginning of algebra, foreign language, or the production of term papers, but this would seem to be a constructive idea. The whole sequence has been repeated, in whole or in part, many times in the past half century.

Although in America two names, Orton (1966, 1937) and Gillingham (1968), stand out in the history of dyslexia education, this by no means points to a personality cult nor a panacea solution, which would have been the antithesis of their spirit. The roll of scientists, physicians, psychologists, and educators in many lands is long.

Schools with programs for meeting dyslexic children's needs have been of several types. Independent schools came first, perhaps because in the early days children were most often referred from and to them and because they were freer to innovate. More and more, public schools are finding a solution here to some of their problems (East 1969; Hall 1974; Ley and Metteer 1974; Saunders and Malin 1971; Slingerland 1971). There have been special education schools for severely disabled youngsters which have devised departments and programs for dyslexic children. Day and boarding schools especially designed for dyslexic children are not entirely novel—we know one which has a record of more than 50 years, but most of them are of more recent establishment. There have been, and are, several good summer camps and summer school programs especially planned for dyslexic children. Hospital-related clinic schools go back to Orton's original multidisciplinary group at the Iowa State Psychopathic Hospital in 1925–1927. There are also nonhospital clinic teaching facilities and more individual therapists than one would believe unless one had been searching through history as I have. Some people go back to the '20s and some have only just graduated from college. Teachers' aides, volunteers, or paraprofessionals, and parents (Saunders and Malin 1970) are beginning to play roles of increasing importance.

People and facilities in all or most of these categories are to be found in other countries, too. Sometimes their activities are comprehensive and well-organized, as in Czechoslovakia, well-reported in the writings of Matějcěk (1971). In other countries they are more fragmentary, and in some places they are falling victim to the current back-to-only-the-regular-classroom-for-everybody vogue, now called mainstreaming.

As we think of the thousands of children who have been rescued from educational and life failure, though, we have no justification for smugness or self-congratulations—we need only think of the millions who have not been recognized or reached.

Teacher Education

Teacher education should have a chapter of its own. It has gone through much of the same evolutionary pattern as have most other professions, but isn't as far along as in many of them. At first it was Samuel Orton or Anna Gillingham on one end of Mark Hopkin's proverbial log and a succession of apprentices on the other. For some of us, who were largely self-taught, finding wisdom wherever we could, even the log was a second-order metaphor. As these arrangements became more formalized, with Gillingham's and other programs giving regular courses and requiring long-time commitment, people began to receive valued but not university-negotiable certificates. College and university credit for work specifically related to dyslexia began in 1959, grew slowly, but is now accelerating. There are graduate courses, perhaps in psychology or learning disability programs but seldom under the aegis of education. More people are getting relevant master's degrees, and there are even occasional doctorates. Since finding the teachers to whom universities are willing to grant faculty appointments has been a serious bottle-neck in the teaching of teachers, we must applaud the present trend.

Short courses, and various institutes and workshops are popular as introductions to the field, which is all they can possibly be. They have both merits and hazards when presented by responsible organizations, such as some associations for children with learning disabilities, the Orton Society through its conferences and branches, and that unusual publisher-with-a-conscience about how the books he sells may be used, Robert Hall of Educators Publishing Service. Some of the introductions lead on into longer courses, with supervised teaching, with or without university credit. Self-education is still very much worth the effort and, with the growth of the literature, more and more feasible.

Educational Management Programs

Aside from what happens in private practice of clinicians, with what sorts of management practices shall we implement our programs, especially in schools? Some compromises with administrative reality we can make, but there comes a time when one must put one's foot down firmly, saying, "Beyond this point we cannot go. These minimum standards must be met, or our effort, too thinly spread, will be worse than wasted. With only one childhood granted him, no child can afford to have it used up that way!"

However we may place children in groups for instruction and for school living, the guiding principle lies in the awareness that people learn as individuals (Rawson 1970b). We may favor a small group for the younger child, unless his disability is severe, and individual teaching for the older student; a class for the mildly dyslexic youngster in a preventive program, and clinical tutoring for the one with severe problems or a history of failure and frustration. We may have one plan where we have qualified specialists to do the teaching, and another where the classroom teacher must learn how, if she has time, or an untrained teacher aide or parent is involved (Jordan 1972; Miles 1970; Roswell and Natchez 1971). We could wish for a qualified tutor for every child in trouble, but with too many children and not enough teachers we will do what we can within the limits of professional responsibility and integrity. Respondents the world over and representing several languages and educational systems have reported both the values and the limitations of each of these arrangements. They are all trying to keep the whole child and the total environment in mind as much as possible and to maintain balance between stability and versatility, scholarly rigor and human warmth, and all the other opposites with which we are all familiar. As an article of faith, and the judgment of observation, we may say that language teaching *is* therapy, but that, on the other hand, unless it is therapeutic in management and in spirit, it will not be effective teaching. The full appreciation of this among dyslexia therapists is a rewarding finding in programs for all ages and in dozens of locations.

Results

But can children who have actually failed, or were predicted to be at serious risk of failure, really learn? A quick tally of the program participants at the first World Congress alone brings up names of at least 47 persons, all on the educational firing line, who could give affirmative evidence, and I have heard from many more in that audience and elsewhere, at home and abroad.

Children themselves think educational treatment works. The reported consensus seems to be, "Boy! It's great. I'm beginning to learn how, and I don't think I'm dumb anymore. [and wistfully] . . . I hope it lasts." Or if they have been at it a while, "I know I can do it now, I'll get there! And it's interesting and even *fun!*"

The parent of a child newly diagnosed and embarked on language therapy often says, "He's a different boy, and our family life and reports of his behavior at school are different, too." Then there was the not atypical phone call a year after therapy had ended: "Do you remember telling me that someday I'd say, 'Freddy, get your nose out of that book and go out and play ball'? Well, it has just happened and I thought you ought to know."

From the teacher of a third grade class of 25 came this: "Last year I had half these children in a smaller class for emotionally disturbed youngsters. They had me climbing the walls along with them, but with the approach I'm using now all but one of them has settled down to work happily in activities from which they know they are learning." (Saunders and Malin 1971) These reports won't surprise those experienced in this field. There have been schools with preventive and re-education programs dating back to the '30s, and there are more of them all the time, public now, as well as independent. They have raw data and case stories which aggregate in support of the statement of one long-time secondary school headmaster (Howard 1974) who says, "I have worked with roughly over a thousand boys during almost 40 years since Dr. Orton started us in this field and I know of *no* [his emphasis] boy whose reading skills were not strengthened. Reading speed rises very gradually in most cases, but comprehension reaches a healthy level. Spelling gains have been more modest . . . "

There is also the reading service director of 30 years experience and unblemished probity who says, "We don't *say* much about the records of success of our full-time 'graduates.' But we do keep careful records, for 'by their fruits ye shall know them.' However, since most people find 96 percent school and job success unbelievable, we long ago decided we'd rather just go on teaching than argue with them."

These statements, which sound so like the testimonials of which we are properly wary, are the more convincing because they are repeated from so many reliable sources. It is dilemma; we do not like to seem to blow our own horn, but neither should a welcome light be hidden under a bushel. We would all agree, I am sure, that these anecdotal facts need to be supported, as increasingly they are coming to be, by comparative scores and controlled studies, with careful description of populations, settings, and methods. Meanwhile, informally and in brief personal reports, we have begun to amass some numerical and descriptive data. From several teachers and whole schools I have received test data of sufficient detail and objectivity to be encouragingly convincing (East 1969; Johnson and Myklebust 1967; Ley and Metteer 1974; Schiffman 1972). There are already a few studies based on larger numbers and statistically reported, analyzed and validated (Herjanic and Penick 1972; Kline et al. 1968; Rawson 1968). Kline and Kline (1975) and others have presented reports of this kind some of which are printed in the 1975 *Bulletin of the Orton Society*. Although at best their number is not large, not all of those published earlier or elsewhere could be included in the reference list for this paper.

Whatever the specifics of instruction, though, with the kind of regime I have been describing, reports generally seem to tell the same story of normal or accelerated progress where before there had been much less or none, or where slower than average growth was expected from predictive testing. The earlier histories of the children and the status of untreated age-mates have provided comparisons and, in some cases, satisfactorily conventional control groups.

Children who are not too handicapped linguistically and are taught in preventive classes, or in regular classes with well-planned phonics programs, may make good progress from the start and may never be aware of the problems they might have had under less benign circumstances (East 1969; Slingerland 1971; Spalding and Spalding 1972). This emphasizes the point that we are primarily concerned with degrees of normal variation, rather than disease or defect.

Most achievement tests by which progress is measured in schools are geared to the traditional basal reader approach to reading and the accompanying language arts programs where vocabularies are controlled by frequency of everyday usage rather than phonic dependability. So it is often not until the phonemic-graphemic or coding skills are well-established that scores on standard tests will show how much learning has taken place. The Gillingham-Stillman-Childs Phonics Proficiency Scales (1966, 1970, 1971) and the new Dallas Benchmark Scales are useful measures of learning of basic language skills. After children show mastery in these tests, they are generally ready to take off into rapidly accelerated independent learning. Their scores on standard tests may then climb steeply and their progress will be limited only by such factors as intelligence and drive, and minimally, if at all, by dyslexia.

Prognosis

These children *can* succeed, if circumstances are even reasonably favorable and if they are given appropriate help over a long enough period. This must be at least a year, and preferably they should have two or three years, because there is much to learn about the language, and often much for the student to unlearn and to catch up on. No dyslexic child, I think we can say, *need fail because of his dyslexia* (Rawson 1968). With appropriate education, there is a way out. It is often long and slow, seldom spectacular in the beginning except for change of attitudes, but with the kind of education or re-education dyslexics need, the process is filled with hope and challenge, interest and deep satisfaction, and progress continues into later schooling and adult life.

This can be shown in the life histories of many individuals known to those among us whose early students are now parents, even grandparents, often of dyslexic children who are now our pupils. There have been only a double handful of long-time follow-up studies. These are usually of clinic populations given remedial help of different kinds with fair to good success, the over-all judgment being, "at least they are self-supporting and a few have done well." The individual careers reported in case histories by my old friends and recent respondents, and the results of my own Rose Valley study, seem to warrant much more optimism. There is room for more and better longitudinal studies and the data exist for doctoral students and retiring headmasters.

As a preliminary to his study, one headmaster says, "About 90 percent of our former students and graduates have continued their educational training with success, . . . I estimate that approximately three-fourths have bachelor's degrees, with several master's and even doctor's degrees . . . Perhaps partially because of their earlier disability, students have developed greater than average perseverance and habits of industry to cope with the academic challenge" (Howard 1974). Perhaps it is that in learning to meet the demands of organized language, well-taught dyslexics themselves become better organized for all of living.

Even with the best of help, our students will always be somewhat dyslexic, I suspect, for this is a matter of constitutional type. They may continue to be unreliable spellers, but the range and quality of their reading is generally in line with their other competencies, if not always so rapid as they would like, and their writing (or typing) can be at least legible. They are likely, on the other hand, to continue to show high aptitude in spatial and visual thinking and creativity. They can make use of other nonverbal, and often verbal, aptitudes of a high order, and other useful qualities such as we have seen in many of them. Hundreds, thousands, of them have learned to cope with language and generally to make it do their will well enough so that they can achieve in school and life in accordance with the full range of their endowment—a truly favorable outlook.

Further study will bring improved understanding and practice, but we need not wait for tomorrow. We have already learned enough to teach almost all children to read well.

Guidelines for the Future

If space permitted, I should set forth at some length our need for carefully designed, statistically validated, and widely published research studies, and for making use of the material already gathered. We might talk about the refinement of instructional materials and the improvement of teaching practices, about assimilation of the new into the framework of the old and tried—enriched structure, not superficial eclecticism. There is also much to say about recruiting both older and younger people as teachers, about educating them well, and about preparing for appointment to university faculties persons who could teach teachers increasingly well.

In the field of public education, which is a major concern of the Orton Society and the professions its represents, there is challenging work ahead for everyone—for professional workers involved directly with dyslexic persons and for members of other professions, including knowledgeable and forceful parents. We who are conversant with the field would do well to remember that it may be hard for others to hear and accept an approach so different from the ones to which they have long been attuned. Rather than being impatient with them, we should simply say and do what we can as forcefully and effectively as we know how, with determination but with restraint and understanding in the manner of our presentation. Then, perhaps, when they hear the *next* paper, or *their* child turns out to be dyslexic, they will be *able* to hear, having absorbed more than was apparent to them or to us when we talked with them.

There is exciting new knowledge about the language function and phenomena to strengthen and enlarge our concepts. In our field we who have focused on specific development dyslexia *do* have something very good to offer. Children, older students, and adults continue to be rescued from the personal and social devastations of failure, and restored to academic, social and economic effectiveness, to self-confidence and human dignity. Increasingly, appropriate early language intervention and teaching are preventing trouble for many language-different children. Programs are flourishing in many settings and in many lands. The world seems increasingly ready to hear what we have long been saying and to see what we are doing. We need not be too modest about promoting our ideas and programs—*except in the manner of our doing so.*

The field of language and language education is as interesting and rewarding as any there is. May it keep growing, and may our next quarter and half century of helping it do so be as exhilarating as have been the first 25 years of the Orton Society's life and the whole period since Dr. Orton's pioneering presentation of 1925. [This paper was written after 1974, before word-processors were available. Ed.]

3

The Meanings of "Reading"

I believe it was John Henry Newman who once said, "Nothing is more common than for men to think that because they are familiar with words, they understand the ideas they stand for."

Now, there are at least two kinds of words that make trouble for us in understanding our world and in conveying this understanding back and forth between any two of us. One kind might be typified by the word *reading*, so familiar that its importance in our lives is the focus of several important national meetings each year. The other, puzzlement about which brings some of us together is *dyslexia*, which is in some way or ways related to reading.

There was a time when I considered both these areas of thought as what W.B. Gallie calls "essentially contested concepts," but for myself I have sorted out the most troublesome concept dispute about *reading*. *Dyslexia* is harder, but perhaps it, too, may prove at least somewhat tractable. In the interest of reducing the temperature of the body politic in the educational world, it seems worth continuing effort.

The simple solution, once you have seen it, to the talking at cross-purposes about reading is to realize that there are not one but two concepts involved, for which we have but one noun. We are talking about getting a message of some sort from one mind to another through the medium of the written or printed word. If I get it from your friendly note or William James' *Psychology* or Hammurabi's *Code of Laws* I am reading, in this sense. The other meaning of reading has to do with decoding the graphic symbols we can see into the spoken code we know to stand for the ideas, in the language we have learned to speak. Reading is, then, a word standing for two processes, both of which are learned, not innate, and so must be taught. If one has not learned the decoding type of reading, he obviously cannot translate the word seen into the word understood, though there are some persons with a special knack for doing so who can say the words they see without understanding them. Any skilled decoder can do this in unfamiliar subject areas if he needs to, as when reading to a blind friend. How well one can do either of these types of reading, for which we have only the one common word, depends on many things, and there is still room for much discussion about their many aspects, but this bit of definitional clarification makes it possible for each of us to know what the other is talking about, so that our talk can have a better chance of leading somewhere.

When it comes to dyslexia, perhaps because the word has been around for a shorter time and because it is a kind of specialists' word, we have much more difficulty in associating it with a common set of ideas as we talk to one another. Some people give up, saying that dyslexia is an abstraction from fantasy, like certain famous ghosts, and does not refer to anything in the real world. Yet, anyone who has known a classroom full of children, or has known with any intimacy the intellectual lives of a number of people, knows that there is something in the field of language that most people who use the word dyslexia are thinking about. Perhaps this often amorphous entity is spoken of by other people in other terms, but the chances are also that these other terms, if often used, engender the same kind of disputacious atmosphere. It is not the word which is at fault, but the ill-defined idea. For, as any good General Semanticist will tell you, "The word is not the thing," it is just the symbol which gets caught in the cross-fire. If there is shooting going on, any substitute for the slain dyslexia would be an acceptable target.

"Reading," in either sense that we have discussed, has variable relations with "dyslexia." Other sections of this book may suggest context for both words, considering either word in analysis and practice.

4
Decoding and Comprehension

Reading with complete, or even moderate, comprehension requires, almost by definition, full competence in decoding; including segmentation, association, and synthesis.

Decoding competence is a large factor in the receptive process of reading. To achieve comprehension of the graphic, verbal message, which is to say for accomplishing the basic purpose of reading, decoding is essential, although it alone does not guarantee understanding.

One may decode at the word level or even sometimes at that of a familiar longer utterance, as is common most of the time to fluent readers. The ability to process graphic symbols at this level has advantages of speed and facility in the use of context, but the burdens it places on memory and self-assurance are great. The eulexic or natural reader seems to catch on easily, often very early, at this level.

The mid-range or slower-learning reader finds some or, perhaps, inordinate difficulty with using this processing method to start with. It does not give him the security he needs in facing forgotten or unfamiliar words. Learning of syllables and observation of their likeness and differences, together with contextual clues and inferences, may provide the immediate ease in decoding facilitation he needs, especially if he is at the upper end of the middle range of language learning facility.

Eventually the capable reader will make use of syllabic skill, but it cannot be the court of last resort, nor for initial learning by most persons with limited natural language acquisition facility. The latter, particularly, need to go back to basic phoneme-grapheme correspondences. Quite commonly the person with severe ineptitude, the dyslexic, can take hold at the beginning in no other way.

This route makes use of the alphabetic-phonetic structure of the Indo-European and some other written languages. It gives an initial "set" or expectation for regularity and structure and for the exact ascertainment of the intended meaning of the message. It minimizes guessing associated with sight recognition and context methods. It can markedly relieve the anxiety associated with proneness to failure of rote memory which generally characterize nonfacile learners of reading skills.

It should go without saying that the structured alphabetic-phonic decoding (and encoding) skills need to be taught with the greatest possible expertness and with full appreciation for the realities of the language to be learned and individual needs of the learners. For example, a "set for diversity," that is, toleration and management of the irregularities of English, should be introduced, not first but early, as soon as the general susceptibility of graphic language to decoding is established. Pacing and manner of teaching, too, should be determined by each learner's needs. One should go, in Gillingham's words, "as fast as possible but as slowly as necessary" for useful and stable learning; with sensory emphases again determined by need.

Decoding, properly taught, is the way to the reception of the printed verbal message; we cannot read without it. The other side of the coin, the apprehension of meaning which is the reason for reading, is the business of all of education. It is connected intimately and inherently with the process of learning to read and of reading itself, from beginning to end—from initial decoding to creative participation with the author and his work and its effect on the reader.

Decoding is, then, the essential beginning of the process of reading for comprehension; and segmentation is an essential part of the decoding process.

5

Education and Dyslexia: A Comprehensive View

In this paper we have set out to think about how education as a whole can nourish the full potential that achievement of language competence helps to liberate when we offer what the dyslexic especially needs.

We have been considering the achievement of language competence by the whole person of whose make-up dyslexia is one component. Some of us have spent many hours—even years—trying to learn about the nature of this syndrome, or complex of patterns, identifying the persons who need to come to terms with it and helping them to do so. The Orton Dyslexia Society's statement, "What is Dyslexia?" is pertinent for us because of its relevance to the common needs of particular students, patients, or clients, and because it provides us with a common starting point in that special field. Let us think about this whole person and how he is to profit from education.

This paper might be further subtitled with one of the epigrams I find most conclusively compelling: "Mind is the Master." In the present context that means to me the whole of Mind, as it is represented or implemented by the human brain and its carrier and instrument, the corporeal human being—the body—complex-entire, not just its language function, however universal is that aspect of its being. With so overwhelmingly large a subject, however, we must keep a tight rein on ourselves, else we shall find ourselves launched on a volume or more instead of a short chapter.

We can still begin on the familiar ground of our special interest in the dyslexic person, whom we already know so well, and his education, expanding from there. In one sense, he is his own kind of person because of his special needs in language learning. Still, our primary concern is with his entire development as a complete and singular individual. This directs us into considering the broad educational process as it is used to help each newly created child to use as fully as possible his capacity for growth toward self-actualization and membership in his own culture, as a member of the human species, and in the life of the planet, in each of which he is a functioning part.

Our responsibility, again for now, has to do quite practically with his education, especially as a child and youth. What should it be? How shall we make it fully available to him? What do we need to know and how do we need to act to fulfill our responsibilities as tribal elders? There have been basic-level teachers—at least trainers—ever since mammalian life began, and genuine educators since the Cro-Magnon painters. Written records tell us of conscious principles and deliberate practices as far back as we have recorded history. Many lines run from, say, the dicta of the Chinese *I Ching* and the dialogues of Socrates, who, being as much of a nonwriter as some of us, needed his Plato to publish his wisdom. The names of giants and journeymen that have followed them are many, through Mark Hopkins on his log and John Dewey in his lab and lab schools, to today's Wise Men of modern science, technology, the arts, and pedagogy. They, and experience, provide our sources. John Dewey gave the directive for the use of all this wisdom when he said that the democratic ideal for our responsibility for childhood education should be that whatever the best and wisest parents want for their child our schools should provide for every child. Some of the authors of P.L. 94-142, we know, were hearing that drummer.

When I am considering the broad subject of education, I am often glad I have no single overriding professional identification, for this may make it easier for me to, as Henry Geiger of *Manas* (1970) puts it, "write as a philosophical human being." On the other hand, I do have a strong interdisciplinary interest in one subject—language, its functions, and their attendant problems.

One can, even must, be both holistic and particular. It is possible to think in both ways at once, though we must express these views in turns, the nature of verbal language being what it is, if our words and their sequences lest our words get lost in the shifting text and context of a kind of part-song. And so, let me speak first as a generalist about all of education (of which language education is a part), of all learners, (including the subset of dyslexic learners).

As I see it today, there are two main categories of the educational enterprise: understanding (in its broadest sense) and mastery.

The full achievement of wisdom requires that *Homo sapiens*, as a whole species, stand firmly and walk purposefully, with coordinated control, on both legs. So we may say that we need both liberal education for understanding and training for mastery.

Often we hear, or even use, "training" when we are talking about comprehensive preparation for life, and we object, justifiably but for the wrong reason. The term needs rescuing, and our thinking needs straightening out. Knowing "how-to" (tool-making and using, the opposable thumb, and the rest of what's needed) is as much part of what makes us human as is "knowing what and why" and being able to talk about it, but we should know which ideas we are invoking so our actions and evaluations will be appropriate. To object to having courses or colleges for "professional training" or for "teacher training" is not to object to the training aspects of these preparatory provisions; they should be done and done to high standards of excellence. Even after one is intellectually convinced, it is hard for a descendant of Mary-and-Martha and of the citizen-philosophers of Athens to shake off the feeling that the verbally conscious and facile mind is the "real mind" or the "higher intellect," and that the technologies are near the fringes of respectability because of their contamination by so much "mere training." A study of history, examination of the works of Leonardo Da Vinci, readings in the recent brain research papers on hemispherical specialization, and a summer as apprentice to a certain plumber-home-improvements-craftsman I know might be one prescription for liberation from such enthrallment.

Among many objectives, the fullness of education should be designed to help us live with paradox, the seemingly irreconcilable but undeniable inconsistencies of life, and to do so both effectively and graciously. Beyond this, education does more than show us how to reconcile opposites constructively. It should also aim to help us to live with alternatives which are not just opposites on a single dimension but deal with different kinds and levels of the dimensions themselves.

Scientists have learned, at least for now, to accept light as both waves and particles, attending to one aspect or the other as the specific lines of their inquiries demand. They have not given up the attempt to reconcile the opposites of the digital and the analogous into a comprehensive general theory. Einstein was working on this until his dying day and others, like the brilliant Stephen Hawkings, are still hard at it. Meanwhile, they all go ahead as if both views were not only possible but actual. That different aspects or levels of truth may be simultaneously applicable shows up, for example, in the usefulness of Newton's Laws in most of terrestrial living, whereas on the submicroscopic and the cosmic scales we have to be concerned with quantum mechanics and indeterminism or with Einstein's relativity. Newton can be subsumed under Einstein, but not the other way around.

Similarly, in terms of human reality and philosophy, we have not yet addressed such problems as the ultimate relationships of mind and brain or the actuality of determinism or free will, but go on living anyway and either choosing, or feeling as if we make choices. If opposite views in educational theory and practice are followed to their respective conclusions, fundamental conflict result. Often we see them in the extremes of authoritarianism and permissiveness and their effect on the climate and the content of learning. Of necessity, some accommodations are arrived at on the separate dimensions and levels, ranging from one extreme to the other, or at some part-way point. This process, and the human tendency to ride pendulums—(with stop-overs)—has been endlessly observed and discussed. The effort always seems to be toward finding some one, and only one, acceptable position which can be consistently defended (preferably with statistics and citations) and applied throughout an educational enterprise. The rationalist or the purist in us seems bent on the search for a Position in both theory and practice. In the name of consistency, we just must make a series of Custer's Last Stands ("Dyslexia doesn't exist"), be "born again" (to the latest panacea), "live in the world superficially" (make it till Friday), or feel guilty about the inconstancy of our loyalties.

I wonder, however, whether a more tenable and useful course is rather to find a way to accept more than one answer where we can do so without violating our deeper convictions. Perhaps this is a matter of how we relate to dimensionality. Are we thinking of nature *or* nurture, for example; of givens *or* of modifiability? Or both at once? Even when we think, "Let education be determined by the nature of the person" (if we can determine what that is), we are immediately faced with the complexity of persons. Similarly, if we consider the modifiability or growth of that person, we have to ask what his, or any person's, growth potentials are and how we can properly affect them, and whether our predictions are matters of objective or subjective judgment. ("You just can't teach some people to read!" or "A dyslexic will never learn to spell." "And what about Pygmalion?")

In education there are personal factors involving human differences, for however we treat people in groups, it is always as individuals that they actually learn and change. They respond as whole individuals, made up of parts, fractions, aspects of themselves influenced as unique persons by their own complex of experiences.

On the other hand, people, as people, have common needs, shared to greater or lesser degrees with others, and sharing in each instance, on one or another configuration or dimension with those which may apply to their fellows. These characteristics may be such general ones as basic food, clothing, and shelter on the physical side, or emotional security as young family dependents, or equality of opportunity in many areas of life, or they may be specific to more circumscribed groups. All these are, in varying ways, precursory conditions to satisfactory education of individuals either as persons or as new or developing members of their respective cultural heritages. We must think of many kinds of needs at once and of many parallel or intertwined routes to their fulfillment. No wonder the challenge seems complex; it *is!*

The next section of this paper if carried out in full would have to follow a labyrinthine route through a series of apparently disparate mini-outlines, looking at our subject and ourselves from what would look like a hodge-podge of points of view. We would surely not be able to follow obviously interconnected lines of thinking in neat logical sequences. Understanding and mastery, for example, are in a different world of discourse from right and left hemisphere functioning and the connections between them. Age-level developments and their cyclical and spiral variations—physical, cognitive, and psychosocial—as well as personality typologies and their contributions to life styles, would be part of our thinking and planning. So would the relations between language and reality, and our perception of either in terms of the other. Much more would have to be said about the traits we know to be reliably related to brain structure and those that seem to be dependent on each other. Whole areas of responsible scientific literature exist, often isolated from awareness of one another.

The complex subject of interpersonal sensitivity, awareness, empathy, and appropriateness of social interaction seems almost to be a "Third Hemisphere" in significance, (though neurologists tell us they have a location for it in the right). It absorbed a whole chapter-section of my background essay-notes for this paper. My folders are, in fact, full of the records of just such local brainstorms, but the task of making a comprehensible model of the whole is, at least for me, a virtually impossible one. The networks become too tangled and complicated. Simplifications clear enough to be grasped and understood by themselves are clearly inadequate to the reality, with which, however, the human brain still seems to be able to deal subsconsciously in a manner more sophisticated and effective than any computer yet devised, or some say ever likely to be devised. Our views reflect the lenses through which we look at life, whatever their hues or complexity of facets.

We are made up of many factors and forces, but however tempting it is to identify ourselves with any of them ("You are what you eat"), we know that in a sense we are all of them and none of them. Perhaps we can say with the Zen masters: "*You* are not any of these things; you are the person who makes the choices." That brings us back to the purposes of education as helping novice persons to see possibilities and make choices. I land, you see, with my center of gravity on the free will side of the fence.

One of the questions which concerns all of us, is the implication for education of the findings of scientists of the several relevant disciplines. How do they, or should they, influence the practical procedures of education? This is important across the board, but especially for persons with learning difficulties of various kinds. To be specific in the light of our own concern, let us consider the case of the neurosciences and the treatment of dyslexia.

If Orton, Masland, Benton, Duane, and the rest, and now Geschwind and Galaburda, are right, differences in people can reflect differences in brains. Maybe the brain of a person, to the extent that he is dyslexic, is in some specific way or ways different from that of the person to the extent that he is eulexic. What difference would that make? Suppose that the rest of what Geschwind, in particular, said is also true: that this difference may well be developmental, associated, for one thing, with the flow of testosterone to the fetus during critical weeks of gestation. Then the events which may impoverish, distort, or delay developments generally in the left, predominantly rational, time-ordered language, hemisphere, may well be associated with a corresponding enrichment of well-organized growth and development elsewhere, say in the other hemisphere—the one that is holistic, spatially oriented, artistic, creative—but speechless. Perhaps this is the reason for dyslexia comprising that range of variation which at best is a nuisance and at worst if untreated leads to a crippling disability. Should we, then, seek a cure or a prevention? Should we try someday to get rid of the dyslexia, if we can, by genetic or chemical intervention, changing the make-up of the individual for his own good?

But Geschwind points out the likelihood that this imbalance of growth may have a positive aspect, one that is to man's long-run evolutionary advantage, the generator of other variations and talents that enrich the human race. To tamper with the process might well cost more than it would come to. An imbalance leading to important superiorities could be sacrificed to uniformity, perhaps to mediocrity. Inborn talent may be a complex of innate abilities. This seems likely.

All this is speculative, of course, but we are not left without a constructive course of action, one that has bearing upon our attitude toward dyslexia as a form of desirable diversity, rather than as a defect. Dyslexia may, after all, turn out to be a problem with a very positive side—what Geschwind (1982b) calls even "a pathology of superiority." (We accept the idea of superiority, anyway, even lacking enthusiasm for the term "pathology.")

We have learned much through dealing with aphasic patients and still more while teaching apparently undamaged—may we say "normal,"—dyslexics. We know that the organization of behavioral and language skills generally comes easily, naturally, to the eulexically talented. With moderate but reasonable effort these behaviors can be taught to and learned by most people. Perhaps people are ranged along a continuous scale of these aptitudes, as my Rose Valley series of 1968 seemed to suggest. Under our present pedagogic practices, there is the not inconsiderable minority whom we call dyslexic. For them, carefully organized, step-by-step educational procedures are called for, demanding expert management and tuition in language and in practical living. Furthermore we know from experience of at least the past 60 years that this approach can be counted upon for success in liberating even the extremely dyslexic person into effective skills in the world of words. He need not be condemned to illiteracy and a sense of deprivation and incompetence.

While we may not be ready to say, "Be glad you're dyslexic!" (for dyslexia can be a frightful impediment), we may still rejoice that the difficulty with which we are faced in this arena is one that is so largely susceptible to constructive treatment, educational treatment. This leaves intact the natural riches and variety of the brain, while it helps build in, in a rationally prescriptive way, skills which develop the individual's talents for language that are insufficient but not absent.

Moreover, come the millenium, if the called for special attention be wisely and generally administered in the school, it will do nothing that is at variance with the natural tendencies of those others who are blessed with what we may simplistically call left hemisphere talents. Fortunate children need not be belabored with work they do not need. (It might even be that they should be working on "remedial shop"—or enjoying the riches of the library on their own.) If we know, for example, that a child is genetically predisposed, or shows tendencies toward, either the dyslexic or the ill-organized cast of mind, we can begin in the cradle by giving all the freedom he can use and yet setting the stage for system and regularity in areas where that is needed, as in the routines of living. In reasonable measure, this helps *any* child by freeing him from responsibilities which should not be his so that he can put his attention on more important matters of experience and learning. Some children respond easily to what has been called provision for "kindly conformity," whereas others need more scaffolding to achieve the same benign conditions. And so it goes throughout education—by leaps and bounds, or step by guided step, as is appropriate to temperament or stage of development.

When it comes to language, too, some needs are universal and some learnings can be interesting as part of one's heritage, even though they may not always be essential to current functioning. Everyone should have good speech and semantic models if he is to use his language with grace and precision. The sequences of metalinguistic awareness—"What is a sentence? A word? A syllable? A speech sound?"—are interesting as the facts of language life, and in preparation for taking on reading readily. Here as elsewhere, what can be incidental and nonconscious for many people requires a carefully built up brick and mortar basis for those who lack a natural aptitude. We do not thus prevent or cure dyslexia, for it is not a disease but a kind of mental organization. However we can generally prevent the unfortunate consequences of inadequate understanding and lack of needed training. As Sarason says, "Changes occur when certain ideas gain currency in relation to a social problem that has appeared intractable to traditional methods of remediation." Surely dyslexia is a case in point.

We have been exploring the nature of things and people and education in a very generalized way, but what we are perhaps most interested in is how all our theories apply when we are sitting across the table or standing across the room from the real people on the other side of the educational equation. How does all this work out in practice?

There are many examples from which we could draw for description, ranging from very early childhood projects to elder hostels. Their variety in forms and objectives is just as wide as their age ranges. Some programs are partial, some comprehensive, some have failed, some succeeded, and some have just muddled along. Here, as everywhere, we have a pluralistic society, with some of its members being well-served, most getting partially satisfactory care, and many, alas, being ill-understood and sometimes very badly hurt by the things that happen to them in the name of education. We see some changes as far as the dyslexic population and its needs are concerned, but it seems likely to be a long time before general practice catches up with what we know could and should be. There are schools that really meet the needs of this kind of child. They are few but growing in numbers. Already bright with promise and with fine results evident, they feed our optimism for the future.

For our encouragement and stimulation, let us choose one among the good ones to look at. It is good for our present purposes because it exemplifies some of the things we have been talking about and does so in a kind of cross-cultural context of dyslexia and education on the broad scale.

About a dozen years ago, Jemicy School, which I have known not just from its birth but almost from its conception, was an experiment planned precisely in accordance with our current topic. As an almost deliberate exercise in the "living with paradox" of which we have spoken, it was designed both top-down and to grow up, in a democratic spirit, from its roots. This meant that the parents, the board, the teachers, and the children used both need and philosophy as the bifurcated taproot. At the same time it was to draw, if you will, its photosynthesis and airborne nourishment through its physical plant, its organization and its program. The sapling was planted, and once physically transplanted, it has grown, with the ups and downs of a uniquely developing identity, even more satisfactorily than could have been foreseen.

Two plans converged in the grand design of this project in education—those we have referred to earlier as liberal education for understanding, and training for mastery. The latter was particularly called for to meet the language learning needs of this school's dyslexic clientele. The specific way is, of course, familiar to you: the Jemicy Variant of the Orton-Gillingham Approach, if a name is needed. To manage this training well was the need-mandate under which the school came into being, but the rest of the program was of equal concern from the start. For the "Philosophy," by which it really lives (see page 170), the school is deeply indebted to the School in Rose Valley, in Pennsylvania. This guideline, produced at the request of the adults involved, predated the opening of the school, and has been the guide of its life.

So this is the successful example of the kind of ideas we have here presented. Of course there are other schools similarly operating. I could name several, but I use this one as the working example because I know it best. Despite its inevitable human imperfections, it comes as close as any I know to being an embodiment of what seems to me the essence of education for all persons, whatever their age or nature.

We have taken a general philosophic look at education as it applies across the board, at special provisions for those with special language learning needs, and, finally at one among several exemplary schools designed to meet the needs of a specific group of dyslexic children. It is particularly important, I think, for the entire school family to be dedicated to the inclusive proposition with which we started, that education for these, as for all children, is firmly grounded in the development of broad, deep *understanding* of life and *mastery* of the skills needed to live productively in today's world. Here, as in other educational endeavors, we can report that this kind of education is encouragingly effective.

6

Beyond the Alphabet:
From Competent Reader to Avid Reader

This paper is addressed to those who know, as I do, how vitally important it is for people to become competent readers. We are the convinced. We need not reiterate that it may even be literally a matter of life and death, of school and economic survival, of any sort of employment or vocational success, of staying out of jail or hospital, of driving a car, of protecting oneself against exploitation, of reading a menu or a mail order catalog, or of just having something to do while awaiting one's turn at the dentist's.

But survival is only the first step. If that is all we are working for in life, perhaps it is not worth the effort that we and our students put into the struggle against tremendous odds. Some people have thought so. However, we do know two things that can make all the difference. First, we now know enough to be able to teach everybody to read at the functional or survival level and beyond. Second, we know that learning how to read is just the beginning of what can be a fascinating "good trip" in life—a trip that, if you have the competence, you will be free to take if you want to. Will you want to? To make reading barely possible is one of the basic jobs of education. To provide the opportunities that will help the young person find out what life is like, what is in it for *him* or *her*, is the other aim of education. It is both concurrent and all-embracing. This major job begins with the child's beginnings, takes the rest of his life, and can provide some of his richest experiences.

Experience for understanding and training for mastery work best as partners in the language education of dyslexic children and young people. For them the careful training aspects may take more attention than is needed by those who are naturally gifted in the learning of verbal skills, but the very process is designed to be cognitively oriented and full of its own satisfactions to the growing self. We need to obey

Reprinted with permission from The Orton Dyslexia Society from *Bulletin of the Orton Society* 29:191–204 1979.

Anna Gillingham's admonition, "Teach to the intellect," for it is, happily, stronger than the rote memory, and so we lean on it, finding real virtue in necessity.

Let us go on from "Supposing that I *can* read," to "Why should I *want* to?" There are several reasons. If the first response is, "Your sense of duty as a school child," that will not get anyone very far. Says Emerson, "When Duty whispers low, 'Thou must, the youth replies 'I can!' "But perhaps he says instead, "Oh, damn" or even, "Why should I?"

Another reason to read might be utility—a means to an end. That is a bit more compelling than duty, though perhaps not enthralling. There are many kinds of utility, some of them genuinely ego-supportive and not bad fun. But there must be more to it than this.

Emily Dickinson, in her poem, "Bequest of Wings," metaphorically, says it all.

Bequest of Wings

He ate and drank the precious words,
His spirit grew robust;
He knew no more than he was poor,
Nor that his frame was dust.
He danced along the dingy days,
And this bequest of wings
Was but a book. What liberty
A loosened spirit brings.

From *First Series, Life, XXI, A Book.*

Another title, this time of a program, *Reading is FUNdamental*, marries the two, utility and delight, and helps to get the young person *Hooked on Books*, another seminal title and an aim of the first importance.

We can surely agree that we need to be scientific as well as humane. In our context, what does that mean? To describe, explain, and perhaps to predict; to know what works and why. A book edited by Arnold and Virginia Binder and Bernard Rimland, *Modern Therapies*, considers these aspects of therapy and goes on to discuss ways of measuring success. These depend, they say, upon one's goals.

One can judge by rating students somewhat subjectively, based on a single instance ("How did he come out?") or comparatively ("Did he catch up with the others? Do better? Lag behind?"). One can use rating scales, still with a considerable complement of subjectivity and sampling limitations (grades, class standing, and the like). One can use the standardized tests, psychological or educational, normative, or criterion-referenced. If appropriate, one may use the more exact measurements of physical growth, strength, or certain kinds of behavioral functioning. As criteria of success, one can use relation to norms, or one can look at intra-individual change and growth toward the more general goals of competence and enthusiasm for living and for continued growth.

To these authors, it seems unlikely that a given therapy will produce beneficent change simultaneously in all of the three dimensions of cognition, emotion, and behavior; but in the Orton-Gillingham framework I have seen this happen so consistently that I think of it as the probable outcome. If it does *not* all happen, we want to know why and to do something about it ourselves or call for appropriate additional help. We may not always be able to see the process through to the end in our own time with the student, but if we have not attended to all the dimensions as far as we have gone, we have not done our job. If, however, we have kept all three balls in the air as long as we have been at work, life can and often does take it from there, as we find when we encounter our ex-student years later.

Now to focus again on our title, going "beyond the alphabet" is something for which we are glad to be noted—even notorious. One needs, in fact, to go beyond it in both directions, to prereading and post "training," if, along with intellectual challenge, the spirit is to be fed and the thirst for life, as found in and through books, is to be developed to the full. Logically, love of spoken language, with its fruits, comes first and provides the matrix of the love of books. Experience with print, in turn, enriches spoken language and thought and extends and enlarges vocabulary and the capacity for living, both vicariously and directly. As Dr. Ralph Sockman has put it, "The larger the island of knowledge, the longer the shoreline of wonder," and we might add, the more will be the "peak[s] in Darien" and the harbors in which to come snugly to anchor. And so any competent reader profits from becoming an avid reader.

Of course, what is good education (in the comprehensive sense) for the eulexic is good for dyslexics and vice versa. Everybody, whatever his language-learning aptitudes, rates "the bequest of wings." By the time the dyslexic-type starter gets really underway, the same principles apply to both, though the details and the pace vary with the needs and tastes of the individual. While the child who has learned to read easily may come readily and eagerly to the literary hearthside, the child burnt by failure and a sense of ineptitude may need more inducement and helpful companionship as he learns to enjoy his birthright. He is the one we, as therapists, must find some special ways to approach. That is part of the art and science of the whole of education.

We should repeat, for we must keep it well in mind, that as much as training is a necessary component of education, so are understanding and enjoyment, with the functional integration of the two approaches as our aim. Therapy of both kinds begins on day one of our contact with the delayed reader, with diagnosis and explanation, and goes on through the achievement of functional literacy to competence, self-confidence, and independent, purposeful school and lifetime learning and enjoyment. There is a scenario, with variations, and there are ways to set the stage and keep the play moving. You know most of the standard ones and have developed many of your own or, as I have, can do so—devices for enriching vocabulary and engendering enthusiasm, selections of sequences of books that lead to that benign addiction to print, and so on. Most of all, we want to keep the pace right. And we want to see that our students have fun—not as a distraction, but as an integral part of the growing process. Little children seem to have a "set" for going at it this way, and we want to keep that attitude alive in the younger ones who come to us at the prevention stage and to restore the older ones to it according to each one's need.

In its particulars, the scenario is not detailed, but it is broadly outlined before the language learner ever gets to the beginning of reading-as-decoding. The love of books is best caught, rather than taught. It is best if the first exposure comes early, in the nursery, from a person who is a "carrier," who genuinely enjoys children, is enthusiastic about his or her own adult reading, and either already has a taste for children's books or is open to the development of such a taste.

The advice to read to children books that *you* like, *too*, needs emphasis on the modifier, *too*, to keep things in perspective. Sometimes the absurdity of omitting that little word is obvious, as when the science historian, George Sarton, gave to his little daughter, May, an elegant two-volume English-French, French-English dictionary, which served *him* long and well, but her only many, many years later. (Who is it who plays with Junior's elaborate electric train set?) On the other hand, there was 5-year-old Holly who named her kitten "Hamlet" because, said she, "he wears a customary suit of solemn black!" Her actress mother explaind, "When I read to her, I read things I like to read," and she read so well that Holly really did like it, too—and for always, and with deepening understanding as she grew up.

For most of us, the options are less spectacular—say to present Marjorie Flack's *Story About Ping* rather than to get entrapped by *Ducky Daddles and Jimmy Joe at Breadcrumb Pond*. You'll have to read whichever one it is three scores times and ten. For both adult and child it might better be Wanda Gag's *Gone is Gone*. Need I say more? And if engines are to be personified, why not share the delight of Hildegard Hoyt Swift's *Little Blacknose*? Forget, if you are allowed to, the banal moralizing of *The Little Engine That Could* and banish the demoralizing falsity of *Tootle*. (If you have escaped that one and wonder at my vehemence, consult David Riesman in *The Lonely Crowd*.) I have just had the fun of introducing a whole new family, parents and children to Blacknose, and they love him as much as my children did 50 years ago and as their children did later. If this engaging little pioneer has nourished one's mind, spirit, and literary taste by the auditory route, he may be just the one to guide the eyes into reading a first "real, long book," already familiar, when skill has come to that point.

Now, whether the future bookworm is a natural reader, a preventively nurtured dyslexic, or an older child being rescued from failure, frustration, and refusal to have anything to do with print, let us assume that he is now getting the graphic form of language straight, "as it is." He has the alphabet and its clusters of letter-sound relationships "down cold" and, beginning with $a + t = /a/ + /t/ = at$, he has been learning about blending sounds and syllables and longer and longer words. Simultaneously, he has been combining words into sentences and sentences into paragraphs, phrased and read like talking. At first he has met the *Fat Sam* type of sound-controlled vocabulary booklets. He knows these are only a kind of "finger-exercise" reading—but what is wrong with playing *Three Blind Mice*, or practicing throwing spitballs, until you get the hang of things? That is how skills are built, to begin with.

Is this child really a bookworm-to-be? Very often we can make a good clinical guess, but I think it works best if we first assume that he is going to *want* to be a reader. We can then leave the rest to him, with whatever good press we can give to the activity. I remember Freddy. He looked like a future literature addict to me, so I predicted to his mother that she would someday be saying, "Freddy, get your nose out of that book and go play ball!" 'That," she said, "will be the day!" Sure enough, a year or so after our lessons had ended, she called me, chuckling, "Remember what you prophesied? Well, it's just happened and I thought you ought to know."

Someone, regrettably a noted reading teacher (from the *Dick and Jane* school) said, "I believe in nurturing individual differences—everyone has the right *not* to read." "A half-truth," said I. "How can you *choose* not to read unless you are *able* to read?" That stopped her, at least for then, I am happy to report. Of course, for some people like Pooh-Bear, exercise means "falling off the ottoman [without] the energy to clamber back." For some, the access to literature comes via the Saturday morning television, or even *Masterpiece Theater* of the Public Broadcasting Corporation, to which all honor.

There is the true story of Mason, a clinic patient, 14 years old and a complete nonreader, despite the IQ of 110 brought out by the WISC I was giving him. You may remember the question on the Information subtest, "Who wrote *Romeo and Juliet?*" Said Mason, thinking hard, "I ought to know that . . . " [How? I wondered.] " . . . I think he lived in olden times . . . and his name had 'spear' in it . . . Allspear? . . . Something like that!" "How did you know?" [As tester, I dared not also teach.] "Oh!" said he, "I saw that play on TV. It was really good!" And he told me about it—well enough to pass a high school comprehension test. Was he exercising his "right not to read" Shakespeare but to watch the tube that night? *I* might have been, but *he* had no choice. He could have learned to read and wanted to; but at that time there was no program open to him and so, though he is a successful, skilled workman—a mason—he is still cut off from the world of books.

Supposing the person can read, will he want to? He cannot choose intelligently and freely until he has experienced what may be in it for him—and that part of his teaching, too, had better be extra wise and positive so that it can supplant the negative conditioning of his earlier failure. His hope and his enthusiasm, once aroused, can hardly afford more than a very occasional "dud" or boring book experience. Many things will need to happen concurrently as he moves "beyond the alphabet"—or elementary skill learning—to being enthusiastically "hooked on books" and launched on a lifetime of use of printed riches for his own purpose.

He may need continued help in skill development. Eulexics seem to gain without much help the needed facility in word deciphering and recognition, a growing vocabulary of understanding, familiarity with complex sentence structure, flexibility of attack suitable to varied texts, and increased speed and power. Dyslexics, however, may need continued help for a long time with one technique or more, or periodic "booster shots" at crisis points in their schooling. Generally, I have found the best promoters of good comprehension, which so many people worry about, to be the degree of interest, felt need, and the quality of educational experience. Given these, the only limiting factor, seems to be basic general intelligence.

Sometimes, however, some students need specific supplementary help with specific skills of understanding. Perhaps problems in mathematics need to be made real, with words translated into facts in sequence; history can be brought to life; science or art forms can be experienced; metaphor as a literary device can be brought to conscious awareness—all beyond what teachers need to do for others in the class who seem to get there mostly by themselves. These are what Weaver (1978) referred to as schemata for increasing comprehension. If they are needed, of course they should be brought into play.

Certainly, it is vitally important to make sure that the student meets the books that are right for him at the right time, as Vail has made so clear (1978). Nothing in this essay is as deserving of bold-face capital letters as this! I have always been glad that I started my teaching career as a limited-budget librarian for a school. With only 50 or 75 dollars a year to spend, I had to borrow and read a couple of thousand children's books so that I could know which few we could afford to buy when they came on the second-hand market. What is more, I knew that we, as churchmousely administrators, could afford very little junk. Neither, was I to learn, could the slow-starting reader afford to spend his limited time on inferior volumes when—and this is important—he could get all the profit and more of lasting satisfaction from the high quality ones. There are those who say, "Let him read all kinds so he will have a basis for discrimination." That is one route, especially if he is a facile reader with a large library available. I'd not stop him, but I believe one can find virtue in necessity, as we had to—a place for critical adult review before offering selection, but not done in a spirit of censorship. Ed's experience is an illustrative example.

Ed's first 12 years, at home and at school, presented him with a nourishing literary diet, controlled by budgetary necessity and parental choice in use of available resources. His junior high school library had no such restrictions. The very first day in seventh grade, its bursting shelves nearly overwhelmed him with joyous excitement. He discovered the Ralph Henry Barbour series-type school stories in which I too, his mother, had reveled at his age. He polished off one the first night. With the second one-night stand came the heady announcement, "Boy! There are 27 of them and I'm going to read them all!" Two weeks later I asked, "Isn't that third Barbour book due today?" I was mean enough to add, "And what about the other 24?" "Aw," said he, "I've had enough. You read one, you've read them all!" So, in developing literary taste, as in skinning the cat, there are more ways than one. As an adult, Ed is no pedantic snob, but he *is* a discriminating reader.

When I became a reading teacher—a language therapist, in fact— it stood me in good stead to have used juvenile literature instead of adult who-dunnits for some years of leisure reading. It helps enormously to be able to say, "Here are two or three stories that kept me awake half the night when I read them. They are about [this and this and this] which are up your alley. You might like to consider one of them next. Take your pick." If your youngster has found your previous suggestions rewarding, and you have to see to it that he generally does, he'll feel helped, not manipulated, by this reasonable narrowing of the field. If you have guessed wrong, of course, you have to be genuinely ready to alter course. Some people thrive on *The Wind in the Willows*, but it is not everybody's dish and may, anyway, be better listened to than read to oneself. But *The Phantom Toll Booth* is an almost sure-fire success with its delicious mixture of fantasy and modernity. It is fun with words at Dictionopolis and with the Mathemagician, and all the other ways that Norton Jester, with help from illustrator Jules Pfeiffer, has found to play with character and philosophy and the high adventure of outdoing evil and rescuing princesses. There is something exciting and amusing happening on every page. But you do not *start* here.

In pursuit of the goal of fluent—not merely functional—literacy for the dyslexic and enthusiasm for the hitherto reluctant reader, I generally though not invariably follow some such line as this:

1. First comes the *therapy of diagnosis*—taking the language differences seriously, trying to understand the student's pattern and the difference it makes for him, and explaining both it and the treatment rationale.

2. Then I make the *promise,* as a probability prediction, that if we tackle the job "this way" and take advantage of the *scientific* approach to language, describing the Orton-Gillingham techniques, it won't be too terribly long before he will be reading real books about things he is interested in. No more of that baby-reader stuff for him! It will go slowly at first, and I'll give him a lot of help with figuring things out for himself. Then, as his power grows with skill and practice, he'll do more and more for himself and do it more easily and faster.

3. Then comes the "alphabet chapter"—technique, well and thoroughly done. It works; ask those who have used it.

4. As soon as possible, I like to substitute a tried and true sequence of *good,* so-called "trade books" for the standard or even the special reading texts. Adult reading aloud is mixed more and more with the student's oral reading in the books we are enjoying together, leading eventually to independent silent reading and an expansion of power and a sense of growth. I don't ask the student to read any words for which he does not have the skills to figure out on his own. There may be only a few he can do as he begins *Liang and Lo* or *The Outside Cat,* but there will be more by the end of each volume. It is a great morale booster when he realizes what is happening, as you see that he does periodically.

   There will be as many of these brief, wide age and interest range books as he needs and wants, followed by those at the level of *Billy and Blaze, High Water in Arkansas, Little Blacknose, Max* (a realistic story of a bear cub and a boy), *Greased Lightning, Honk the Moose, Homer Price, The Enormous Egg, Mr. Popper's Penguins, Farmer Boy, Nuvat the Brave, Call it Courage, Justin Morgan Had a Horse,* and so on through more and more challenging but always interesting pieces of the world of reality, adventure, fantasy, humor, beauty and other joys. There are dozens of winners at every level until at last you are "on your own," with only as much help in selection as you want.

5. *Concurrent and advanced skill techniques* and encoding (spelling and writing) are parallel and cross-connected. Still, however difficult and time-consuming are the writing skills, one should

not get so carried away by their obvious importance that reading and its joys are supplanted or neglected.

Then there is the whole question of what is sometimes called *bibliotherapy.* From my viewpoint, just becoming a competent reader is
perhaps the most important bibliotherapy there is for a dyslexic, potential or confirmed. As the term is usually used, however, it refers to
the deliberate choice of books with certain content for the student to
read because of the contribution they are likely to make to his mental
health, to the solution of his emotional or social problems.

A great many of the best books give us a golden opportunity to do
this and I am all for using them. However, we are no longer in the era of
"Goody Two-Shoes," the laughing stock of even my youth. If bibliotherapy is to work, it must be subtle. Pointing out the moral, or even
drawing it out of the reader, will not adorn the tale, it will probably kill
it—and your relationship with the student, too. It is, if anything,
worse than studying Shakespeare by dissection or insisting on the rote
mastery and acceptance of Mao's Little Red Book. The discussion of
feeling, ethics, and social relations is certainly not taboo and merits
frank, sensitive, and respectful handling. But that is a different matter.
One has other reasons for offering or choosing a story, and the psychosocial therapy, while it is often intended by the adult, ought to seem
"serendipitous" to the youngster or should enter his world without
benefit of conscious identification or acceptance. To achieve this is not
so much manipulation as the high art of ministry and a mark of able
therapy.

Some of the themes are universal, whether they are personal like
fear or broadly philosophical like the age-old struggle between good
and evil. There is the need to belong, to be accepted. Who of us has
read *The Outside Cat* without identifying with Samuel who desperately
wanted to be an inside cat? Samuel labors persistently in his own way
to bring this about and, still true to his feline nature and dignity, finds
his way to happy acceptance. Certainly, no dyslexic unwillingly excluded from the most important life of his world, its language, and
longing to be a full participant, can fail to identify with Samuel. Kate,
in *The Good Master,* and many another in both real and imaginary time
and circumstances—notably Madeline L'Engle's older young people
—touch this theme, and through it the inner life of their readers.

Or is it the sense of identity, the "who am I and why am I here,"
that concerns us? Little Blacknose, sometimes puzzled and often triumphant, finds out as he lives through a hundred years or so into the
history of science and technology. So do David, in *It's Like This, Cat,*
and preteen Margaret in *Are You There, God? It's Me, Margaret,* to contrast divergent settings. It is a universal theme we find everywhere,
often in the current rash of problem-oriented novels too explicit and

obvious for the literary taste but apparently acceptably helpful to young readers.

Are you beset by fears, amorphous and terrible or specific but perhaps unmentionable? You, too, will welcome with Wagtail Bess, the therapeutic ministrations of Angus, the irrepressible, sympathetic Scottie dog as he helps her to get over being afraid and to "wag [her] tail and *smile* as an Airedale should." When the tiger who terrifies Liang, Lo, and their erstwhile intrepid water buffalo turns out to be a paper structure (*you* knew he would, from the pictures), you are suffused with a warm glow of amusement, laced with unadmitted relief at the jolly homecoming paraders' acceptance of the destruction of their festival paper beast and their friendly invitation to "come back next year . . . creep into the tailpiece and make it wiggle." From here, all the way through the terrors of the road to the rescue of the Princesses of Sweet Rhyme and Reason, relieved with humor in *The Phantom Toll Booth*, and almost unbearable in the climaxes of *A Wrinkle in time*, *Narnia*, *The Lord of the Rings*, and Alexander's *Taran* books, you learn, if you are ready, to face terror and live in triumph. But here is an area in which great wisdom is called for in the mentor. Some hardy youngsters seem to thrive on such challenges, but it is possible to push matters too far and too fast for a vulnerable child's tolerance. *The Hobbit,* just right for some people at some times, can bring on nightmares, as can as innocent seeming a tale as *Karoo, the Kangaroo,* when wild dogs almost overtake the mother kangaroo, terrifying a too frightened 5-year-old imaginative identifier. It is well to read for oneself and re-read with *this* child in mind when one is walking the thin ice of therapeutic prescription.

Or are you a little girl, by turns glorying in and cramped by the chromosomal chance that made you female? *Joan Wanted a Kitty* (beautiful but in first reader vocabulary) or *Caddie Woodlawn* or *Roller Skates* may be your meat—being a girl can be great fun. Or *The Golden Horseshoe* and *Master Skylark*, and later, *As You Like It,* can give you the thrill of delightful, and eventually triumphant, masquerade.

Small may not always be beautiful to you, but you can have recourse to Tom Thumb and his tribe, and all those put-upon third sons and daughters who star in the old tales; to *Paddle-to-the-Sea* and other artifacts, toys and animals come-alive; to *Stuart Little;* and to that heroic humorist, 6-inch Peter Peabody Pepperell III and his "airplane," Gus the Gull, in their exciting *Fabulous Flight* and its hilarious preliminaries.

Dyslexic children needn't, praise be, think of themselves as "handicapped," but it helps to know such people as the characters in *Little Magic Painter,* David in *Two Children of Tyre,* Mary in the *Little House* series (before the media got hold of the *real* Ingalls). Time was, perhaps still is, when there was a lot of tear-jerking about people's physical and social-economic misfortunes, but it is not hard nowadays

to find whole boys, girls, and adults living lives with aspects of wholeness and often super-humanity where once there were but sentimen-
tal Lame Prince-Little Matchgirl stereotypes. But don't take them from
memory—read them afresh before you introduce them. They may be
worse than "dated!"

One characteristic frequently met among dyslexic readers merits a
special look because it may have to do with the special capacity many
of them have to think, perceive, and solve problems globally, as whole
chunks of reality, rather than analytically and verbally. They have a
thirst for realism. Perhaps, as the reading of Samuel C. Florman's *The
Existential Pleasures of Engineering* suggested to me, it is because some
books give our "right-hemisphere-active" youngsters just the kind of
vicarious experiences in living they can feel most at home with. They
can see and feel themselves making use of the artifacts of Nuvat's Arc-
tic ancestors with him. They can milk cows and train steers with Al-
manzo in *Farmer Boy,* fight blizzards and grasshoppers and bears with
Pa and Ma and Mary and the others in the (real) *Little House* sequence.
They practice woodlore and camping with Dickon, as he lives with the
Lenape Indians, and they can climb the rigging in Alan Villier's
schoolships.

Florman points to *The Iliad* as a source of aesthetic satisfaction as
well as practical interest to the adult engineer, who relishes its exact
description of construction details of ships and buildings and other
vivid bits of reality. Perhaps it has the same bihemispheric appeal to
dyslexic boys, such as those to whom George Hayes read it at the Linden Hill School, their natural bent attuned to his Homeric enthusiasm.
An imaginative inspiration (and an enabling grant) gave him and his
older boys a chance to explore the real Troy, sail the Aegean, play soccer with boys in Rome, and experience the Pillars of Hercules for themselves. It did not, in all likelihood, make epic poets or civil engineers of
the boys, but neither they, George, the Board member who photo-
graphed it all, nor those of us who have seen the film, are ever likely to
forget the reality of that experience.

I think of Ralph, as bright and as dyslexic as they come at age
eight, who became a voracious and independent reader of all the sea-
going stories we had by eleven, made and more or less mastered his
own shop-built sextant at twelve, and by fourteen, had become a
knowledgeable authority on naval matters—history, ship design and
marine lore. For him this was an intense but passing phase; he now has
a double doctorate and a professorship in medicine and biochemistry—and a son as dyslexic as he was himself. One reads for many purposes—to learn how, to satisfy curiosity, to extend experience, to enjoy life, and sometimes as a precursor to a career. Ralph might have
gone on, as did his younger look-alike, temperamentally twin fellow-
alumnus who has sailed the waters of Southeast Asia in a small boat

and, along with becoming a physicist, has written sea-going sagas himself.

Much, much more could be said about the uses to which one can put reading experience, but this is enough. Let us turn for a moment to the general criteria appropriate for selection of books for "our" children. Where can you get help in looking? You can ask the "voice of experience." There is none better than Dorothy Tower in her letter to her grown-up daughter, "Books and Children". Or, for fuller treatment, there are those standard library references: May Hill Arbuthnot's 1977 edition of *Children and Books; * Annis Duff's *Bequest of Wings;* and Constantine Georgiau's *Children and Their Literature.*

These and many others tell what books are available and what they are about, but they do not tell—because most librarians and their guides do not know—which volumes are for which dyslexic readers. For this there is no substitute for doing it yourself. Some librarians can be very helpful, others moderately so, but they are very much worth consulting, especially school librarians. So are some teachers; but the final judgment rests on your informed and responsive experience and your students. You will build your list of books, as I have mine, and they will be among your best and quite indispensable teaching tools. Certainly you should not lean heavily on *my* guidance, especially for specifics.

I have told you somewhat autobiographically of just a few of the well-worn volumes I would pull again from my own shelves. In principle, I'll vouch for the choices, but your world and its children and its resources are different. To some extent, that is as it should be, though I find it an impoverishment that many young librarians and modern libraries are unaware of the still viable treasures with publication dates before 1969. This is as true here as it is in professional bibliographies, where only an occasional reference over 15 or 20 years old is cited, and even the products of the 1970s tend to be put in the half-price, stale-bread sales bins. On the other hand, you have undoubtedly noticed that most of the books I have referred to by title and most of the ones I have listed as the larger set I want to take to my desert island school for all-aged dyslexics are very much out of date by publishers' standards. Such are the unfortunate facts of publishing life that many of the best books are out of print and not always available in even rather good libraries. Quite a few of them, a knowledgeable author of children's books tells me, would probably not be read spontaneously by most modern children, who really want—are sure they do—more of the here and now, social problem stories, and more science fiction. I agree with them on the merits of sci-fi. I am, in fact, quite a fan and have been since the early days of Heinlein and the rest. Still, I think I could sell almost any of my enthusiasms to the right child at the right time, just as I saw a fine male therapist at a summer camp some years ago enjoying that social satire, *Fatapoufs and Thinifers*, with a 10-year-old boy in just the way I used to do forty-odd years ago. The principles are basically timeless. So, what does one look for in a good book?

In the first place, I don't think I could have a valid opinion on books for children unless I kept on reading adult books for my own information, growth, and pleasure. In literature as elsewhere, "What do they know of England who only England know?" One needs to encourage the "open personality" and a wide range of taste, at home as well as in the classroom and the clinic. I'll be attracted to a book if it is well-written by adult standards, with clear, felicitous prose (or verse, about which I have not spoken, though not for lack of enthusiasm), well-planned plot and characterization, accurate but well-assimilated and usually unobtrusive background research, clear explanation if its purpose is to give a matrix for further information. I'll be likely to use a book with students, and enjoy it myself, if it has humor and imagination and is alive and paced appropriately for its subject and readers, with the right amount of print on each page and chapter and between the covers. It should, of course, be appropriately printed, bound, and illustrated with pictures of artistic worth and essential conformity to the facts of the text, and so arranged as to enhance without being intrusive. Then one can enjoy it aesthetically and physically as well as intellectually. Genuine sensitivity, not sentimentality, is important. It takes the genius of E.B. White to address with satisfying subtlety, as he does in *Charlotte's Web,* such great moral issues as good and evil, justice and mercy, appreciative acceptance of one's own self and the precious difference of others, the whole business of how to meet the joys and vicissitudes of life, and the growth of real people in real and satisfying ways. But it is this kind of excellence we are looking for in a book for any age or reading ability.

Can books really touch the lives of children? I think Edward Eager knew when he gave his children in *Seven-day Magic* the experience and the words we may well listen to. Here is Barnaby, the prime idea-man among the five quite real, not quite prosaic, children who were returning to the library with the book itself as a flying carpet, using the library roof as their heliport. The children were following Barnaby's lead. As the story goes from there:

> They went down a ladder and found themselves in the upper part of the library, where they had never ventured before because only grown-ups were allowed.
>
> "Think of all those books we haven't read yet," said Abby [the poet].
>
> "Maybe some of *them* have magic inside, too!" said Fredericka [the youngest].

"*All* of them, I should think," said Barnaby, "one way or another."

Barnaby already knew, and perhaps said better than any of us, that if man cannot transcend himself and partake of the nature of his growing, innovative kinship with the Universal—his full humanity— it will not be for lack of stimulation and liberation provided *par excellence* in books. Those people, be they few or many, whom we teach to read with skill and enthusiasm and who use their skills to give them touch with their heritage and to feed their minds and spirits, make our game well worth the candle.

7

The Structure of English:
The Language to be Learned

The material in this paper has been culled from many sources, especially in psychology, semantics, linguistics, and pedagogy. This organization of the structure of English with an eye to maximal rationalization of its spelling is only in small part my own. First there were the pioneering insights of Orton, then the prodigious work of organization and detail of Gillingham and Stillman through seven editions of their manual from 1930 till 1970—a monumental contribution. Sally Childs, through her Spelling Curriculum, supplemented by other works, has focused attention on reorganization of approach and refinements of pedagogic technique in line with new developments in psychology and linguistics. Their work has enormously facilitated the practical implementations of the designers of texts, guides, materials, and workbooks. They have inspired and guided the programs of schools and clinic services and such complete programs as those of the Texas Scottish Rite Hospital Language Unit in Dallas, the Remedial Reading Center in Rochester, Minnesota, and the Massachusetts General Hospital Language Clinic.

Those of us who have come into the field on tributaries from the '30s to the present day have been able to join the main stream, each in his own way, for such is the structured flexibility of this approach that there is ample room for individuality. The constraints are provided by the nature of the language to be taught, the ways a human being learns, and the unique needs of language-disabled learners as a group and as individuals.

The focus in this paper is on the first of these constraints, especially the spelling patterns of English, with accommodation to it, in the light of the other strictures, by one teacher and pupil working together. Within practical limits one never can—nor should one try to—

Adapted and reprinted with permission from The Orton Dyslexia Society from *Bulletin of The Orton Society* 20:103–123 1970 and Reprint No. 35.

tell it all. If what Dan and I have coordinated here, with the help of those on whose shoulders we gratefully stand, is of help to some readers and their students, we shall be glad. Better yet, other teams can improve and elaborate what we suggest here. The field is open.

Our subject here is the anatomy of the language we speak—the beautiful, venerable, and complicated English tongue. What we do about it all depends on how we see the problem. At its broadest, language is the vehicle—the symbolic carrier—of meaning from one mind to another, through intervening space by some means—waves of sound, electricity, light. For now, we are concerned with the message itself, the meaning and especially the form in which it is transmitted.

Language may be of art, music, or the lovers' or the mother's touch, but here we confine ourselves to *verbal* language—the system every fully human being must learn and, please note, must be taught by other human beings.

We are all troubled about this difficult language our children are struggling with. Most of us adults are in the linguistically underprivileged generation—too young to have been well-taught in the old, classical tradition. (It wasn't all good, by any means, but if we were academically apt we did learn how to use language tools and to sharpen up our subjunctives.) We are also too old to have profited in our schooling from the recent advances in scientific linguistics and computer technology; they will be for some of our younger children and our grandchildren. Even those of us who have studied the subject as adult professionals, however, might like to refresh our minds on some facts of English language life.

First of all, we should remind ourselves that, as the semanticists say, "The word is not the thing"—it is only a sequence of noises that stands for the thing, or the idea, or the experience. "It means," in Humpty Dumpty's words, "just what I choose it to mean, neither more, nor less." Well, that's what *my* words mean to *me*. What they mean to *you* depends on you; and whether I convey what's in my mind to you depends on how much of our background experience is alike and whether we symbolize it in words the same way. If we all speak English (or Eskimo or Urdu) we do have much in common, but never quite enough—witness the hassles we get into over definitions— "What do you mean dyslexia? There's no such thing." "There is, too. I ought to know. I've got it!"

Let's look at the spoken language a child from a middle-class English-speaking family brings to first grade.

It consists of meaningful sentences of from one to many words, like this long, written one, or like "Scram!" The words are in the right order—they must be in English, "Fido bit Junior" (too bad, better get the doctor); or "Junior bit Fido" (unlikely, better get the psychiatrist).

This is still acceptable as English, though, as is the even less believable headline: **Former Resident on the Moon Helped Land Men.**

The child uses the right word forms too. "I hit him, (and am I glad!)" or "He hit me (and am I mad!)" but not "Him hit I." Plurals and tenses are generally conventional by five or six, with only an occasional "Will you helpen me? I loozed my ball." In other words, the child knows, without knowing he knows, grammar—syntax, word order—and morphology—word form. If he doesn't, the kindergarten teacher and the speech therapist will work on it with him and his parents. His sentences may be short and simple or tangled, and ours perhaps should be shorter than they often are, and clearer—a lifetime job, for him and for all of us.

He has a good vocabulary, too, several thousand words (5,000 or more is a conservative estimate), with which to make his meaning reasonably clear and there are other words that he can comprehend, well or dimly, but not use. As an educated adult he will use about 17,000 words other than his occupationally technical vocabulary, so he has a good start on words in their grammatical context when he gets to first grade—from a middle class home.

Normally, no matter what his background, by six he is ready to learn to read anything he can understand when he hears it from outside his head, or from within, in his thinking. He has mastered one code—the system of translating into ideas the sounds-in-sequences which you and I know as words. You notice that influenced by modern linguistics, we *begin with the spoken language* which is then written down in letters which *tell people what to say*—not with printed "letters which *have sounds*" or "say a"—(Letters are the signals, not the speakers.) To apprehend a writer's message in our system the reader must be able (whether he actually does so or not) to speak the word for which the printed or written form stands—the one which the writer dictated to himself as he wrote.

This translation into the speech of the writer is neither necessary, nor often possible, if writing is pictographic. In this "thing-writing," ♀ can be /man/, /homo/, /hombre/, or whatever you are accustomed to, but the vocabulary is small. With ideographic writing, like Chinese, the minds of sender and receiver of the message meet in the understanding of the sign-pictured thought. They might not be able to talk together, but it doesn't matter. This is a very useful attribute of the parallel-code languages—as anyone who has driven by international highway signs appreciates. But if one wants to use a powerful and versatile language like Mandarin Chinese, the graphic vocabulary and the visual memory load are staggering to most learners, about 22,000 characters.

But fortunately once, though apparently only once, in man's history (among the Phoenicians or their forebears, perhaps), the alphabetic principle was invented. A sign or letter came to stand for a basic sound, or phoneme. The word-sign for ox—aleph ⊲ —became henceforth the sign for /ä/* which the Romans and we were to write A. By this simple principle we Indo-European speakers can encode all our languages with just a few letters. In English, we have only 26 symbols, though we need many more to represent at least 24 consonant and 14 vowel sounds (some linguists distinguish more) which make up the basic sound units (called phonemes) of our stream of speech. We make up the lacks in our symbol repertoire with spelling conventions so that, for example, s and h take care of /s/, /h/, and also /sh/ for which we have no symbol. The ways we write the more variously spelled vowel sounds with six or seven vowel letters, singly or in combination, are more complicated, but still, if you know enough, the system is over 85 percent predictable. You can do even better if you realize that such de-mons as *was* and *laugh* are only partly nonphonetic or irregular. If we match a usual or possible sound to each letter we get an approximation which is often close enough, especially for reading, where we fill in with what one student called "good, tame guesses."

This makes the mastery of the English code possible, learning 26 letters, which are as dependable in identity as 10 numerals (almost, because letter type fonts vary more than numerical ones). Even learn-ing the necessary additional letter-sound patterns and the coding prin-ciples leaves us with a much easier task than learning a large vocabul-ary of sight words. Our 26 letters, properly combined, generate all the combinations necessary to produce Webster's Unabridged, with as many possibilities left over for foolishness as we can want, such as Jab-berwocky, and "turbo encabulator" (that engineers' nonsense instru-ment with the "reciprocating dingle-arm").

It is time now to consider the structure of verbal language in a condensed sequence. First we'll take a general overview, then a more particular one. Even so, much will have to be omitted lest this become a volume; let a sequence of instances represent the grand design.

First, in the history of the race and the development of the individ-ual, as we have said, comes *speech*. This is *Code 1.* (Refer to Figure 2 on page 62 or Appendix.) As shown on the left side of Figure 2, audible language comes into the listening ear and goes out through the speak-ing voice. The linguists break it up this way: The elements of spoken sound, as heard electrically in the acoustics lab but not consciously rec-ognizable by us, are called *phones* (sounds). We, as ordinary but acute listeners, begin with *phonemes,* the sound units that make a difference in the identity of words, the ones we teach as phonograms, like /b/, /ă/, /ch/ and the like. These are blended together as in *batch*, into *morphemes* (words and word-parts to the likes of us, as for example, *boy* and the s

---

*Letters or words between slashes, / /, indicate spoken sounds.

in *boys*). Morphemes are the basic units of *lexical* meaning, to be found in the dictionary, "the words themselves," we say. *Utterances,* from a one-word sentence like "Scram!" to phrases, clauses, sentences, paragraphs, and so on, are the carriers of *semantic sense,* the meaning for which the verbal message exists (the inner language of the diagram). In polysyllabic words, and in longer linguistic units, *stress,* or accent, helps with identification and/or meaning (compare pres'-ent and pre-sent'), as do *pitch,* the rising and falling patterns of utterance (Yeah! or Yeah?), and *juncture,* ways of interrupting the stream of speech between words and phrases ("Not every white house is a White House"). Semantic meaning also requires us to use the culturally agreed upon word *inflections* and *word-orders.* When we speak according to the above structure, we *encode thought,* and when we listen to speech, we *decode it into thought.* It is important to note that *speech is verbal sound arranged in time-sequence.*

This, in brief, is *Code 1,* for the transmission of thought from mind to mind.

Now for *Code 2,* speech recoded into visible writing or print, in *space-patterns* mapped, or nearly matched, to the sound patterns of speech, and often defined as a *second-order symbolization* of thought. This is shown in the right half of Figure 2; printed words come into the mind through the eye and go out through the writing hand.

Here we, as English users, begin with the *alphabet,* with its 26 invariant *names* and their variant *forms* (printed and written, capital and lower-case). These *letters,* each *space-oriented* singly (*b-d-p-q-g*), or in groups (like *ch, ou*), are the linguists' *graphemes,* the visible units which represent (not "say") the audible phonemes. *Spatially ordered,* they signal the temporally blended phonemes which make up the morphemes, the words we read, and at the next level, the *groups of words* which stand for longer and more semantically complete utterances, written, of course, in the order in which they would be spoken. Punctuation and other devices help with vocalization, as do context and style with semantics.

This, then, is *Code 2,* relating sound and print. When we encode speech, we write; in order to read, in the primary sense, we decode into speech, whether or not the vocal organs and the air waves participate.

To recapitulate even more briefly, the way to get the semantic message (inner language) from mind to mind may be through the audible route (Code 1) of speaking-to-be-listened-to; or it may be with the visible route (Code 2) of writing-to-be-read interposed between mental speaking and mental hearing. (See also "Developmental Dyslexia: Educational Treatment and Results," p. 59.)

Now let us narrow down to the relation of the two codes to each other, and consider not reading but spelling—encoding from speech to print. Why do we follow conventions and how do they pattern?

Why conventions in spelling? We want to get the message across to the reader with the most information (relevant signals) and the least noise (or static) we can manage. There are two rules, or codifications of useful behavior, to serve this end. First, "If you hear it, spell it." Second, "Spell it the way the educated reader is used to seeing it, so he won't be distracted from your message by what he will think of as your 'spelling errors.' " In emergencies, of course, just do the best you can. Even Dogpatch spelling (strictly phonic) can get an important message across, just as the doggie stroke can get you through the water if you don't know a more effective one. But it is useful to learn to swim, and even to spell. It's a complicated system, but it is a system which will repay a closer look. But first consider a couple of written instances.

Figure 7 gives a sample of Tom's writing to dictation. Although he was 14, and bright, he was spelling at a less than Dogpatch level of efficiency. To remove the static from the puzzle, here is a translation:

Truly the hour when he was compelled to develop a composition seemed the longest and grimmest of the whole week. He fretted, chewed his pencil, regretted that he had not applied himself earlier, and thought of other ways he would have preferred to spend (or was it 'have spent'?) the hour. In fact, he underwent every form

TOM

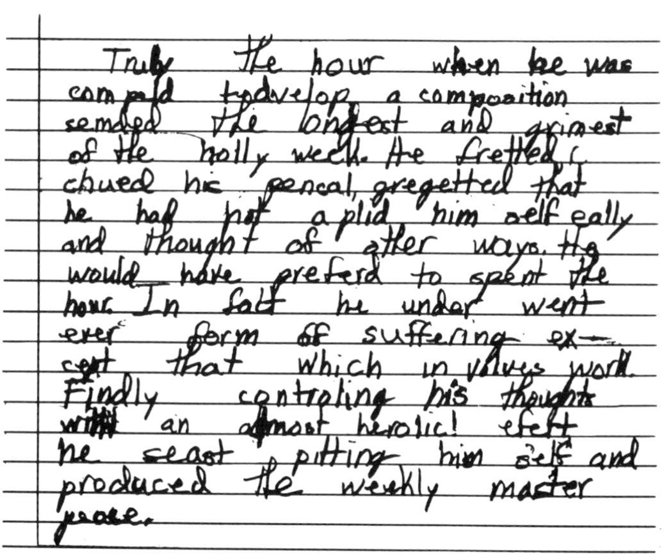

Figure 7. *Dictation sample by Tom, an extremely dyslexic, bright, 14-year-old.*

of suffering except that which involves work. Finally, controlling his thoughts with an almost heroic effort, he ceased pitying himself and produced the weekly masterpiece.

(There is, you'll be glad to know, a happy ending, Tom did learn to spell well enough to get a top-university degree, in English which he is now teaching in a first-class secondary school. But it took a lot of ingredients to pull it off, a very important one of which was one of Anna Gillingham's most expert graduates.)

The second sample, free of static, needs no interpretation (Figure 8). This boy, Dan, at the end of Grade 7, had already had the help Tom had needed and had been able to assimilate it better than Tom, the more severely dyslexic of the two, ever did. Dan co-authored the spelling book from which most of the other examples in this paper are used, with his permission.

It might be of interest here to note that at 11, Dan's WISC score was good but not remarkable. A left-hander, he wrote at first in the hook position, but all work here shown was done after he had changed to the standard position. How did he learn to spell—to master this aspect of "the language as it is?"

First he worked on the *phoneme-grapheme correspondences* (Linkages 7 and 8, familiar to those who use the Gillingham Manual) until he had the simpler ones automatic and the multi-choice ones (like long vowels)

DAN

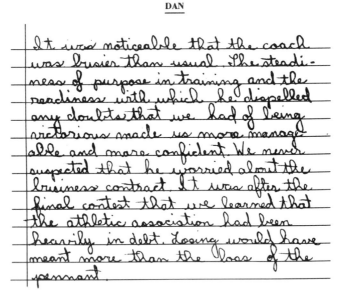

Figure 8. Dictation sample by Dan, moderately dyslexic, age 13, IQ comparable with Tom's (Figure 7), after two years of systematic spelling instruction.

well in mind, with their probability behaviors in usable form. While he was doing this, of course, he was applying each new item of knowledge and skill to written words and longer sequences. He learned a lot in his first year, as a sixth-grader. All of it was fitted together, first in his teacher's mind, and then it went into the total system as Dan built it into his spelling book the next year, as more and more of his spelling vocabulary moved from the unknown to the sound-spelling and rational categories (Childs and Childs 1963). Some of his pages were review and some new work, and there was a lot of reference back to early pages as he went along, with new or problem words being entered where they belonged. The pedagogy? It was systematic but flexible. Its structure and sequences came largely from the Orton-Gillingham approach. Sometimes he was "just told," (quite didactically) but wherever it could be managed he was helped either to generalize from the evidence (by induction, sometimes called discovery) or to solve spelling problems with knowledge he already had (deductively). The concepts were introduced in appropriately and consciously interrelated minisequences. Arranged logically for our review, here is what he had to master, largely summarized in Table I (p. 114) and briefly described below.

Base Words

1. The *closed monosyllable* (ending with a consonant). First came the many little ones with a short vowel sound followed by a single consonant sound, spelled with one letter each—the two and three letter words, like *bit*, as a sound pattern simply spelled, or as a morphemic or pronounceable nonsense unit. ("Bit" as the information theorist's unit of input was a pun our computer-age Dan appreciated.) To these simplest graphemes were added *consonant diagraphs* and *consonant clusters* or blends, up to the complexity of *splash*.

2. The *polysyllable* of two, or more, *closed syllables* like *gambit* or *rabbit*, up to and beyond *establishment*, but with emphasis on two-syllable words. (–v̆ c·c v–)*

3. *Gillingham's Rule 1.* This is a left-over from history, when many present-day short-vowel monosyllables were dissyllables, had final *e*'s or *e*-suffixes, and a doubled consonant was needed as a signal, "First vowel short, syllable stressed." When no longer necessary, the second consonant was generally dropped, along with the by-then-silent *e*, as in *bad*, *leg*, but in some cases the second consonant was kept, as in words ending, now, in *ll*, *ff*, *ss*, often *zz*. Here Dan added *ck*, *tch*, and *dge*, because, functionally, they are doubled consonants, too, and follow the same spelling pattern. (v̆ c c)

---

*v = vowel, c = consonant, · = syllable division, – = other letters.

Table I

Partial Outline of English Spelling

BASE WORDS
1. Closed monosyllables: *bit* to *splash*
      Pattern ŏ c [vowel + consonant(s)]
2. Polysyllables closed: *gambit, rabbit, establishment*
      ŏ c'·c v, ŏ(c'·c)v
3. Monosyllables with double (or "reinforced") consonants: *bell, batch*
      ŏ (cc)
4. Final-e, long vowel: *safe*
      −v̄cȩ, an instance of −v̄cv
5. Open syllables, stressed, long vowel: *me, po'-ny*
      −v̄ or v̄'·cv
6. Patterns for 2-syllable words
      a. *gambit* (−ŏ̱c'·cv−)
         rabbit (ŏ c'·c v−)
      b. *pony* (−v̄'·cv−)
      c. *robin* (−ŏc'·v−)
      d. *begin* (−v̇·cv') (an unstressed "long vowel" sounds "half-long")
7. Two-syl., cons + *le* words. See patterns 6a, b, above and Figure 9
8. Consonant-spelling choices
9. Other spellings for long and variant vowel sounds

DERIVATIVES
10. Plurals
11. Possessives
12. Addition of suffixes
      a. After final consonant (Table II)
      b. After final *e*
      c. After final *y*
13. Addition of prefixes; assimilation (Figure 10)
14. Word building: simple compounds, root compounds; affixes; etymology

GENERALIZING SPELLING EXPERIENCE
15. Double consonants, summary (Figure 11)
16. Relation of syllabic stress to vowel quantity and spelling signals; dealing with *schwa*
17. Functions of final *e*
18. Four principles for spelling long vowel sounds
19. Customary usages: *y* and *i* as alternative spellings for vowel and consonant sounds
20. Vocabulary of language terms

---

4. The *final-e, long vowel* pattern. This was not called *magic-e*. It is, in fact, a signal to tell the reader, "Make the long vowel sound," and does not "make the vowel say its name." This pattern leads to the principle or convention that a vowel is usually given its long sound if only one consonant stands between it and the next vowel. These so-called

"silent *e's*" were formerly sounded, but now they are kept only for their signal-value. ($\bar{v}$ c $\cancel{e}$)

5. *Open syllables*, stressed, ending in single vowel, which is long, as in monosyllables like *I, me, go* (there is nowhere else for stress), and *po'·ny* and still longer polysyllables, but with emphasis on two-syllable words. ($-\bar{v}$, or $-\bar{v}'$·c v)

6. *Standard patterns for two-syllable words.* (This is easier for children than for adults, I find.)

    a. *gam'·bit* (spelled as sounded), *rab'·bit* (second b silent, but a useful signal to readers). See principle in 3, above ($-\breve{v}$c·cv$-$)

    b. *po'·ny*—see principle, in 5. ($-\bar{v}'$·c v)

    c. *rob'·in* ($-\breve{v}$ c'·v$-$) there are a good many of these and the fact that a given one *is* of the "robin-type" must be learned; they sound like rabbit types but look like pony-types. A second try gets you out of the reading problem they pose, but in spelling that may not work, because spelling depends on visual memory. "When you *hear* only one consonant after a stressed short vowel in a base word, as a best guess, use two—or better still, the dictionary!"

    d. The o-mit' and be-gin' words are a third-choice pattern for reading but make no trouble in spelling—until you must recognize them when adding suffixes—see 12a.

7. The many 2-syllable, *consonant + le* words, almost always follow patterns 6a and 6b. That is, they are "rabbits" *(rabble)*, if they are not "gambits" *(gamble)*, or "ponies" *(stable)*. (Figure 9)

8. *Consonant spelling choices* dictated by: etymology (*f* or *ph*, etc.); convention (final *ge, ve*); probability (likelihood of initial *c* and final *k* spellings of /k/, with many predictable variations); etc.

9. *Other* ways of signaling *long and variant vowel sounds*, including diphthongs. Note: 8 or 9 have many mini-sequences, mostly taught earlier but structuralized here for convenience.

Derivatives

The foregoing words were unitary, not derivatives. In forming variants, the principle is to be as logical as possible in giving signals to the reader—but there are exceptions he will be expecting you to know; don't let them throw you. (A "set for diversity" has its values.)

10. *Plurals*—regularly add *s*, sometimes *es*, (always if you hear /ez/, and often using the rule developed in 12b below).

11. *Possessives*—add an apostrophe ('), and an *s* only if you hear it *added* in speech.

12. *Other suffixes*. Three most useful rules in spelling. They are

Consonant- le Words

"Pony" type	"Rabbit" type	Others
tā́-ble	bríl̄-ble	săm-́ple (sounds)
brū̄-́gle	lit-́tle	nee-́dle (2 or.)
stifle	struggle	tremble (s)
rifle	apple	tumble (s)
cradle	bottle	tangle
stable	riddle	people
able	pickle (ck=double)	trouble
	buckle	wrinkle
	pebble	double (2 or.)
	bubble	syllable (accent)
		feeble (2 or.)
		eagle (2 or.)
		Robin type
	whistle (stle=ssel)	treble
	rustle	triple
	castle	
	wrestle	

Figure 9. Sample page from spelling notebook of Dan (see Figure 8), grade 7. Classification of 2-syllable, consonant + le words.

better presented, or better still, developed, as diagrams than as verbal rules, or even formulas.

  a. If there is a *final consonant on the base word*, just add the suffix unless you need to double it to fit the "rabbit" pattern (see 6a, above.) You are concerned with the last (or only) two syllables of the *derived* word; make a "rabbit" if you need to, never a "robin" which could be mistaken for a "pony"; your reader needs to know whether you are *beginning hopping* or *hoping* for an *opening*. (Table II)

  b. If there is a *final silent e*, just add the suffix unless it begins with a vowel which can take the *e's* place; use the principle in 3, above. (*a, o,* or *u* cannot signal "soft" *c* or *g*; *e, i,* or *y* can do so.)

Table II
Scheme for notebook page: Adding suffixes to base words which end with consonants.

If suffix begins with	Most words	Word Patterns 1, 1, 1 or 2, 1', 1
Cons.	I *Just add* (encampment)	III *Just add* (shipment) (unfit'ness)
Vowel	II *Just add* (ending) (headed) (lim'ited)	IV *Double cons.,* *then add* (A. shipping) (B. begin'ning)

Code:

1, 1, 1 means:
1 syllable
1 vowel
1 consonant
   after vowel

2, 1', 1 means:
2 or more
   syllables
1 stressed
   vowel fol-
   lowed by
1 consonant in
   last syllable
   (next to last
   syllable in de-
   rived word,
   which, thus,
   "ends with a
   'gambit' or a
   'rabbit' ")

Examples

Just add	Double
(Specify: I, II, III) heartless I greatest II badly III +	(Specify: A. or B.) hotter IV A. omitted IV B. +

Stated differently: If you still need the *e*, keep it; if you don't, drop it.

c. If the base word *ends in a sounded y* not part of a diphthong (that is, a *y* preceded by a consonant) change the *y* to *i* before adding the suffix, unless the latter begins with *i*. *Principles*—1. two *i*'s together make a non-English pattern. 2. *y* is the preferred, almost invariable, final spelling for its several sounds, but *i* is the preferred, though not invariable, non-final spelling for the same sounds; many changes are the result of this English convention.

Important caution: Look at the base word! If conditions demand it, there is one thing, and *only one* you may do:

1. A final *consonant* may be *doubled;*
2. A final *e* may be *dropped;*
3. A final *y* may be *changed to i.*

Especially, *don't* drop a *y* as long as you hear it, nor double a consonant after dropping a final *e;* a word can't end two ways at once! Dan worked out diagrams similar to Table II for 12a, b, and c.

13. *Prefixes*—are either simply added or have a final consonant changed for euphony, as in *assimilation,* which is both an example and the name given to the procedure (*ad* becomes *as*). Similarly, *syn* changes in *sympathy, syllable.* "Chameleon" prefixes. (Figure 10)

14. *Word building,* for change of basic meaning or grammatical function; simple compounding *(fishhook),* root compounding *(photograph),* addition of affixes (*affixes,* itself). Etymology, with consideration of Anglo-Saxon, Latin and Greek roots, prefixes and suffixes begun at this point, is too involved a subject for the present outline but proved interesting and useful to Dan.

Some Other Groupings Which Generalize Spelling Experience

15. *Doubled consonants* can be expected in six situations, which take care of 90 percent of that problem. (Figure 11)

16. How *vowel quantity* and, hence often sound, is *related to stress.* The more stress, the longer the long sound and the more clearly identifiable the short sound—the less stress, the closer they get to the short-

"Chameleon" Preffixes - Assimilation

	Double	Not Double
ad	accident (ch.)	
com	connect "	coincident
dis	difference "	
ex	effort "	emit
in	illuminate "	incident
ob	office "	
sub	supply "	
syn	syllable "	
	addition (co.)	[co. = coincidental
	commission (co)	doubles]
	dissolve (co.)	
	obbligatto (" irreg.)	

Figure 10. *"Chameleon prefixes," showing doubled consonants resulting from* assimilation. *From Dan's spelling notebook.*

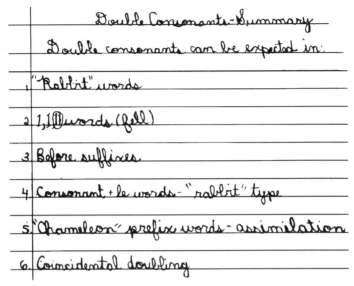

Figure 11. Notebook page summarizing about 90 percent of the occurrences of "double" consonants in English spelling.

est sound of all, the *schwa*, or even to the vestigial /t'l/ (of *little*), or /t'n/ (of *often*, if you don't say /off'n/, or *captain*). Sometimes an exaggerated, or "spelling pronunciation," approach helps here.

17. *Final, "silent e"* can be expected in six situations where it is functional, in addition to the "no-job e."

18. There are four common *principles for spelling long vowel sounds,* some more likely in some places, some in others, but it helps to have a starting inventory when one is eliminating unlikely ones, narrowing the choices. See Gillingham lists for probabilities. Dan developed lists for 17 and 18 similar to Figure 11.

19. There are contextual and historical clues to the uses of *vowel-y* as an alternative to *i* or the reverse and of these two letters to spell the *consonant-y* sound.

20. It helps to know the *vocabulary of language-about-language* (meta-*language*, it is sometimes called); this improves the communication between mind₁ (student) and mind₂ (teacher). Dan's list: (Figure 12)

Danny didn't know all there is to know about all this, of course, and he did know quite a few additional things that were easier to learn, and even to use, than they were to squeeze into this summary outline. Teaching, as well as learning, is a multi-dimensional affair. While we, ourselves, are keeping the structure of the language in mind, we need also to remember the learner's need for a program that is at once: *structured, sequential, cumulative,* and *thorough.* It is to be kept constantly in mind, also, that we want both education, for understanding, to make

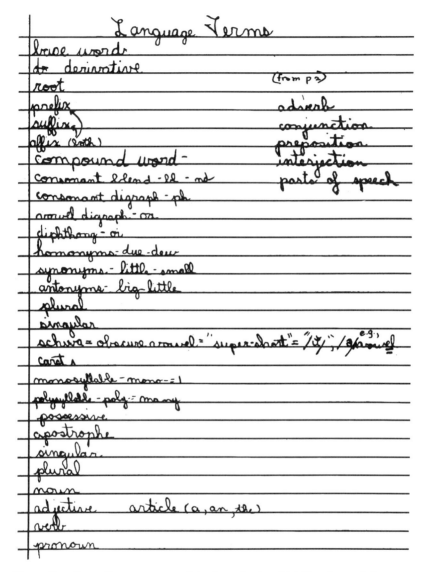

Figure 12.   Some "language terms" in the order in which Dan learned them.

the principles clear, and training, or practice, to make the elements stick and the processes automatic. The skills are to be learned through all the sensory avenues of learning open to the student—*visual, auditory* and *tactile-kinesthetic, in interaction* (our familiar multisensory approach). But although we use all the input and output modalities, we do it with the full realization that clear vision, sharp hearing, and controlled muscles are the necessary servants. *Yet the mind is the master.* It is, in the end, not the eye, the ear, the voice or the hand, but the brain which learns both to read in order to understand, and to write that others may read. And so we teach the language as it is to the child as he is—a human nervous system with a unique configuration, a thinking, learning person. This will take all the knowledge, skill and wisdom we can muster in the years it takes to become professionally competent, an endlessly fascinating life-time challenge.

(PS 1988. Dan, a church pastor with two academic degrees, reports that he still uses the "standard" hand position for writing and many of these spelling principles—when he is not relying on his computer.)

Part III
The Orton Trail

1

The Boswell Function

Everyone who does not keep a detailed journal needs a Boswell, but this link with posterity is more important to some than to others. Society may need for there to have been such a recorder, especially if the Johnson in the case has made significant contributions through his life work. The need is even greater with this (or, indeed, any) person who has died "in the traces" or has brought his life-work to the punctuation point of retirement but has died before having had time to review and make a considered evaluation of that life's findings.

Among our pioneers, Norman Geschwind fits the first category and Samuel T. Orton, and, in some sense, June Orton and Anna Gillingham fit the second. They were too busy *doing*, and thinking about other people's lives to give reflective written consideration to their own cumulative experience. Fortunately, there are still enough people who knew them and they did enough writing in their fields of interest so that their "posthumous Boswells" may have at least some chance of keeping their spirits as well as their written works alive for the future.

Samuel Orton, the leader of the leaders in our field, had his first interpreter in his wife, June L. Orton, without whose biographical summaries and personal reminiscences much of significance would have been lost. Roger E. Saunders, Lucia Karnes, and I were among those fortunate enough to have these recollections direct from her. Several people who were personally associated with Dr. Orton have also shared their memories and associations with me, and I even have a very few of my own. For me, every contact with Dr. Orton was memorable. Other people have reported the same experience.

David Charnow, who is reading the entire file of Samuel Orton's records, now housed in the Medical Library at Columbia University, has found the personal essence of the great physician and scientist there. Charnow, during a sensitive, yet fully aware, *de novo* immersion in the Orton past, has been able to bring almost to life the man himself. He appears as he practiced medicine and truly cared about his patients, while continuing to develop and mature his scientific understanding of the central interest of the last half of his professional life. Charnow purposely undertook his explorations without the mind-set that extensive prior literature search might have given him. (His mind was well-prepared in other ways for this unique approach.) What he has discerned from the original records squares extremely well with the accumulated findings to be derived from other sources. In fact, there are numerous point-to-point relationships between the personal records and the ripening of Orton's views to be had from an intensive study of his papers published from 1925 onward.

It is, in fact, Charnow's experience that has suggested to me the need, and the remarkable possibility, for a kind of unknown interpreter to play Boswell to someone he has not personally known. This is the kind of service that life and the best of history really owes to a person cut off from the opportunity to formulate during his latter years the wisdom that is in him. In the end, we all benefit.

Roger Saunders and Lucia Karnes, who knew June Orton perhaps better than any of us, would doubtless be able to add not only substantially (as I could myself) but *essentially* to what I have said this year, but for whatever it may contribute, my offering is in the "Trail" paper (see p. 136).

Anna Gillingham did have her Boswell in Sally B. Childs. She also had partners like Bessie Stillman, Orton himself, Paul Dozier, and Paula D. Rome, Jane McClelland, and others who knew her well, but it was Sally Childs who was her designated professional heir and who did a comprehensive job of collecting her works, writing her history, and keeping her invaluable teaching materials in print and available. I knew Anna Gillingham well but very briefly almost at the end of her life when she might have been finishing her life-appraisal if she had not been carrying on her work to her uttermost. Still, in some ways, I have known parts of her background better than others could, and these I have attempted to contribute to the "Trail," together with some overall comments.

So, to some extent, the preliminary "Trail Papers" from which the conference paper for November, 1986, took its origin, are under the influence of Boswell, in disguise.

2

Orton: The Educator

What little we know, what little power we possess, we owe to the accumulated endeavors of our ancestors. Mere gratefulness would already oblige us to study the history of the endeavors, our most precious heirlooms. But we are not to remain idle spectators. It is not enough to appreciate and admire what our ancestors did, we must take up their best traditions, and that implies expert knowledge and craftsmanship, science and practice. (George Sarton 1931, 1956.)

The immediate ancestors of the approaches to teaching set forth here are Samuel Torrey Orton (1879–1948) and Anna Gillingham (1878–1963). Orton and Gillingham came together in 1931 in the Neurological Institute of the Columbia-Presbyterian Medical Center in New York. Each was prepared in his or her own way for a collaboration in which one might say that *primarily* Dr. Orton was the scientist-physician and Miss Gillingham was the educator—"engineer." While they shared philosophy, ethos, and expertise, he specialized in finding out the possibilities and she in ways to achieve their goals with their patient-pupils. In this paper, I shall focus on Orton's influence on the diagnosis and educational treatment of those we call dyslexics.

Orton

Samuel Torrey Orton, an intellectual, a scientist, and a humanitarian was a giant among the initiators of professional treatment and understanding of dyslexia. Beginning in 1925, he provided its first major understanding, expertise, and impetus. Like other creative contributors to the richness of human life, he had a particular combination of innate and cultural roots from which he sprang. He pursued his interests and enthusiasms in his unique era, nourished by his personal and professional associates and activities and strengthened rather than defeated by the difficulties and oppositions he met.

As a compassionate physician his primary goal was to foster the well-being of his patients. Understanding their needs, alleviating their difficulties, and educating others to work toward these ends and to pursue them progressively into the future were his way to serve that purpose.

The details of Orton's biography need not concern us here; there are ample references for those who wish them (see, among others, J.L. Orton 1966a, 1975; Rawson 1987). What is of present interest to us are the scientific background on which he based his clinical appraisal of his patients' difficulties and the educational practices he proposed as consistent with that background.

The problems of those of his patients with whom we are here concerned were specifically in language and its learning. Hence he concluded that their treatment should be based in the nature of the brain as it processes language and in the characteristics of the language the young people he saw were striving to master. Since human language and its learning are complex and each learner is unique, there is an almost endless variety of ways in which the process can go wrong or can take a course so different from the one expected as to *seem* wrong to those in charge.

Whatever the pattern, it was Orton's belief that as careful and complete a diagnosis of each patient as possible was the necessary prelude to successful treatment. Only such belief and practice would be consistent with this man's professional orientation, whether his prescription called for a medical or an educational regimen.

Paul Irvine was to say in 1969, in his series of profiles of "Pioneers in Special Education":

> Samuel Torrey Orton: With brilliant tenacity, he sought solutions to the perplexities and the dilemmas posed by children who should but could not read. Seeking specific determinants and causes, he never lost sight of the total child. Hewing to a medical etiology, his remedial approaches were by and large educational. His voice, uncertainly and hesitantly heard in his day, rings clear and vibrant in ours.

The medical etiology that Irvine refers to was that of a neurologist, for Orton was a broad, yet thorough, student of the best of brain science of his day. It seemed reasonable to him to look to that organ of the mind, the brain itself, and how it works, to find the answers to his questions about how each human being can master the language of the culture in which he grows up, or how and why he may fail to do so.

It was already accepted knowledge in the medical world that language, at least in right-handers, was dependent on proper functioning of the left hemisphere of the brain. Gross localization of various aspects of the function within the hemisphere was accepted by most neuroscientists, including Orton. Little was known about the purposes of the right hemisphere, except in those left-handers whose language processes apparently took place there.

Orton observed that the motor preferences of more of his patients than would be expected were for the left side, or that they were ambidextrous or ill-established in their choices for either side. It seemed to him that this and other aspects of their spatially unpredictable behavior might have something to do with their language problems. It seemed to him probable that the cause might not lie in either of these phenomena but that they might have some common cause further back in developmental history.

Either hemisphere could process language, but one should be and generally was, in charge. Orton reasoned that failure to establish such dominance might well be the primary factor in most forms of specific language learning difficulty.

Orton's so-called cerebral dominance theory was by no means his sole contribution to the field, but, because it is so different from the common opinion, it is the one for which he is most often known. Its validity has quite generally been questioned, although some recent Harvard-Beth Israel research data suggest that it may, after all, have been rather more correct but ahead of its time than naive or over-simple; we still do not know and may never be entirely sure.

In any case, Orton's treatment prescription makes sense on educational grounds even without the hypothesis. It should be noted that he did not (as is often mistakenly said) try to change the innate make-up of his patients; his aim was to devise a treatment regimen that would enable each of them to function well, making the best possible use of his initial endowments. This involved self-insightful (we would now say metalinguistic) understanding and systematic practice to build dependable language competency. If the student's external behavior made any change in his brain organization, it would be in the establishment of skill patterns through reinforcement of what Orton called "the physiological habit of use."

Many times in the history of medicine, as appears to be the case here, treatment practices have been successfully used for a long time before their rationales have been established through proof that satisfies the strict canons of modern scientific research.

Thanks to advances in medical technology and research methods, much has been learned since Orton's time. Yet so many of his other hypotheses have been vindicated by neuroscientists in the intervening years that Norman Geschwind (1982b), in his paper, "Why Orton Was Right," could list thirteen of them from the neurological field. As an educator, I have proposed a fourteenth—the one likely to be of special interest to readers of this book.

The approach of most of those who have developed programs emphasizing decoding and the structure of the language is substantially based on logical outcomes of Orton's views (and usually Gillingham's as well), modified to meet their personal needs and styles of practice. It would be hard to see how a systematic, multisensory approach to teaching language in our country could fail to take this "ancestor" largely into account.

In other countries our colleagues report arriving at closely similar answers to the same questions of human language and problems encountered in its mastery, whatever the tongue. This seems reasonable, and so adds to our conviction of the viability of that fourteenth point: Orton's treatment prescription, which the fifty years of my own experience tells me, also, is "right." In a book designed to expand the understanding of dyslexia, I think we are justified in looking in some detail at Orton's educational strategy and tactics (Rawson 1983). The following, I think, is the essence of his advice:

An Ortonian Prescription

1. Analyze the language to be learned into its smallest useful elements—the sounds we hear and speak and the graphic symbols we use when we read or write. This reduces to a minimum the necessary memory load, a major problem for those who find language learning difficult.

2. Teach these elements thoroughly, to the point of useful (i.e., near permanent) automaticity.

3. Teach thoroughly all the appropriate senses, associated simultaneously and coordinately.

4. Synthesize what is learned—immediately, progressively, in practice—spoken, read, and written.

5. Use the cognitive, purposeful approach—"teach to the intellect" (Gillingham's words but Orton's advice, also). The language has its own system, to which we who would master it must accommodate.

6. Involve all the participants actively, reinforcing their understanding of the problem. Engage pupils, parents, and pedagogues.

7. Be fully aware of the social and emotional factors in order to mitigate the negative and reinforce the positive forces in each learner's life.

8. With relation to the problem, be at all times both open-minded and critical, both flexible and structured, both scientific and humane.

9. Remember always that understanding is basic, treatment

is obligatory, and the long-range goal is the prevention of disabling consequences of the anomalies or variations of the language function which are themselves part of the human condition.

10. Focus clearly on the ultimate aim: the good of the person, be he patient, student, client, or however designated. The rest, important as it may be, is secondary.

Many references in Orton's writing could be cited. There is ample supporting evidence for the viability of the recommendations of "Point 14" in 60 years of their practice. This verification is to be found in the literature, in people's files, in knowledgeable, experienced heads, and "out there" uncollected.

The experience accumulated has been reported descriptively in case studies of individuals and of clinical and school teaching. Increasingly, reports are being presented in terms of the scientific paradigm. Individuals have published materials for classroom use, with accompanying guides for teachers.

Orton's detailed case records are now being carefully reviewed by David Charnow at the Orton Library, College of Physicians and Surgeons, Columbia University. These records give abundant examples of the importance Orton placed on the individual wholeness of each patient and the specificity of his needs. His patients, although predominantly of school age, ranged from very young preschoolers with spoken language problems to adult men and women, engaged in their academic, vocational, and personal-social lives, but still needing help with the printed word in all its forms.

Some of Orton's instructions were broad and general, but some were specific and detailed, as those given to me by one of his graduate trainees in a short practicum as I, the 1935 greenhorn, began working with a sixth grade virtual nonreader Dr. and Mrs. Orton had just evaluated. I followed the Ortons' lead as well as I could learn how and, also on their advice, adapted procedures to Peter's singular needs. From such beginnings grew many a later success—in Peter's case a Harvard doctorate and a university professorship.

Perhaps it would not be amiss to give a sample of the kind of instruction on which this boy seemed to thrive. I could not have *written* it out then, although it was what I learned to *do*.

Because the process worked, meeting Peter's needs, I kept on in the same vein, just becoming more articulate, until 30 years later (and that is now 20 years ago) I wrote the following typical daily lesson for a very similar boy, about halfway through our two years of intensive sessions. Some items, by that point, took little of the hour—just enough review to keep them as near-automatic as a dyslexic can ever get. More attention was paid to those activities on the cutting edges of his learning achievement, for example, age-appropriate reading and vocabulary and below-grade spelling and writing. Whatever the age, stage, or appropriate teaching idiom, the language we use in our culture is a constant system, so this "chunk out of the middle" really is typical, albeit in a very summary way, of the whole range; a complete account would take several volumes. (Compare especially: Gillingham 1956, 1960.)

Typical Language Lesson for Don, Written in 1965:

1. Drill cards, recognition, multiple sounds, emphasis on "shaky ones." Almost all now instant-automatic.
2. Word building—cards, syllables, word packs for analysis and synthesis.
3. Auditory training—hear and sound, hear and spell.
4. Spelling—notebook, theory and etymology as appropriate; phonetic words, "think" words, sight words with sounding-tracing.
5. Dictation.
6. Handwriting—attention to: "left-hand-hook," pencil and paper, letter forms and connections, tracing, copying, writing-looking and eyes-averted, kinesthetic recognition.
7. Vocabulary—cumulative list from reading, for secure, smooth sounding.
8. Oral reading—interest level "trade book."

To get all this took careful timing, but it was our standard operating procedure. Interest and progress were good during "training for mastery" and Don persisted in his wider education through college and graduate school into social work; never an outstanding student but always acquitting himself creditably in the mainstream; some periods of discouragement but eventual success and confidence—all as prophesied by Dr. Orton for a boy of his type—and one more reason for me to keep practicing and teaching others to practice this approach.

However temporarily all-consuming were the detailed demands occasioned by his patients' difficulties, Orton never forgot, and urged others to remember, that each learner was a total person with, inevitably and desirably, a wider range of interests that should be encouraged and nourished. The individual comprehensive and detailed programs he laid out for treatment were as diverse as the students, the teachers who were available to carry out the instruction, the parents, the objectives, and the settings in which everyone had to function.

Samuel Orton was a man of strong, closely-reasoned convictions, but no dogmatist. He could hold his ground, but when circumstances proved him to be in error, he was secure and modest enough to say so and make changes. (Charnow 1985). As Norman Geschwind (1982a) said of him, "He represented a great tradition, a tradition that insisted that for comprehension of behavior it was necessary to cast one's intellectual net widely."

3
Guidelines for Teaching

In 1982, the Board of Directors of The Orton Dyslexia Society adopted an official statement, "What is Dyslexia?" which I drafted for them. The statement advocates educational approaches which recognize the following essentials:

1. Its teaching is planned to meet the differing needs of learners who are similar to each other but no two exactly alike. It is **individualized.**
2. It draws on the knowledge and skill of experts from many fields—education, medicine, psychology, social work and language theory. It is **multidisciplinary**.
3. It uses the learning pathways we all share of seeing, hearing, feeling, and awareness of motion, brought together by the thinking brain. It is **multisensory**.
4. It takes advantage of the letter-sound plan on which our language is based. "Words which carry meaning are made of sounds; sounds are written with letters in the right order." It makes sense to learn this **alphabetic-phonic** system.
5. The sounds of the letters can be blended into words for reading, and the words can be divided into the sounds they are made of for spelling and writing. We call the process **synthetic-analytic**.
6. Words and sentences are the carriers of meaning. Based in proficiency, fluency with language pattern serves **linguistic power** as full literacy is achieved.
7. Material is organized and taught in a way that is logical and fits the nature of our language. The procedure is **systematic.**
8. The learner moves, step by step, in order, from simple, well-learned material to that which is more and more complex, as

___
Reprinted with permission from The Orton Dyslexia Society from *What is Dyslexia?* 1982.

he or she masters the necessary body of language skills. The teaching is **sequential.**

9. Each step of the way is based on those already learned. The process is a **cumulative** sum or cycle of growth.

10. The student is helped to understand the reasons for what he is learning. Then, when necessary he will have the confidence that he can think his way through language problems instead of counting only on memory—"The mind is the master." —a **cognitive** approach.

11. The purpose of it all, from recognizing a letter to writing a poem, is getting meaning from one person's mind to another's. **Communication is paramount.**

12. The person's feelings about himself/herself and about learning are vital to education. A sense of confidence in oneself comes from true mastery which takes away tensions and makes a person want to achieve at his or her best. Such an approach is **emotionally sound.**

As we see it, these are the primary and essential ingredients of a scientifically effective way to set the dyslexic free to make full use of his or her many gifts and talents.

4

The Orton Trail: 1896–1986

. . . New things, new views are of little use until they come to use
through someone who describes them reasonably well, and who, if
his vision goes farther than the intellectual horizon of the day,
adds to his experimental achievement the import of his addition to
man's welfare. (Drinker quoted in Bowen 1970.)

1896

Those of you who know me and the Orton Dyslexia Society know
that our intense interest in anything having to do with language does
not by any means cover our whole interest in life. We're far from perfect, but narrow-minded we emphatically are not! But, just for this session, our defined job is specific; to hold a mirror up to our selves, turn
on the linguistic and sequential functions of our brains and see something of how we got to be what and where we are.

"The recollection of the past," says an old Latin aphorism, "is the
promise of the future." In that spirit, let us consider the history of our
Society's field. In the title, under the influence of Orton's "strephosymbolia," I transposed a couple of numbers to get back, by a kind of
numerical time machine, from 1986 to 1896, when "congenital word-
blindness," the immediate precursor of dyslexia as we know it, began
to be noticed in its own right. By that year, it seems that three well-
informed men of medicine in Great Britain were simultaneously ready
for the concept.

Dr. W. Pringle Morgan (1896), an English ophthalmologist, picked
up the idea of *word-blindness* (acquired) from a late 1895 paper by Dr.
James Hinshelwood, an eye surgeon in Glasgow. Could this be related
somehow, Morgan wondered, to one of his own adolescent patients
who had "just never been able to learn to read"? (Does this make us feel
like seers, foretelling Orton's "M. P." experience, 30 years down the

Reprinted with permission from The Orton Dyslexia Society from *Annals of
Dyslexia* 37:36–48 1987.

road? It should.) "Could there be," asked Morgan, "such a thing as congenital word-blindness? Here is what a patient of mine is like." Then he described a 14-year-old boy, blood-brother to the ones we have all known—a very recognizable dyslexic. Named Percy, the lad fortified the diagnosis by signing his name *Precy.*

"That's it!" said Dr. Hinshelwood. "I've known several just such." Thereupon he published his own first case description, giving Morgan full credit for naming the syndrome. Dr. James Kerr, school physician, gave an apparently independent presentation of the same phenomenon, too. The three men made 1896 a base-line year for us.

We do not hear of the other two again, but Hinshelwood continued for another 21 years, with 13 short papers and two small books. He was, by all accounts, a very able man, a distinguished professor at the University of Glasgow, a surgeon of high repute, a careful scientist and a compassionate physician. For him the study of what he insisted should be called *congenital word-blindness* was one absorbing interest within a large and varied practice. In his last, and summarizing, book, *Congenital Word-Blindness*, in 1917, he reported having seen altogether 31 such patients, "from all over the country."

Of the patients in his defined category, he says, "The cases we have been considering in this book are pure cases of congenital word-blindness, where the defect is confined to the visual memory centre only, in an otherwise normal and healthy brain, and it is to these cases that my remarks apply. . . ." The defective area he located as (generally) at the angular gyrus of the brain's left hemisphere. Had the condition been other than innate, there should have been optical symptoms, which he did not find, in addition to the manifest cortical ones. Through the latter, his logic led him to identify his syndrome and find what eventually proved to be one correct point of language origin in the brain.

Two other domains than that of his special interest he excluded as both incorrectly identified with it and confusing. For them he finally proposed names. The term *congenital dyslexia* he thought might appropriately be reserved for those cases whose "degrees of aptitude" showed not "as pathological conditions but simply [note that!] as examples of physiological variations in the degree of development of the areas involved." These children "simply lag somewhat behind their fellows in acquiring the visual memories of letters and words . . . where a little extra time and effort overcomes the difficulty." (That simplicity has great appeal; people still adhere to it!)

If, however, thought Hinshelwood, other areas of the brain, such as those controlling auditory or kinesthetic aspects of language, seem pathologically deficient, this must be considered as "part of a general cerebral deteriorization" and might well be called "congenital alexia." It was, he thought, "practically irremediable," of a piece, it seemed, with what used to be called "feeble-mindedness." (Here's another idea that dies hard.)

The word-blind population, in clear contrast, must be limited to those "of high degree of defect and of perfect purity of type." Further, he wrote, "all . . . I have recorded were bright intelligent children, [otherwise] quite intact. . . ." Given these conditions, Hinshelwood felt justified in a favorable prognosis, borne out by his long, arduous, personal experience in teaching the word-blind, and also he noted, those with acquired, as well as congenital, symptoms. His attitudes and many of his multisensory procedures have far broader use in all of education than he seems to have envisioned.

Although he found "look-and-say" teaching of reading quite unuseful for his patients, he seemed to know as an alternative only what he called the "old-fashioned method of 'spelling out,'" or naming aloud, each letter of each word or syllable, as in "double-u, e, es, tee—west." (Truly old-fashioned; my grandmother learned, and taught, that way in the 1840s and '50s.) Still, with patience and perseverance, and some of the multisensory and synthetic techniques that some of us still commonly use, it worked, probably, Hinshelwood thought, as a result of training the unaccustomed "other hemisphere" to take over for the deficient one.

Hinshelwood's beautiful clinical expertise seems not to have extended outside his deliberately self-imposed limits, which, to be sure, did not seem constricting to him. He simply "drew a circle and kept [the others] out"! It was a self-limited beginning, but it contributed to the later work of many people in Britain, on the Continent and in the USA, a kind of ancestor for the ODS International.

The Times—1900–1925

For the most part, education and psychology, during the first quarter of the 20th Century, were getting ever further away from medicine, with which they had scarcely been in tune, anyway. The professionals in education were going back to Horace Mann, friend of Gallaudet, or perhaps even to Rousseau and the French Revolution. They thought they were listening to John Dewey, William Heard Kilpatrick, and others at Teachers College, Columbia, and in Chicago and Boston. Despite the clear and well-disciplined thinking of many of those leading innovators, the new Progressive Education was too often misunderstood as giving free rein to permissiveness, rather than as a freeing of creative energy and vision to "learn through doing" to live more wisely in a "changing world."

Proponents of the new curriculum were calling for a modernization of reading methods, away from "dull and sterile" phonics and

"Goody Two-Shoes" readers into the bright, new, "look-and-say" world of Dick and Jane—the direct and easy way to master and learn to love reading, with immediate adult-type expertise. True, there were problems; there always have been. They were most frequently ascribed to emotional causes; Freud was new and right. Or they were so-ciological—drunkenness and family problems; calling for the trained social worker, or the hospital clinic, or perhaps the new Binet test. Within the ranks of education, there were some specialists—like psychologists Durrell (once of Orton's Iowa staff) and Dearborn, and particularly Augusta Bronner and Leta Hollingworth, who wrote about children's disabilities and how to educate the gifted. In the US, Montessori was little known and less followed. Psychology was mostly testing or university laboratory experiments. In education, anthropology was not noticed and linguistics as a discipline was barely even a gleam in Jakobson's or Sapir's eye. Psychiatry was a medical discipline, and by no means the household word it was soon to become.

It was Kilpatrick's "changing world," with even greater changes in store. Still, anticipating our future, it should be noted that by 1920 Anna Gillingham, at the Ethical Culture School in New York, was considerably ahead of her time in both psychology and education. She was well-prepared for Samuel Orton when he came along in 1929 to validate her practice with his science.

The Ortons

After the manner of Genevieve Foster's excellent children's history series; THE WORLD OF . . . (say, Abraham Lincoln or some other historic personage), we might use our imaginations by picturing "The World of Samuel T. Orton," from whom our Society takes its name. He was born Oct. 15, 1879, 107 years ago, two years after Kussmaul, the neurologist, invented the terms *word-blindness* and *word-deafness* and eight years before Berlin introduced, and etymologized, *dyslexia*—both of them thinking of the acquired disorders. Young Sam Orton lived on the campus of Ohio State University, where his geologist father was President, and where he himself was later an undergraduate. Meanwhile he had "prepped" at his Uncle Horace's Taft School in Connecticut, been junior assistant on geological vacation field trips, and decided in favor of medicine rather than mechanical engineering as a career. He earned his medical degree here in Philadelphia, at the University of Pennsylvania Medical School, in 1905. At that time, Hinshelwood was still in vigorous practice in Glasgow, and the field of neurology was in a state of growth.

When we try to understand what manner of man Samuel Orton was to become, it helps to know that he came under the influence of several excellent medical role models in his early practice through 1912: for example, Simon Flexner at the University of Pennsylvania, Adolph Meyer, and neuropathologists Frank B. Mallory and E. E. Southard in Massachusetts. At the same time, he garnered a Master's degree and some teaching experience at Harvard and taught at Clark University about the time Freud was making his American debut there (1909). The year 1913 Orton spent in the laboratories of the already famous Dr. Alzheimer in Germany and in learning about neurology overseas. By 1917, when Hinshelwood was laying down his pen, Orton was near the end of four years, here in Philadelphia again, as pathologist and scientific director at the Pennsylvania Hospital for Mental Diseases.

By 1919 Orton (now not quite 40) was searching the country for top-flight staff members for his next job, and finding them. The challenge offered him was to build and direct a State Psychopathic Hospital System for Iowa and head the medical school's department of psychiatry, with freedom to develop an innovative program. Some 55 years later, June L. Orton, formerly June Lyday, Orton's chief psychiatric social worker, was to recall with nostalgia both the organization's excellence and its *esprit de corps.*

My contemporaries among you can remember what cars and roads were like in the 1920s. A travelling Mental Health Clinic seemed a good idea to Orton and his staff, to the rural people so far from Iowa City, and to the Rockefeller Foundation in New York which supported the program. For the first such clinic in the country, in January, 1925, Miss Lyday had gone to Greene County to set up the appointments. All her life, June Orton vividly remembered the interview with the teacher of the 16-year-old who was to become the famous M.P. It went thus:

> "Is he dull, perhaps of low IQ?"
> "No, he seems quite bright—does well in arithmetic."
> "Is his behavior a problem?"
> "On the contrary, he's a very nice chap, of a good family."
> "Then what IS the matter?"
> "That's what puzzles me. We just haven't been able to teach him to read!"

"Dr. Orton, not his assistant, must see this boy," thought Miss Lyday. And so he did. He saw, also, 14 other problem readers who were registered for the two-week clinic, but it was M.P. whom the doctor invited to the Hospital for further intensive and sensitively understanding study and who became the classic case.

By January, 1925, Orton must already have thought a lot about this language problem, for by May he had his now famous landmark paper " 'Word Blindness' in School Children," with case material about M.P.

included, ready to read to the 51st Annual Meeting of the American Neurological Association in Washington, DC. By November, 1925, it was in print.

By this time Orton was 46, in mid-career, a one-man team and team leader in neuropathology, psychiatry, aphasiology, and general medicine; a state mental hospital director, a medical school professor (voted "best" by the students), and still active in the brain research laboratory. He was about to receive the first of his three Rockefeller Foundation grants, and was enough of a writer to have published 28 papers in 20 years, on a variety of subjects—but none of them on language. (Of his 33 subsequent publications in the next 23 years, only 10 were *not* on language.)

He had found his specialty, logically and scientifically of a piece with his earlier history. The recital of his accomplishments is impressive. We have a founder we can look to with pride.

Orton left the Iowa post in '28 and spent a busy sabbatical year. A widower with his three children already away at school, he first wrote his Rockefeller report, then went to Europe. (Was this when he consulted Henry Head, leading neurologist of his day, about cortical function? I think so.) When he returned, he and June Lyday were married and they prepared for the move to New York in 1929. There he was to practice psychiatry, specializing in the language disability problem, teach at Columbia University's College of Physicians and Surgeons, and continue to do pathology himself and to direct research at the New York Neurological Institute.

In 1929, also, he served as President of the American Psychiatric Association and later of the American Association for Research in Nervous and Mental Disease, and helped edit their journals. He also traveled to see people and give talks, to visit schools to which he was referring students, and to carry out other responsibilities.

The records, now at Columbia, document his work with over 2000 patients (and I know, myself, of others unrecorded). People who knew the public Orton seldom knew much of his large concurrent private practice. There are accounts of many warm and admiring friendships, evening and Sunday seminars with teachers and tutors, and some jolly weekends at "Hwimsy," the home he was building, by hand, up in Dutchess County. It was there, just after his retirement in 1948, that he met with the accident that caused his death.

There are references to serious and persisting health problems, but no details beyond regret at the interruptions to his varied and absorbing activities. Perhaps his continuing laboratory work, his mechanical interests and his migraine headaches would have interested Norman Geschwind. He was certainly not dyslexic himself, but what of the cast of mind? He was exceptionally able to see life through the eyes of his patients.

142   THE ORTON TRAIL

There was one more very important factor in Dr. Orton's personal career, his good partnership with his wife, June. She brought into their collaboration a basic (though sometimes dissembled) preference for being, as she said, "the vice-president, never the president." The labors of such people can often be overlooked by history.

Before she went to Iowa as June Lyday, she was already a professional in her own right (Bachelor's from Vassar, Master's from Smith College School of Social Work [one of its earliest]), with casework and administrative experience that gave her a firmer grounding in reality than was often apparent until one knew her well. She was intelligent, well-organized, informed, and had high standards of excellence, and she was thoroughly versed in diagnostic testing and record writing. She was a gifted writer and editor and participated, no doubt most tactfully, in preparing many of Dr. Orton's manuscripts, as far back as the Iowa days, and in the writing of letters that went out over his signature. In short, she was a full partner in practice, indispensable to his career. We are forever in her debt, for her biographical pages and oral memories have given us a wealth of fact and insight.

It is not necessary, I think, to tell this group, at least in this session, what were Orton's scientific and educational premises and conclusions. We have already discussed them many times. Geschwind, in his "Why Orton Was Right," and I, by adding "Orton's 14th Point," have summarized some of his major work and pointed out where time and technology have proven him wrong, and on what judgments "the jury is still out."

Orton's development in the specific language disability field refined his judgments so that they seemed as secure as he could make them, but that he was open-minded, not doctrinaire, is evident from this statement of his position in his last published paper (1946):

Whether or not our theory is right, I do not know, but I do know that the methods of retraining which we have derived from that view point have worked. I do not claim them to be a panacea for reading troubles of all sorts, but I do feel that we understand the blockade which occurs so frequently in children with good minds, and which results in the characteristic reading disability of the strephosymbolic type of childhood.

Gillingham

How did Orton do all these things himself—just one person, with one partner? The answer: by not doing them all himself, although he knew how to do them (as well as why) when he needed to. The mark of

a good Chief is that he can show his Indians how, any time. Orton was
the coordinator, simultaneously, of several many-person programs.

While June L. Orton was Orton's executive partner at his own office, many others collaborated in each of the programs at the New York
Neurological Institute, uptown. There were doctors, like Cole, Dozier,
Chesher, and Wright; educators like John Bigelow, Helene Durbrow,
Elizabeth Peabody, and Warren Koehler, who are still abroad in the
land, and like Charlotte Pardee, Ellen Donohue, Margaret Stanger, Peter Gow, Page and Laura Sharp and many, many others—teachers,
headmasters, new and experienced tutors, parents and all. Some of
them may be among your memories, as they are in mine. Many of them
went on to be leaders themselves, to be your teachers and mine.
Among them all, however, I believe that not one had impact as great as
that of Anna Gillingham, teacher and psychologist, who, with her
quiet, competent friend, Bessie Stillman, worked on educational
technology.

Anna Gillingham, like the Ortons, had quested and studied her
way into this viewpoint, which she found to be so consistent with her
broad approach to the whole of education. At age 50 in 1929, when
Samuel Orton was moving to town, she was an already established
professional there and an individualist who lived her convictions with
straightforward vigor. Her genetic and cultural background and the
nature of her life experiences were integrated in the kind of person she
was, just the right person to give both sound and practical implementation to the treatment ideas Dr. Orton had so clearly formulated.

Anna Gillingham had her deepest roots in the Philadelphia
Quaker subculture, with her Gillingham ancestor on William Penn's
ship "Welcome." She, herself, was born in 1878, a few months before
Samuel Orton, at a stage in her school-teacher parents' westward migration when they lived in Batavia, Il. She grew up on the Sioux Indian
Pine Ridge Reservation and a Nebraska ranch, where she was taught at
home, with reading begun when she was 10. Hers was an experience-
enriched and intellectually stimulating childhood. High School in To-
peka, Kansas prepared her to make an outstanding undergraduate record at Swarthmore College: Phi Beta Kappa and the highest Senior
honor, the Lucretia Mott Fellowship, which gave her a postgraduate
year at Radcliffe, and a second Bachelor of Arts degree. Her first teaching job, four years, was at the West Philadelphia Friends School, with
time for graduate courses at Penn. (Her Master's degree came later at
Columbia.) The family home, and her father's business were now in
Atlantic City when it was still a New Jersey coast summer resort.

Her next move was to New York, where, except for sabbatical
leaves, she was teacher, psychologist and reading expert, by turns, until 1936. Anna Gillingham, as I have said, was more than ready for Dr.
Orton when he came in 1928. She consulted him at once and often

about the many children her Binet tests had shown to be bright but with baffling reading problems. For the first time, someone she could respect had an explanation and a suggested treatment that made sense to her.

It took the redoubtable Anna Gillingham: first, to reason along with and be convinced by Dr. Orton; secondly, to understand and use psychological testing to advantage; and thirdly, to see pedagogical connections here with both education in general and the special needs of children with language problems. Then she and Miss Stillman figured out in detail how to organize teaching in accordance with principles.

Orton, for his part, felt sure he had sound theories to explain the difficulties and a logical educational treatment plan, but he saw in Miss Gillingham someone with the background, intelligence and expertise to work out the details of the plan better than he could do it himself. He arranged for her appointment as a full-time Research Fellow on his staff at the Neurological Institute for the year 1932–33. Work was begun on what was to grow into *The Gillingham-Stillman Manuals* on which teachers can still base their work, and on which a teacher-training program is still growing and expanding.

It is in character that Orton realized that, just as he would not expect Anna Gillingham to be adept with his pathologist's instruments, with her own he could expect her to do better than he. Both appreciated the challenge of this fruitful partnership as they worked together for several years.

We might put it that he was the scientist with engineering proclivities; she was the engineer vitally interested in science beneath the reality; both were practical humanists with first-rate logical minds, open to new ideas, and both were courageous, creative, multifaceted individualists. If they were among us today, they would pursue with delight the new knowledge and ideas that technology, information, and thinking are making possible, remaining too strong to be swayed yet too honest not to set course wherever convictions might lead them in pursuit of developing truth. We are fortunate to inherit from both.

In 1936, Gillingham and Stillman retired from the Ethical Culture Schools, went to Punahou School in Hawaii, and became close friends with Beth Slingerland. They later returned to New York, private practice, and publishing until Miss Stillman's death in 1947. After this, Anna Gillingham developed a teacher-training project which took her circuit-riding four times a year to several schools widely separated over the country, a practice she continued until 1961, that is, as long as health, strength, and eyesight permitted, till long after most of us would have given up. Sally Childs, long a student and teacher with her, a primary colleague, and eventually Anna Gillingham's professional heir, was her devoted friend and care giver until her death at 85 in 1964.

In Defense of Biography

It has seemed important to pause on our trail for these biographical vistas, so that you of the present day Orton Dyslexia Society may learn, or hear again, something more about the underlying soundness of your own and your Society's professional grounding and the sturdiness of the giants whose shoulders we all feel under our feet.

General Progress

As we look now along the scientific side of the trail for mileposts in the neurosciences and psychology, the next important one, I think, is the beginning of the neurological revolution of the late '50s which is still in full cry.

My awareness of this new era began with the publication of Penfield and Roberts' *Speech and Brain Mechanisms* in 1959, and the whole opening up of the right cerebral hemisphere. Somehow it was like the effect of the liberating discoveries of Einstein, Bohr, Born, and their fellows on the physics of the early 1900s. Although the clarifications so far have been more piece-meal and promising than the sweeping clarifications of relativity and quantum theories, the world of the neurosciences was as surely changed. As in physics and chemistry, there was to be no more leisurely complacency and just tidying up theoretical ends, with the answers seemingly just around the corner!

A whole new world was opened for exploration, the tremendously interesting and significant world of Howard Gardner and of our own explorers there, like Masland, Geschwind, Denckla, Galaburda, and a host of others.

The Orton Dyslexia Society was surely one whose heritage had prepared it to participate not only with enthusiasm but in research support. This latter began in the biomedical field, but is now evolving also in the psychoeducational arena. I hope it is not overambitious to project both a promise of support and some appropriate leadership here on the part of The Orton Dyslexia Society as a Society, as well as through its members' work.

The Orton Dyslexia Society's Historical Highlights

So far, I have given you a homonymous hybrid of a *route* (some call it/*rout/*) with a bit of background and some personal *roots* in a terrain of history. I have chosen to do so perhaps at the expense of leaving a specific account of The Orton Dyslexia Society less than its share of the hour, but I did this on purpose, too. The people I have focused upon are, to my mind, not only historic but fundamentally important to our understanding of the basic problem of dyslexia and of the Society that exists to reflect our interest in it. Moreover, the vital statistics of the Society are yours for the asking at its Office, while glimpses into the lives and thoughts of our professional forebears may be harder to come by.

And yet, the ODS has a biography, too, a life of its own. We should put at least a summary account of its roots—as well as its route—on our Trail Map.

Let us picture first the Orton Society as it began, on October 28, 1949, at a dinner meeting of perhaps 30 old friends and associates of Dr. Orton. June Orton as President, Sally Childs as Secretary, and Carolyn Woodin as Treasurer were the officers. Dr. Earl D. Bond of Pennsylvania Hospital and Mrs. Grace McClure of Columbus (Ohio) School for Girls, both old friends of Dr. Orton, gave medical and educational support to the new Society for the continuation of his interests; topmost quality from the beginning. One meeting a year, in New York, one *Bulletin* a year, and an avenue for members' interchange; that's all there was to it! Still, because of its viewpoint and standards of excellence, those few of us who shared it found there vital stimulus and support in a largely noninterested world.

Now think of The Orton Dyslexia Society (so renamed in 1980) as it is today. There are upwards of 9000 international members with an organization grown to meet their active and expanding needs: seven officers, a Board of 17, a distinguished Advisory Council of 25, an Executive Director and supporting staff, an active Research Division, innumerable committees, 37 Branches, chartered or in process, a publications program of professional direction and calibre, a budget and financial operation handling six-figure money. We have organizational collaboration and interlocking activity with other organizations here and abroad, conferences from local to international, a growing place in the public eye and ear through public media and the professional efforts of members, in their personal jobs and activities but ideologically part of our world—out where invaluable services are delivered to real people.

Does that make you dizzy, too?

The Society first grew slowly, from the original 30 to about 250 in the first decade, to 1500 in the second ten years and then increasing rapidly to nearly 9000 by 1986. The nationwide membership also has outposts scattered from Australia to Czechoslovakia.

There are about as many branches now (37) as there once were members, with branch activities connecting with direct services. The largest Branch events occasionally outdo their national opposite numbers. Beyond that, overseas meetings have speakers, official ODS representatives, even occasional co-sponsorship.

We have "moved house" several times, beginning in June Orton's desk drawer, stopping for a dozen years at Rectory School, Pomfret, CT, and now making full use of a whole floor of a small office building. From getting the work done wholly by volunteers, we have become partly paid and highly professional, but the spirit of the enterprise is still the same.

It seems appropriate that the printed word, and its publishing, has always been a major Society activity. I have been so personally involved with our development here that you must beware lest you fall prey to the Ancient Mariner in me. Look instead at the table in the exhibit hall here at the hotel. And I know you are aware of our growth with the times into the other media.

The Society's finances have behaved at times like a fragile cockleshell on a windy sea, but the oarsmen have been able, though we have often wondered how, to see us into port without shipwreck. We've been on the verge of floundering sometimes, but we have kept on sailing under the wings of some quite human Guardian Angels, both paid and volunteer.

National conferences began (1950) with a reported 10-member business meeting followed by a public meeting for 45. By 1970, with attendance persistently outgrowing facilities, it seemed time to start to move from city to city, zigzagging over the U.S. So, here we are now in Philadelphia, 16 years later, for—hold your bonnet strings!—four days of sessions, a couple of days of board, branch presidents' and committee meetings, a banquet, two keynote memorial addresses, 69 numbered sessions, 114 speakers on program, and various other events, and exhibits, and between 1500 and 2000 expected attenders.

Think back again to 1949! You would hardly believe it, June Orton. I hardly do, myself but it's all true. How could it possibly have gotten from initial there to astonishing here?

Regina Cicci, former national program chairman, comments approvingly on 37 years of uniquely combined professionalism and warmth of welcome at national conferences, a spirit that has always pervaded the Society and has much to do with the regard in which it is widely held.

Very few of the ideas we find basic in the organization today were not present, evident or foreshadowed, in the Society's early years, and, in fact, in the thinking and practice of Orton, Gillingham, and their cohorts, well ahead of their times. New technologies (electron microscopes, TV, computers and the like) have permitted enormous expansion and enrichment, but the basic thought and practice were already there. The modern expression of all this you recognize in the Board-approved flyers "What is Dyslexia" and "The Problem of Dyslexia."

Max Born, great originator in quantum physics, made a statement in his acceptance lecture as he received the Nobel Prize that reflects clearly what I take to be the attitude of the Orton/Gillingham outlook. I leave it with you:

> I believe that ideas such as absolute certitude, absolute exactness, final truth, etc., are figments of the imagination which should not be admissible in any field of science. On the other hand, any assertion of probability is either right or wrong from the standpoint of the theory on which it is based. This *loosening of thinking* seems to me to be the greatest blessing which modern science has given to us. For the belief in a single truth and in being the possessor thereof is the root cause of all evil in the world (1978).

Impossible as the task may seem, I have tried to study the history and practices of all the dyslexia, and even learning disabilities, trail in the past 52 years of my involvement with the language learning problem, and I say with great conviction that, in 1986, I wouldn't be anywhere other than right here. It's a good life, full of interest and satisfaction. May you enjoy it!

Part IV
Ways That Have Opened

1

"Fish"
To Teachers of Teachers

"Give me a fish; I eat for a day;
Teach me to fish, I eat for a lifetime."

—Chinese proverb.

But first remember:
    I need to taste fish,
        if I am to develop an appetite for fish;
    I need to experience satisfaction of hunger,
        if I am to appreciate eating;
    I need to catch a fish or two of my own,
        if I am to know the enjoyment of fishing;
    I need to know myself as becoming a fisherman,
        if I am to think of my life as having a purpose.

Help me get started on my way.

You will have liberated both my body and my soul.
    You do not ask reward, but my gift to you,
    As free as was your gift of life to me,
    Will be a bit of your immortality.

Margaret Byrd Rawson
August 20, 1976

2

Prognosis in Dyslexia:
The School in Rose Valley I

" . . . any beliefs definite enough to make observed phenomena surprising or incredible constitute a suitable starting point" for the re-examination of currently held concepts, says J. McV. Hunt in a paper on "Traditional Personality in the Light of Recent Evidence" (1965). The study on which the paper here presented was based was the result of just such a juxtaposition of the prognostic judgment of a well-known clinician and the experience accumulated over a generation's time by a language therapist.

"What do you tell the parents of your young patients with clearly manifest specific language disabilities?" asked the therapist. They were discussing the condition variously known as dyslexia, reading dis-ability, strephosymbolia, developmental language learning problems, and by many names. This difficulty is characterized by failure to learn language skills with facility consistent with intelligence, sensory equip-ment, cultural background and educational opportunity which are nor-mal and often superior.

Said the clinician, "Well, I think it is kindest in the long run to be honestly realistic. I usually advise such parents to lower their academic sights, to substitute other training for college, preferably training in a skilled trade if the patient, as is often true, is a boy with that kind of aptitudes. It does seem a pity, for many of these boys and girls have both high intelligence and high hopes, but they just couldn't make it academically. Why compound frustration and failure with more of the same when a reappraisal, no matter how agonizing, could lead to a reasonably satisfactory future?"

"But," countered the therapist, "what about Peter and Henry and Ralph and Sue and . . . ?" She told him of a chemist, a college pro-fessor, a physician, a nursery school teacher, and many others. Not

Reprinted with permission from *Academic Therapy*:164–173 1966 and from The Orton Dyslexia Society, Reprint No. 13.

only had she tested and taught these young people as children, but circumstances had made it possible for her to follow them as they went through college, graduate school, and into their professions. The case histories which followed struck the clinician as, indeed, "observed phenomena surprising [if not] incredible" enough to warrant a systematic, rather than a purely anecdotal study.

The School in Rose Valley Study

Much of the material from the therapist's private practice and college counseling years seemed to justify a "perhaps they can do it" attitude. However, because of her close connection with an elementary school, The School in Rose Valley, Moylan, Pennsylvania, she thought that this institution might present an opportunity for a comprehensive examination of a whole population of both dyslexic and nondyslexic boys whom she had known, both personally and clinically, in many cases from their infancy to the present, and who were available for current follow-up. The school's records, too, were available. While they had not been kept according to a research design, they could supply important evidence. The outcome was a study which was set up as carefully as possible to use the inherent advantages of the situation and to minimize any biases it might contain.

The school is a small, independent (private) day school, with elementary and preschool programs, in a residential community near Philadelphia. It was founded in 1929 by an already associated group of parents who had a high degree of consensus as to educational objectives. Its policies and its educational climate have continued with little fundamental change until the present, being, in fact, much broader than might be inferred from the largely accidental restriction of its early clientele to predominantly upper-middle-class, white, Protestant professional or business families. This early homogeneity, while decried by most of the participants, has given our study the advantage of a group of children of such similar backgrounds and capacities as to make language learning abilities stand out as a systematically observable variable.

Since one of the fundamental purposes of the school was the fostering of individual differences within a socially functioning group, the language development program was only one of the many ways in which attempts were made to meet individual needs of normal children. *This was not a "special school,"* although an occasional child was enrolled because of the relation of its offerings to his particular needs. In many ways it was representative of the private (as distinct from parochial) school population of the Philadelphia area, despite its ideological uniqueness, and findings from our study can, to some extent and with care, be generalized to such a population. It is however, by no means representative of the poulation as a whole, and this has been borne in mind in interpretation. Nevertheless, it seemed of value to examine what had happened to a small group of adequately known, highly individual representatives of a carefully delineated segment of that population.

Hypothesis

The hypothesis tested was that "dyslexic students, so diagnosed between the ages of six and twelve, necessarily have poorer prospects for success in later educational and vocational achievement than do nondyslexic students." Diagnostic testing and observation were adequate in this school group to determine the language learning patterns of each child, but since the children's needs, in this as in other respects, were always met to the limit of the school's ability, the differential effects of testing, diagnosis, and treatment within the group could not be studied. The nature of the group did, however, provide exceptional control of other variables. A large amount of material having to do with psychological, sociological, and educational backgrounds and outcomes was collected in the course of our study and subjected to appropriate qualitative and statistical analysis. We shall confine ourselves here to the central point of the hypothesis. Did the dyslexics among the boys studied, young men from 26 to 40 years of age at the time of the study, do substantially less well academically and vocationally than their linguistically more facile classmates? Did we, by nourishing false hopes, add to the boys' sense of failure and frustration?

Population Characteristics

The population (statistically speaking) which was chosen for study consisted of *all* of the boys, of the full range of language learning ability who had been enrolled in the school for at least three elementary grade years during the period from 1930 to 1947 when the investigator was a member of the school staff and knew each boy individually. There were 56 boys who met this attendance criterion, considered a minimum time for identification and substantial treatment of the dyslexics among them. The study was confined to boys because the smaller number of dyslexics among the girls and, especially, the difficulty of measuring the extent to which the girls had achieved their educational and vocational potentials posed different and quite difficult problems for the statistician. An examination of the known facts concerning a sample of those boys who were enrolled for less than three years showed that, for the most part, the reasons for their late entry and/or early withdrawal were not substantially more related to their dyslexia status nor to the school's language program than was the case with the group chosen, but rather that exigencies of the Depression and World War II and other factors had been controlling. Those whose later histories are known also seem not to differ much from the more exhaustively studied group. We feel justified in supposing that we have here a true "population" which includes all of those boys who were substantially exposed to the school's elementary grade program, rather than a "sample" perhaps biased by language factors.

The boys, like their parents, were a sociologically homogeneous group. With one exception each, they were white (one Oriental), Protestant-background (one Jewish), living with both parents (one father was deceased), sons of college-educated, all but one with degrees (one eighth-grade educated), with professional or business occupations (one blue-collar father was otherwise typical). Forty-four families were represented by one, two, or three sons each.

The beginning reading experiences were similar for all, being primarily under one of two well-qualified teachers. The school testing and special language teaching were carried out almost entirely by, or under direction of, one person, with a self-consistent philosophy—the Orton-Gillingham approach.

The boys were also alike in being of high general intelligence as measured by the Binet Scale. The IQ range was from 94 to 185, with a Mean of 131 and a Standard Deviation of 18.1.

As we have said, the nature of the population studied naturally limits somewhat the generalized applicability of the findings to other groups. On the other hand, because of their high potential and their own and their families' high educational and vocational aspirations, these boys represent an important, even if small, stratum of the general population, a source of possible leadership, and one whose children are often found in private practice caseloads, but seldom statistically studied. In our judgment such a study has value in its own right.

Language Learning Facility Scale

Similar as these boys were on the whole, the microscopes of intimate acquaintance and careful analysis showed them to be unique individuals. There was a wide gap in language learning ability between the half-dozen most fluent readers, who were also "natural spellers," and the six most language-handicapped boys who, despite good intelligence, required years of special help. Still, it was not possible to say at any point, "Here dyslexia ends, and all the other boys are clearly non-dyslexic." Rather, when we had combined all the evidence dating from the years under study (from test scores, teachers' qualitative reports, and the therapist's judgments, most of which were in written form), we found that our subjects could be ranked without too much difficulty in order of their language learning facility. These were numbered from 1, the most, to 56, the least facile, with borderline cases at the cut-off points of categories.

In studying the records we held particularly in mind certain diagnostic criteria. Generally the first consideration was the initial failure of the boy to learn to read and spell in the first year or two of reading instruction up to levels which were consistent with grade expectations, classmates' performance, and his own general intelligence. Also important were the ways in which he failed to measure up, such as the prevalence in his work of the errors and inadequacies characteristic of specific language disabilities and their relation to other academic achievements. The learning responses to the tutoring procedures often helped to distinguish degrees of disability. The persistence of characteristic spelling inadequacies was almost always definitive of dyslexia. Problems of speech, motor skill, penmanship, verbal formulation, auditory and visual perception and memory (not acuity), lateral dominance, and directional confusion were all taken into consideration. Family histories consistent with diagnosis of Specific Language Disability were noted as far as possible, but were not used in ranking.

Some of the diagnoses were made and others were corroborated by psychological and neuropsychiatric testing or consultation at the Institute of the Pennsylvania Hospital in Philadelphia, whence the school received initial guidance in its language treatment program.

In the end, we felt fairly secure in our individual rankings and in categorizing a High Language 20, a Middle Language 16, and a Low Language 20. The High Language 20 were rated "clearly nondyslexic," although even among the second ten of them we had noted a few scattered symptoms. The Middle 16 included eleven nondyslexics whom we had at some time watched especially or helped a bit because of one or more symptoms of possible trouble and five boys considered mildly dyslexic, who had required and responded readily to considerable special help. The Low Language 20 comprised eight moderately and twelve severely dyslexic boys. Four of the latter had enrolled in the school at grade four or later because its language program seemed likely to meet their needs. (A five-year offering of a seventh and eighth grade curriculum made this possible.) The other 16 of the Low 20 were "home-grown." The percentage of children with language problems, while high, can be attributed largely, we think, to the rather rigorous diagnostic practices, and is not out of line with the number found, for example, in the Walker-Cole (1965) study of a very similar population by similarly fine screening.

Those boys who needed special help were seen in individual sessions, generally every day and lasting from 15 minutes to an hour, over as long a time as their needs required or the school's facilities permitted. The optimum program was not always possible, but the help given varied from considerable to sufficient, in the opinion of the therapist and the teaching staff. Classwork and therapy were generally consistent, often coordinated and well-articulated. The atmosphere was one of understanding and cooperation.

When the boys' language ranks were compared with many other of their characteristics in their elementary school years, only Binet IQ and academic achievement in certain skill subjects showed marked relationships with language learning facility. Figure 13 and Table III show that the Low 20 scored noticeably lower than the other two groups in IQ.

Figure 13 shows that two of the tests considered "unreliable because language-limited" fall in the Low 20 group. Both boys made very high scores on a nonlanguage test given experimentally at the Institute. (The third unreliable test was of a partially deaf boy in the Middle group.) Readers familiar with the 1916 and Form L Binet Scales then in use will recall that they were orally administered in individual sessions but had relatively high verbal content. In view of the high degree of later achievement on the part of our Low Language 20, it is at least permissible to wonder whether these IQ scores may represent the inadequacy of the best test we then had to measure intellectual ability in

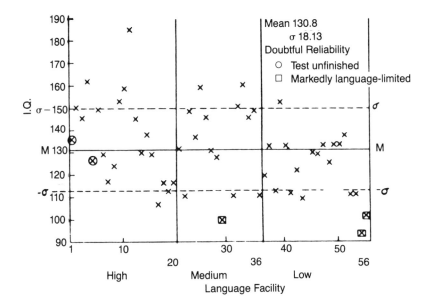

Figure 13.   Binet IQ vs language facility 56 Boys in Rose Valley School—1930–
              1947

Table III
Mean Binet IQs of Three Language Facility Groups, 56 Boys in Rose Valley
School, 1930–1947

Language Group	Mean IQ	Standard Deviation
High 20	136	19.0
Middle 16	133	18.5
Low 20	123	13.3

language handicapped boys, rather than a real group difference in this ability.

At the time of leaving the school, whether or not they stayed till graduation, 80 percent of the High Language group were very superior readers, while, in direct contrast, 90 percent of the Low Language group were very poor spellers—a half year or more below grade level. Other ratings were intermediate. The entire complicated accounting cannot be given here for reasons of space, but appears in the complete study (Rawson 1968). Several boys, representing all language groups, repeated a grade in their next schools, either because of the schools' policies ("every newcomer goes back one" was not uncommon) or because of their own inadequacies. A few boys from the two upper groups accelerated by a year in high school. While the Low 20 were somewhat more often slowed in their progress than the others, it is the eventual outcome, by 1964–1965, which seems to us to tell the most significant story.

1964–1965 Follow-up

In the year 1964–1965 it was possible for us to reach, by interview, 100 percent of our original group of 56 boys, either in person, through a close relative, or in four cases, through a friend who had been in close touch with the boy through the years and had seen him recently. The enthusiastic cooperation of our respondents brought a wealth of data only a small part of which can be presented here. That material having to do with post-high-school education and present occupation, analyzed in terms of elementary school language rank, gives material whereby our hypothesis can be tested.

Higher Education

Reference to Figure 14b will show that by the time the youngest class of the 56 boys was 26 years old and the oldest was 40, all the boys had graduated from high or preparatory school, and each had had

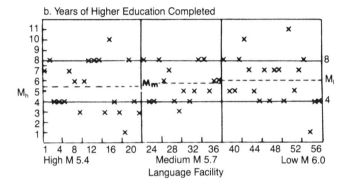

Figure 14.   *Educational and vocational achievement—language rank 56 Boys in Rose Valley School—1964–1965*

some further schooling. Only one boy had not had at least one year of college; he had gone to a trade school only. Seven others had attended college without graduation, although three were still working part-time toward their degrees. Another 13 had graduated from college, while the remaining 35 had also gone on to graduate school for from one to seven years, several of them still being candidates for advanced degrees.

When we compare the boys' subsequent schooling with their elementary school ranks on our three-group scale, we find slight, but statistically nonsignificant, differences in the number of years' work completed. (We are talking here of "college years' worth," not time spent, since service interruptions, part-time work, and other irregularities of attendance require translation into some kind of standard unit for comparison.) If we found no differences at all, this would negate our hypothesis, as would also even statistically nonsignificant differences which favored the higher language ranking groups, though some shade of doubt might still linger with us in the latter case. To our surprise, however, we find that the differences are in the opposite direction. The High 20 average 5.4 years of college and graduate school work, the Middle 16 5.7 years, and the Low 20 6.0 years (see Table IV). Even allowing a margin of uncertainty in each of these figures, their order reinforces the statistical conclusion that the Low Language boys

Table IV
Years of Higher Education Completed by 1964–1965, Three Language Learning Groups, 56 Boys in Rose Valley School, 1930–1947

Language Rank	Years of Higher Education Completed	
	Mean	Standard Deviation
High 20	5.4	2.4
Middle 16	5.7	1.6
Low 20	6.0	2.4

have achieved at least as well as their more linguistically facile classmates by the educational yardstick.

The degree pattern of these Low Language boys holds some interesting surprises. For the trade-school-only boy we transmuted two years of training into one year of "higher education equivalent." One other boy with one year of college and four and a half years of technical schooling without degree was credited with four years as a rough equivalent. Each of the other boys had done all of his work in an accredited college (as had those in the other two language ranks). Four boys achieved their bachelor's degrees; five more added a year of graduate work, and one of these is pursuing his master's degree. Of the five boys who have already achieved master's or law degrees, one has also a Bachelor of Divinity (a post-graduate degree) and three others are candidates for the doctorate, although the geologist among them is wondering whether he will pass his foreign language requirements. Five boys already have their doctorates; one of them has spent two years post-doctoral study, and another has added a Ph.D. to his M.D. He already had Phi Beta Kappa, Sigma Xi, and numerous other honors and publications to his credit. No, he was not misplaced at about rank No. 50 on the language scale, as he himself, would tell you. He was always an ambitious perfectionist and a worker to be sure, but he is also a charming fellow with wide interests, and he is a good husband, father, and friend. Just as deserving of laurels are the two boys whose multiple language handicaps placed them at Nos. 55 and 56, but whose good intelligence, strong motivation, and family support and persistence through years of tutorial help (and doubtless other ingredients) have enabled them to win through to A.B. degrees and excellent personality adjustments.

Vocational Achievement

Vocationally 18 of the 20 Low Language boys have achieved positions which place them in Warner's (1949)(11) Occupational Classes I and II. These are the "upper and upper-middle-class classes," with "high" professional and "high" business positions rating Class I and "middle" professional and "middle" business or management positions in Class II. One of the blue-collar boys is in a foreman's job, Class III, while the other, still in training, can be expected eventually to achieve this status as a "skilled workman in a position of responsibility." It is hard to make meaningful numerical analyses of such ratings; simple inspection of Figure 14a tells the story more clearly. Again, the Low Language boys not only do not fall behind the others, but even seem to have a slight advantage—at least justifying the rejection of the hypothesis on the second count. The Low 20 did *not* turn out to have been poor vocational risks, either.

The reader may wonder whether our language groups are in any way loaded by some hidden factor. We have searched diligently and found none. It is true that age and time out for military or alternate service have made some difference in the boys' educational achievements, and statistically significant difference in the proportions of older and younger boys in Occupational Classes I and II (numbers in the other classes being small and about equal). This is as one would expect—the younger boys have not quite finished whatever graduate work they may plan to do, and they are probably due for some job promotions by the time they are 35 or so. Since, however, there is a near-zero correlation between age and language rank, with boys of all ages about equally distributed through the language groups, these age-related statistics do not affect our hypothesis.

Residual Difficulties

An assessment by our respondents, especially the boys themselves, of present reading and spelling activities and skills shows that most, though not all, of the lowest ranking 25 still have some residual problems. They report varying degrees of difficulty, especially with slow reading and poor spelling. They have been able to compensate, however, by persistent effort and reliance on wives, secretaries, and dictionaries. The content level of their reading was intellectually appropriately demanding.

Relation of Prognosis to Achievement

How far was the school program on the whole responsible for the success of the Low Language 20 in achieving appropriate, generally high, educational and vocational goals? It was certainly by no means the only factor, but we like to think that perhaps it helped, with timely diagnosis and reasonably effective treatment. It may easily be true that one of our most valuable contributions was to the boys' self-concepts. We *knew* they were intelligent, and we *believed* they could come through, though we were sometimes hard put to it to convince *them*.

Certain it is that for only two of these boys was the clinician's suggested advice the right course. For them it would have been really appropriate and helpful. They are functioning well and happily in skilled trades. But had we followed the other 18, and had they and their parents acted upon it, society would have been the poorer by:

Five research scientists—two of them also physicians and two college professors.

Five other teachers—three in secondary schools, one a full professor and department head in a large university, and one of principal's rank and a member of the staff of a city superintendent of schools.

Five business men in responsible positions—Occupational Classes I and II.

One engineer—personnel manager for a large concern.

One lawyer—a partner in his law firm.

One actor—on full-time contract in Hollywood.

Add the five mildly dyslexic boys, who may have been saved real trouble by preventive work, and we increase the research scientists' roll by three, two of them college faculty men, and the business men in responsible positions by two.

These boys "had it in them," to be sure, but let us not do anything to drive it out of such fellows or to close doors in advance for them by unrealistically pessimistic prognoses!

3

Childhood IQ and Adult Accomplishment: The School in Rose Valley II

Contrasts Which Raised Questions

A striking parallel in life histories between the two boys with language ranks No's. 12 and 50 threw into bold relief the extreme difference in their childhood IQs. These boys, not close friends, were about three and a half years apart in age but four classes apart and so not in high school, college, or medical school together. They attended the same secondary school which frequently sent its more able students, including these two, to the same small university. There the boys made almost identically outstanding records (Highest Honors, Phi Beta Kappa, Sigma Xi, and other distinctions) in the demanding premedical course. They attended the same medical school but developed different specialized interests. In 1964–1965 both were engaged in research and appeared likely to achieve distinction consistent with their academic records. The older boy had already begun to do this, with over fifty scientific publications and a national award in his field. The younger scientist had done very well as to publications and recognition considering his age and an extra three years spent in post-doctoral study, but had just accepted his first post-degree position when interviewed in 1965.

The startling contrast of 52 IQ points, based on two consistent Binet tests for each boy, could not be ignored. Subject No. 12, with the higher IQ, achieved his school record with less apparent effort than did Subject No. 50, whose extreme childhood dyslexia left him with residuals such as "rather slow reading speed" and continued "very poor spelling" (his own 1965 appraisal). Still, the harder work was by no means compulsively all engrossing. This young man had a breadth of

Reprinted with permission from Educators Publishing Service, Inc. from *Developmental Language Disability: Adult Accomplishments of Dyslexic Boys*:90–95 1978.

interests and a pattern of personal-social development which seemed consistent with his other areas of superiority.

Admittedly the comparison here was between the "most gifted subject" (by Binet score criterion only—IQ 185) and the "most success-fully rehabilitated extreme dyslexic" (by educational achievement crite-rion only—two doctoral degrees). While such a parallel and contrast was most unlikely to be repeated, it drew attention to the apparent ceil-ing of IQ 135, only once exceeded, in the Low Language Facility group and suggested a comparative study of IQs in pairs of dyslexics and nondyslexics matched as closely as was possible as to educational and career histories.

A Study of Matched Pairs

Given the homogeneity of the population, it proved relatively easy to pair each boy of the Low Language Facility group with a "best match" from among the other two groups on the basis of the history and the 1964–1965 status of each boy. Some of these matches were ex-ceedingly close and all seemed adequate for the comparative study. The criteria used were:

Age— ≤ three calendar years difference.
Years of higher education— ≤ one year difference, except in three cases.
Type and degree of "difficulty" of college and university attended; e.g., Haverford paired with Swarthmore, Harvard with Yale; wherever possible attendance at the same institutions.
Socioeconomic status—generally either the same or minimally different.
Occupational choice—from "identical" to "closely comparable."
No attempt was made to match personality factors.

Since it was necessary to use for pairing only twenty of the 36 boys in the High and Medium Language Facility groups, it was possible to find matching subjects without including the five who had been thought of and taught as mildly dyslexic, the two whose Binet tests were incomplete, the three youngest subjects, the boy with hearing loss, and five others not needed. (Figure 15.)

The range of IQs in the dyslexic group was from 94 to 153, and in the matching group from 111 to 185. In 14 pairs the IQ differences fa-vored the nondyslexic subjects by from 11 to 52 points, with a median difference of 14.3 points, a mean difference of 22.2 points (t-test— $P < .01$), and a standard deviation of 12.8 points. In five cases the IQ differences favored the dyslexics by from 2 to 9 points with a mean of

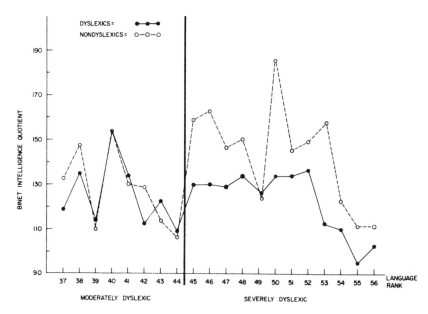

Figure 15. Childhood IQ's of dyslexic boys (Numbers 37–56 on the Language Learning Facility Scale), compared with IQ's of nondyslexic boys (not here identified by number). Subsequent life histories of the paired subjects were closely matched as to age, education, and occupation.

3.6 points (t-test—nonsignificant) and a standard deviation of 3.2 points. In one case only were the IQs of a pair identical, the pair including the 153 IQ mentioned earlier as the sole score above 135 among the dyslexics. The life histories of these two boys were also strikingly similar.

The t-test shows the difference between the mean favoring the fourteen nondyslexic boys and that favoring the five dyslexic boys to be significant beyond the .001 level.

The relationship of childhood IQ to dyslexia is particularly noticeable in the group of twelve boys rated severely dyslexic. In only one case, and there by only two points, was the IQ of the nondyslexic member of a pair below that of the dyslexic. (The match in this pair, while rated nondyslexic, was nevertheless a boy who had difficulty expressing his thoughts in words. It is quite possible that he, too, was underrated by the Binet test.) The mean difference favored the nondyslexics by an obviously highly significant 21.9 points. This subgroup is the major source of the difference noted for the Low Language Facility group as a whole (twenty boys) and of the moderate correlation of IQ with language rank previously noted.

Whenever statistical averages are used some loss in significant detail is inevitable. A closer look at individuals showed this to be probable in the IQ comparison. In nine of the 20 dyslexic boys' scores the investigator felt fairly secure in judging that the Binet test had, in fact, measured the boy's academic potential adequately. In eleven cases among the dyslexics, however, and at least five among those adjudged nondyslexic, the Binet score had not been an adequate predictor of academic achievement.

For example, there was a difference of 46 points between two matched scientists with undergraduate degrees from Swarthmore and Haverford and doctorates from Yale and Harvard. The dyslexic was tested by a very competent outside examiner and the nondyslexic's score was later validated by retest by an outside examiner. Were these two boys as far apart in intellectual ability as their IQs suggested?

Other differences, both large and small, seemed indicative of the effect of verbal factors on test scores which was not necessarily reflected in ultimate academic achievement. In two cases (Nos. 14 and 22), the school may very well have missed opportunities to help two boys with language problems of a dyslexic type. Information suggesting this came to light especially during the follow-up interviews. In another instance, the match of the boy with his moderately dyslexic counterpart was particularly close and the IQ figures equally, and very considerably, seemed to have underestimated the potential of both boys of the pair. Binet scores in the low 130s do not lead one to expect distinction in post-doctoral study and research careers such as describe these boys. The examiner (the author in both cases) was certainly unaware of whatever specific "ceiling factor(s)" may have been operating but recalls having been a bit surprised in each instance that the score was not higher for these apparently gifted and creative youngsters.

Two dyslexics made IQ scores below 120 but later earned Ph.Ds. from well known universities and achieved professional rank on university faculties. Had anyone at the school, or any later counselor, discouraged the boys from academic pursuits or advised their parents to do so on the basis of the childhood IQs, the pressures of the self-fulfilling prophecy might have been added to the language burden the boys were already carrying. "College may be too tough for you; graduate school is a most unrealistic idea." Such a statement, or even the attitude behind it, could have discouraged the boys and damaged self-concepts already vulnerable.

A well qualified psychologist would not have used a single IQ figure this way, of course, but might himself have been influenced in his judgment by a boy's performance on such a justifiably highly respected instrument as the Binet, as the school staff may well have been in the case of boy No. 22, for example. Moreover, not all users of test scores are equally sophisticated, nor are most parents in position to thread their ways among the values and limitations of findings or their interpreters, even if scrupulous care is used in not quoting IQ figures. The Binet test is still a much better instrument to use with a language-disabled youngster than are classroom group tests, but great caution is always indicated in its interpretation.

4

Invent a Wheel—At Least Once

Nowadays it is fairly common practice in education to recognize the psychological value to the learner of discovery *for himself*, through his own reasoning and experience of the elements of reality in his world. Often *we* set the stage so that the experiment, reasoning, and reflection bring to him "the glad surprise of discovery" of a bit of Truth. "Everybody," we say, "should have the experience of inventing at least *one* wheel." If the discoverer finds his "wheel" already in use, or even projected, by others, he has still learned at least two important lessons: (1) Science, technology, and wisdom grow also by verification through replicated experience; (2) The revelation, discovery, and original creativity by which mankind approaches solutions to the riddles of life comprise a continuity in which we can all take part.

If it is new *to you*, you have tasted creativity; it is to that extent *your* wheel. You can usually accept and use the discoveries of others as valuable parts of your culture. Someday it is possible that something *you* devise will be *really new*; fruitful invention does keep happening. Enjoying the quest is part of your being human, so make the most of it.

In my School in Rose Valley study (1968) I seemed to find some measure of further verification for Orton's and Gillingham's empirical approach to the educational treatment of what we had come to call developmental dyslexia. For that I was glad; I have tried to make these findings of value to concerned others. I liked that, and the fact that the study was my own, original work in a unique set of circumstances, and that it had a positive outcome that people are still finding useful. It gives me deep personal satisfaction to have made what I believe to be a contribution to science in this way. Many people have done far more, but this one wheel is very specially mine.

But there was a small, serendipitous wheel inside this one that gave me the *real* excitement of discovery. Many people believe, and a few have produced some evidence for their conviction, that the best IQ tests that we have known how to give are almost sure to underrate the intelligence of dyslexic people. My genuine thrill came from having stumbled by sheer luck on a single item of evidence to this effect in the comparison of two of the 56 boys in the study and *most especially* in realizing the possible meaning of the evidence, pursuing it, and bringing forth a very small jewel of a subsidiary exploratory study. For what it is worth, the number of cases being so small, it has the impact (on me!) of a perfect short-short story. Nobody else has paid it any attention, but that doesn't matter to *me*, for its *discovery* and *creation* have given *me* a tingling thrill, and do so every time I reread those five pages and look at their accompanying diagram. However little it means to anyone else, in me it excites the same feeling I think I would have if I had been an artist and had painted or carved a good miniature.

The whole Rose Valley study gave me the earned satisfaction of honest work, with some added creativity payoff, but the paired IQ fragment produced the glad surprise that was pure bonus. My delight!

Everyone should have such experiences, preferably beginning in childhood and happening every now and again throughout life. Let it happen—to yourself and your charges—and for them, set it up when you can. Life should be like that whenever it is possible.

5

The Jemicy School: A Philosophy

A school should be designed for its children, their present happy growth and their soundly based future effectiveness. A school is established as a *group* in which people are taught or led to learn, but it is as *individuals* that they learn, through experiencing group life and developing unique personal competences and understanding of their world.

Just as, in Aldous Huxley's words, "It is no good knowing about the taste of strawberries out of a book," so each child needs to experience for himself the worlds of city and country, of nature and human culture. These become part of him through all his senses, through emotional and spiritual appreciation and responsible involvement in all the world about and within him, and by the active processes of the ordered observation, problem solving, and critical thinking which we call intellectual functioning.

Each child is born with a distinctive combination of potentialities on which, by the time he comes to school, a unique set of experiences has been at work making him a separate individual, different from all others. At the same time, he is a member of the human family, with certain basic physical, emotional, and spiritual characteristics and needs which he shares with all of us. It is this which makes society both necessary and possible. A school life which promotes the healthy, vigorous, joyful growth of its children should provide a well-planned physical setting and general program. Such dependable security gives a firm foundation and a stable framework within which each child can live a cooperative and rewarding social life while he is developing from dependent childhood into self-reliant adolescence and adulthood.

But this provides only the background for the major interest of the school, which is the meeting of each child's specific needs and the fostering of his strengths and unique talents. The plan which is best for him is the one which will enable him to grow toward achieving his own potentialities. For this he needs a richly varied educational experience in physical activity and sports, in a wide variety of creative arts, in happy social relationships, and in the intellectual appreciation of his cultural heritage.

He needs careful training, too, in the basic skills which are the tools through whose use he will develop competence and a sense of confidence in achieving his educational objectives. Tools themselves are not the goals of education, but just as it is difficult or impossible to construct a beautiful and satisfying building without a set of well-sharpened tools and the skill to use them, so one cannot hope to acquire knowledge, understanding, and vocational competence without mastery of reading, writing, mathematics and the disciplines imposed by shop, studio, laboratory, and playing field.

Children have varied degrees of talent and difficulty in different traits, and so their needs differ. Wholeness of development requires that we know a child's strengths so that we may encourage him to use them well, and know, too, the exact nature of his difficulties so that we may help him to cope successfully with them, and so gain a well-rounded competence as an effective person.

To achieve these goals for the school there must be a staff which itself embodies wholeness of body, mind, and spirit, with a capacity for both loving acceptance and calm firmness. Effective pedagogy requires knowledge and enthusiasm in subject matter, coupled with astute assessment of individual children's needs and capacities and skill in teaching one in his own style and at his own pace, whether individually or in varying groups.

Since none of us is all-knowing, the planning and operation of the school requires not only teamwork on the campus but consultation with outside experts when needed, cooperation of parents, and, most important, a spirit of involvement on the part of the children as they grow toward taking full responsibility for their own behavior and learning.

This is education—a leading forth—toward the full, happy, and effective living we all want for each of our children and for the school community as a whole. This experience of the good life in childhood, with the development of competence and adaptability, is the best preparation we know for meeting the demands of later schooling and of a world of rapid change and complexity. Specific training is obsolete before it is mastered, but intellectual curiosity, skill in learning, and creative flexibility in the face of new problems are dependable resources with which to meet whatever the future may hold of challenge and opportunity.

These are the objectives to which *The Jemicy School* has dedicated itself.

6

Some Thoughts for Graduating Students

You came to this school because you were having some troubles in your other schools. Sometimes people call these difficulties *learning disabilities* (they're *not*, and I'll tell you why I say that later), or they call them *dyslexia*, which is just an impressive Greek way of saying "trouble with language." It's a good word, because it's short and easy to use, and it's different from other words. It has a meaning of its very own, so it may help straighten out some of the mixed-up thinking about the one thing that makes each of you special in the same way as other students in this school.

Labels like dyslexia are useful if you don't make the mistake of thinking that a label on some little part of a person is the person himself. As a whole person everyone needs a lot of labels, like "soccer star," "ham radio whiz," "science fiction fan," and "the guy who can put away more ice cream cones than anybody else on campus." But if one of his labels is "dyslexia," and he's lucky, he may end up at this school.

I promised I'd tell you something of what dyslexia *isn't*, and how people are often wrong about it. Of course, anybody can tell just by looking at you that it isn't a disease that you've got, as if you had measles. It isn't a defect, either, like having a hand or an ear missing— and (as the psychological tests show) you've got all your marbles. And it isn't a *learning disability*, though some lawmakers and people who assign tuition funds may find that label useful. Sometimes labels don't really describe what's in the package. You people are very sharp learners—bright guys and gals—in all sorts of ways. You know that and so does this school or you wouldn't have got in, and so do your parents and a lot of other people.

You have had some problems, and they are very real, beastly ones. When you came here I suppose it wasn't far wrong to say that your troubles with catching onto reading and spelling and writing and

---

Adapted for Jemicy School from talks given at Linden Hill School, Northfield, MA 1981 and Armstrong School, Menlo Park, CA 1981.

maybe math had you limping or sitting on the sidelines in the class-room game, just as if you'd pulled a ligament and some trainer hadn't known what to do about it or had done the wrong thing. For the time being you really were *disabled* in your *school learning*, but that didn't have to last. You know that from what you have already been able to accomplish here and what you've seen other people do.

Dyslexia isn't something you, a victim, have got so you have to be cured of it. It points to the kind of mind you have, and it's a very good kind of mind, too. Lots of great people have been wired up in their brains the way you are, like Albert Einstein, Thomas Edison, former Vice President Rockefeller, Bruce Jenner, and hundreds of other peo-ple, not necessarily famous, but doing very well in life.

Everybody has some of the traits and abilities and quirks we're talking about, some one way and some another, some a little or a few, and some a lot, some in ways that help and some in ways that hinder, at least till somebody finds the right way to deal with them.

Whatever the mixture you have, it's your kind of mind, and it's yours for keeps. There are all sorts of ways that you can make it work better for you, better and better all your life. Whoever sent you here knew what they do at this school and thought it was a good match for what you need to help you make the best use of many, many talents you were born with. They were right, and you know it now, even though, possibly, you weren't sure when you came.

It hasn't been easy. Some of it, like spelling, may never be a walk-away. But if the hard work pays off, then you work hard—and in the end you win. People have told me about lazy kids, stubborn kids, clowns (in the wrong places), trouble-makers, dreamers (at the wrong times), and all sorts of kids who, they said, "didn't care" and "wouldn't work." I always say, and almost always I or some other teachers have been able to prove, "If he's not sick, just let us have a good chance to convince him by his own experience. Then he'll show you that he *can* learn, and learn *well*, and that he'll work at it as hard as he needs to, often harder than the other guys. What's more, he'll get real satisfaction out of the job, and a lot of his other troubles will clear up, too."

It looks good enough now, you admit, but perhaps you wonder if it will hold up after you leave this school. Will it really help get you where you want to go in life? My answer to that is, "Absolutely, *yes!*" Of course, it won't just come to you by wishing or dreaming or putting quarters in the slot. It will help a lot if you have the adults who mean most to you believing in you, but it is *you* who will do it, now that you have begun to learn how and know that your work and practice will pay off.

I know this for a fact, and I'd like to tell you just a little of how I know it. I've been a dyslexic-watcher, and sometimes a regular teacher, since before even your parents were born. I could spend the rest of the day—but don't worry, I won't—telling you about George and Ralph and Barbara Ann and the rest of them I've known, and I'll bet you wouldn't even be bored (except with the sound of my voice). But here's a very small sample.

Take Harry. I saw him first when he was 14 and knew just 14 simple words on the test. He wanted to become a mechanic and have a garage of his own, but he couldn't get into the training course or even get his driver's license without first learning to read. He did—enough. People in our town now say he's the best mechanic around there, especially with foreign cars, and he's now gone on to run his own business with, when I last heard, eight big trucks, some fine looking buildings and 20 men working for him. He's a nice guy, too, and the kids think he's a swell Road-E-O manager. He is happily married and his two kids are in high school.

Take Ralph, a very different sort of fellow. When he was eight he couldn't manage to spell c-a-t = cat, or read it after he wrote it, but he wanted to manage everything. We got that straightened out, just the way you've been learning to, and he became the No. 1 soccer man in his school and an authority on naval history by the end of eighth grade —but he never won any spelling bees and couldn't to this day. He went on to high school, university, medical school and then got a second doctor's degree in biochemistry, believe it or not. Now he teaches in a medical school, and has a son, Stanley—with the same set of language problems his father had—who is a struggling sophomore and a swimming star in a famous university.

Take Jeff. You know what hyperactive means? At ten Jeff was like the 3-year-old who is into everything and most of it trouble. Everything, that is, except school work. It was a long, slow start, but he was game. In prep school it was a little better and he'd made the Honor Roll by graduation. In college he got to the Dean's List as a Junior. In graduate school, in business administration, he'd found the place where his talents were, got a few Bs but mostly As and ended up No. 1 in a class of over a thousand! But you should see his notebooks. I did. They are as messy as they ever were, and as hard to read (I couldn't begin to *understand* them—hard economics and such). But now he has a super job, a new one as a sales manager in a big firm where he just got a $10,000 raise. I can hardly believe it, even yet. But he was smart in another way, too. He married a girl who could spell, and she writes his personal letters, as his secretary does his business ones. There's part of the recipe for success for dyslexics. Moral: get through school as well as you can, however hard the going; get a job that rates a secretary, marry a girl who can spell!

Take Tom. Right from the start, in nursery school, he had all the problems in the book. He tried hard, and so did I, but we were both discouraged enough, almost, to give up when he was nine—and moved away. He had a lot of help from good people, but it never seemed to work, except barely to keep him in his right grade. Then just as the great Dr. Orton himself, who saw him at nine, had said it would, the payoff came, with an excellent Orton-Gillingham type teacher, when Jeff was 17. He graduated, but then it took him five years to get through a top-level university—because he had somehow to pass Spanish, finally and with a D −, but he majored in what he liked best, English Literature. Every now and then I come across his trail when I meet a boy from one of the prep schools where he has taught. They like him, admire him as a skier and a sailor, get a lot of help from him in photography. What does he teach? You guessed it—or maybe you didn't—English! Of course. That's what he's interested in, that and boys he can help. You'll like him if you are lucky enough to go to his school. Don't ask me which one it is. I don't know. Teachers move around, and I haven't heard from Tom for a while.

Take Barbara, to represent some of the girls. (They are fewer, have the same problems as the boys, and are every bit as important.) Many, many years ago, after left-handed, dyslexic Barbara had one year of the kind of tutoring you know all about, her mother said, "Yes, I know she *can* read pretty well now, but please go on until she can do it so easily she *wants to,* just for fun." We did, and then she moved away. Forty-five years later I met her again. Meanwhile, she had gone on through the University, married a classmate, seen both of her sons (one of them also dyslexic) through college and into scientific management of the family's big Midwestern ranch. Still a "great reader," an active citizen, and a prize-winner in crafts, she had just been named Woman of the Year by her state's Governor.

Of course, these are just some spectacular success stories, but Tom, Jeff, Ralph, Harry, and Barbara aren't all that unusual among grown-up dyslexics. My files and your school's alumni records, and a lot of other people's lists could match them many times over and add even more men and women who have done satisfyingly well, if not spectacularly. It's the rule, not the exception in our experience. They still run into problems, who doesn't? They still work—even the most talented musicians and tennis players practice for hours on end. But they do what they want to do, make a pretty good living at it, and they live the kinds of lives they want to. It's not that there is any magic in dyslexia that makes sure of this. In fact, it has sometimes slowed them down a bit, but there is nothing that says it has to stop them. They are the kinds of people you'll be glad to grow up to be like.

What's more, all these people I know felt good about themselves as of course they have a right to. They don't strut around about it, just feel satisfied inside that they are basically all right people. If they think about dyslexia at all, they think of it as a natural, OK, something about them, like Ralph's left-hand writing, Harry's amusing cartoons, Jeff's interest in his church, and Tom's knowing, by sixth sense, where the wind is coming from as he pilots his small plane, and Barbara's weaving or business skill. Each of you will, too. You will keep on learning. You'll work at it. You will do whatever is in you to do, what you want most to do. And you'll feel good about yourself, and so, of course, everybody else will feel good about you, too.

What's wrong with dyslexia? Sometimes it's a nuisance, but look at your friend Jack, from your school. He's just great. That's *you!*

(P.S. 1988: *Harry's* business has grown and prospered. For fun he restores antique foreign cars—*Ralph* is still practicing medicine and teaching medical students; his research interest in biochemistry wins him grants and occasional appointments at the National Institutes of Health. *Stanley* got his university degree and has a good start in banking. For fun, Ralph sails, Stan swims—*Jeff* soon became Vice-President for Marketing. Now he has his own business, with clients all over the U.S. and in Canada. He flies a Bonanza (plane) for business and for fun. *Jeff, Jr.*, "dyslexically" very like his dad, had the kind of preventive help Jeff needed; he reads easily, works hard to keep up in math and spelling, uses a word processor for papers–but prefers soccer—I have mostly lost track of *Tom*, though I believe he still has the same occupation and hobbies—*Barbara* and Jim (her husband), on vacation last summer, stopped at my place "for 20 minutes" and stayed all afternoon. Their sons run the ranch, but in busy seasons Barb and Jim pitch in, and they help with the computerized management through their modem up in Big City. For fun they travel, and Barb weaves and runs a scouting program. She's still *my* Woman-of-the-Year—or one of them —Dyslexics generally keep right on with whatever it is they want to do.)

7

The Dyslexic College Student and the Arts

Dyslexic students are still dyslexic when they get to college. Now, I've been working on language problems for a good many years, and I think I can recognize and even describe the patterns I group together as dyslexia, and identify them when I meet them in students of many ages, backgrounds, and temperaments. I am more than glad to talk with art educators about the subject. I believe we have a lot of friends in common. And we need to know more about dyslexic art students and what they are up against if we are to help them to be all they can be.

Here is a group of young people whose aptitude for mastering language skills is not consistent with their other general or special abilities. How come? How shall we recognize them? What will that tell us about how to free them for the best they can assimilate in education?

You all know these students. I'd be willing to wager that you have a lot of them—probably a higher incidence in your liberal arts programs designed for college students than we'd find at most other colleges and universities in the communities you represent. There are several reasons for this.

In the first place, let me clear the decks. I don't think what we call dyslexia *is* a disease. On good authority, from Orton (1925) through Thompson (1966) to the Silberbergs in (1972), a case can be made for the view that the learning of language skills, the aptitude for facile use of language forms, is a trait like any other. It is really a complex of many subtraits working (or not working) together, and so, in the end, it gives a distribution which ranges, approximately on a normal probability curve from high aptitude to severe ineptitude. Compare it to artistic or musical ability, inventive genius or other creativity, engineering giftedness or mechanical talent, physical skill or prowess, interpersonal giftedness or any other of what Thompson (1966) calls "the capacities of man." What, then, is the difference which makes us focus so much attention on the language function and its disorders or people's consti-

Adapted from a speech delivered to the Union of Independent Colleges of Art. Baltimore 1973.

tutional differences in respect to it? Simply, I think, that in our culture everybody must have at least a functional command of language skills if he is not to be unduly penalized in his passage through traditional education and through life.

If a student is drawn to the world of the arts and applies to one of your schools, you look over his records and his portfolio. You may ask him to demonstrate his aptitudes by formal or informal test. You look into his objectives and motivations and other personal factors and try to decide whether he has what it takes to make use of what your school has to offer. If you think he has, you give him a chance. If you think not, you suggest that he explore other pastures where the grass may be more likely to give him nourishment. If you don't accept him, he may be disappointed, perhaps even greatly disappointed, but neither he nor anyone else is likely to discredit his intelligence or other aptitudes because he is not artistically talented. If the field were music and he lived in Vienna in the 1800s, perhaps his ego would be more vulnerable to rejection by a musical academy, but probably not much more so. Who can blame even a son of Bach if he has not been favored by the gods with a gift for music? Of course his parents or teachers may say, "You could if you'd only work at it. Everybody can carry a tune if he tries," and so forth, but the whole culture would not find him a defective in a general sort of way.

With language it is different. There is a universal expectation, especially in a literate culture. *Talking* most people manage reasonably well, but *reading* and *writing*, too, are essential. If one is as inept in mastering these skills at the accepted time and rate as some of us are at the keyboard or the drawing board or the potter's wheel, the people to whom language comes easily (many of whom go into academic teaching) are apt to conclude that one is stupid, lazy, or emotionally disturbed. One just has to learn to read and write. (Of course, fortunately, with proper teaching, one can, just as, if it is important enough for his survival, I am told that almost every child can learn to carry a tune.) Of course, too, there are linguistically inept learners who are also stupid (whatever that means), underprivileged in various ways, and handicapped in physical or sensory modalities. This makes the problem more difficult, just as it is harder both to diagnose and to treat a child who is incubating measles while he is beginning to bark with whooping cough. There is almost always emotional involvement, too, sometimes as a result of the frustrations of language learning failures and sometimes concurrent but from a different cause. This complicates, but rarely causes, the dyslexia problem.

Studies of the incidence of difficulty have conclusively demonstrated that the dyslexia pattern is at least familial and probably genetic. Similar studies of linguistic giftedness would probably show the same thing, much as we find musical families or those with high general intelligence.

When we study the lives of eminent persons (see Thompson 1969) or when we test children (I suggest that you read the Symmes and Rapoport 1972 paper about this)—we find that there is no demonstrable correlation between language learning differences and the relative presence or absence of other traits, such as intelligence, creativeness, and the like, with a few exceptions. Family tendencies there do seem to be, and differences in ability to hold in mind auditory or visual sequences of random materials, like numbers or speech sounds or letters in a word, long enough to imprint them on short or long term memory, and so to have them clearly ready for processing into remembered words for reading, spelling, or writing.

There are several patterns of general intelligence that we find in giving Wechsler intelligence tests to people of all ages, and these are borne out by findings from other tests. Some people process problems for solution well in words (spoken words—no connection, it may seem, with reading and writing), while some do poorly with words but well in spatial relations of some or many kinds. We find dyslexics in both groups and also in the group which does equally well in both areas.

There is some evidence of engineers who do not handle language well, and, from such biographies as Einstein's, evidence that these visual-spatial individuals form a particular subgroup of very able people with a sort of imbalance of aptitudes. I should expect to find that your Art Institutes would have more than your share of them. There are, too, the people who say it best in action, but most tests identify this group only indirectly.

I am reminded of Gary, now a graduate of a college of arts and a fabric designer, whom I knew as a child. I did not consider him a dyslexic then, and I guess I still do not, but he did have a language problem which I have glimpsed but not understood. In a play about the American Revolution Patrick Henry himself could not have portrayed Patrick Henry more convincingly. It was a superb performance for an 11-year-old, or an actor of any age. And Gary's painting of a Bessemer converter and the Pittsburgh scene still has me feeling the heat and hearing the sound of the fire. An engineer-artist who saw it was full of admiration. But when I tried to talk with Gary about either the historical or the experiential content of these apparently very meaningful experiences, it was as if he really didn't understand them cognitively at all—almost as if he were the unconscious channel for some unidentifiable artistic force. Perhaps the explanation lies in the functioning of the right, or non-self-conscious, hemisphere of the brain, understanding of which is [in 1973] the newest and most exciting breakthrough in

brain science. I could well believe it. I mention Gary because I am sure
you have met his like. Is he dyslexic? Or does it matter? He must have
mastered language well enough to get by the collegiate requirements
for he got his art institute college degree. I wish I could have known
and tested him as a Freshman.

I spent a number of years at Hood College, in Frederick, Md.,
wearing two hats. One of them had a band which said, "Sociology."
When I was wearing the other, I was working with the students on
what I have always thought of as "the Dean's *other* list." Of the three
dozen or so young women I saw each year, usually for nowhere near
enough time, I have estimated that perhaps half a dozen would qualify,
based on extensive individual testing, as true dyslexics—students
whose major stumbling block was inadequate mastery of their mother
tongue. One or two of these would be severely handicapped from this
cause. If this had been a men's or a co-ed college, or a college whose
curriculum was specialized in art or engine design, the numbers would
have been higher and, perhaps, the proportions of mild to severe difficulty different.

There were other problems, too, of course, as there are in your
student populations. Some Freshmen are badly prepared for college
level work, either because their high schools were inadequate, or because the students themselves were too bright for their classmates. In
the latter case, they may have found it easy to be valedictorians (or to
get by with Bs and Cs), but when they get to college with a half a class-
ful of valedictorians and where the academic demands are proportion-
ately higher, things change. Sometimes they rise to the occasion, with
or without help, and sometimes they don't. The freedom and necessity to plan one's time, to resist too great temptation to major in extra-
curricular activities, may be more than they can handle, at least at first.
There may be family disturbances that take their toll in emotional energy, or broken hearts or roommate troubles. But when all these are
accounted for, there are still some who are primarily dyslexia suspects.

Perhaps a couple of cases of such students will interest you. I have
chosen two young women and a young man from my files because they
are, particularly, your kind of young people.

Laura was a girl who, unfortunately, was not identified even by
her mother, an elementary-school teacher, as having a major reading
problem. The indications were plain, against the backdrop of other
kinds of schooling, but Laura was by all odds the brightest girl in her
rural high school class and had been the brightest all the way through
school. She listened well in class, was intelligent, stable, and responsive, so nobody, not even she herself, realized how much trouble she
was having until she got to college. She was, by several points, the lowest scorer in her freshman class on the Nelson-Denny Reading Test and
later made very typical dyslexia errors in individual reading and spell-

ing tests. Her IQ of 128 on the Verbal part of the Wechsler test, with a special strength in abstract reasoning, should have permitted her to do college work well above the average level, but despite her best efforts— and she was a conscientious worker—the first semester grades brought her failures in English, History, and Home Economics (which demanded more reading than one might expect); she had dropped Chemistry. Art brought her a B, however, (and an A at year's end), with a comment from her teacher about her exceptionally fine "abstract intelligence" (in which she had shone on the Wechsler verbal test also) and her creativity.

Why these discrepancies between native ability and academic performance? With reading and spelling achievement at the low 9th grade level, slow speed, and innumerable errors and confusions, it would have been surprising if it had been otherwise. During the year, with some, but not adequate, tutorial help, she learned a lot about her language and was ready to make rapid strides in a well-tailored University summer school course. She was, not surprisingly, dropped from Hood, and was unable to enter the University until she should have gained a C record elsewhere, so she entered a school of interior decorating in a nearby city and when last heard from was doing very well. Whether she ever returned to college, as she could have, I do not know.

As far as we were concerned, it was the not unfamiliar case of "too little, too late." She could have succeeded in the academic program if we had been able to get to work on it even a year or so earlier, and in the right school in her own field, after some work in language, too, she did do well. As it was, the best we could do about her Freshman year was to help her succeed as a *person,* although she had failed as a student, as the following summary, written at the end of the year, indicates.

> Laura has, of course, had many unhappy hours over her academic failures, but she has faced them with courage and come out whole, I think. As a student she knows she has not been successful, but she has had some good experiences at Hood and has many happy memories to take away, too. She has certainly grown as a person and will, I believe, make both a loyal ex-student and one we can someday be proud of having salvaged from the kind of "failure" she might have been had she started out in a less personalizing kind of college.

Then there was Lewis, who came around when he was 16, a Junior in high school, but very much your kind of a boy. Nobody thought too much about his indifferent school work until his 11th grade English teacher gave him what turned out to be a therapeutic F. This galvanized his mother, a former English teacher, into action. She had known about my work for some time, as we were old friends and our husbands were close professional associates, but she just didn't think it had any connection with Lew. It decidedly did. On the basis of the school's group intelligence test IQ of 110, and in view of Lew's preoccupation with making beautiful and elaborate architectural scale models, the school had decided that he was of average ability but just wasn't interested in school work, and they had been undisturbed by his mediocre grades in an average section of his class. He had a history of reading and spelling difficulties in grade school and other troubles with foreign language and algebra, but there were rationalized explanations for each of these. As his scientist father said later, the parents had no frame of reference in which to understand Lew's scholastic record as a whole.

The facts, as they came out on the tests, showed how wrong a judgment based on inadequate evidence can be. Far from being of average intellectual ability, Lew achieved a Verbal IQ of 125, with a top score (20, where 10 is average) in abstract verbal reasoning; a Performance IQ of 138, with one top and two very superior scores; and a Full Scale IQ of 134, a "very superior" rating. He made only high average scores, which were still well below his *own* average, in auditory rote memory and symbol manipulation—a pattern classically typical of dyslexia. His achievement test responses were almost unbelievably "classic," including such errors as "A dog had a boy," instead of "A boy had a dog," and with no awareness of the error!

When the dyslexia situation was explained to Lew, and he realized that he was neither stupid nor lazy, as he had been led to suppose, his feelings of guilt disappeared and his self-confidence improved. He was, his parents reported, a different boy. His father, an eminent biological scientist and an understanding father, realized that he, himself, and two of his three sisters had had almost the same problem. He had managed to get through an easy mid-western college, beginning to find himself about midway through. He had really hit his stride in graduate school, and most wisely, married a faultless speller who still acted as his secretary when he had papers to prepare.

Lew's building models were superb. In the school's Science Fair he made second place for a model of a heavy water plant and would have placed first if he had been able to explain it to the judges. They thought he had had help from his father, but he had not. He was just too shy to explain, and, he said, later, after he knew the nature of his language problem, he was too afraid that the words he might utter would "come out all wrong." Just the diagnosis of his difficulty and its explanation, however, so liberated him that a few weeks later when his cutaway model for a proposed addition to the local hospital was turned over to the appropriate committee, we have a newspaper picture of him explaining it to several of the town's leading citizens with a relaxed and easy assurance.

There were a few weeks left in the school year by the time the tests were finished, so we laid as much groundwork as possible and sent Lew off to a special summer camp for dyslexics. The family moved and Lew had no more opportunity for help. He repeated grade 11, struggled through, got work with an architectural firm, studied part-time, later won his degree, and is now an architect. We are filled with admiration, yet regret the unnecessary hardness of the way.

And now, lest you think I do not believe it possible for *you* to do something about *your* dyslexic students, when you meet them first in college, let me tell you briefly about Jane.

As a Freshman at Hood, Jane was neither so badly off as Laura, nor, like Lew did she have to move about during the time following her identification and the implementing of an appropriate plan. She was about as able as Lew and had the same kind of understanding and support from equally able parents who had been just as baffled as had Lew's father and mother.

She was identified first by a knowledgeable French teacher before she got her first semester grades—4 Ds and one F. A diagnostic study showed high intelligence, typical dyslexia (if there is such a thing), and yet a favorable prognosis. She substituted a course of Orton-Gillingham-oriented tutoring for a three hour course for each of the next two semesters, with further, but less intensive work through her Junior year. She gradually brought her average up to a point where she had some margin over the minimum for graduation and even got a few As and Bs. She worked for a year in a social work job (her first choice, with high personal aptitude). She did so well she was offered a fellowship at a graduate school which is among the best in the field, and was soon rating high in her class. Her M.S.W. came to her with a rank of No. 3 in a class of 80 candidates. She worked very successfully and has married a physician. One summer, after having found a high incidence of language difficulties among the children in the settlement house in the housing development where she worked, she joined my graduate school class for therapists. As she had in my sociology course when she was an undergraduate, she did very well, but her reading rate was still low, her spelling was far from perfect, and her written expression was not either effortless or flawless. In other words, she was still herself—a dyslexic sort of person with high intelligence, fine professional qualifications, a charming personality, and, now, glowing health and a radiant kind of beauty. Like Lew after the diagnosis, she was "a different person," in many good ways, from the defeated Freshman I had first known eight years before and a good example of what can be done if circumstances are favorable. It has been done many times, and can be accomplished for many of your students, too.

(PS 1988. Jane is happy and productive as a citizen with a wide-range of volunteer activities. Neither of her teen-age sons has had roadblock-level school problems.)

8

Case Histories as Evidence in Dyslexia

"One swallow doesn't make a spring," we are told. Case histories are too anecdotal, incomplete, circumstantial—and do not have proper controls. Hence, they are not acceptable as proof of much of anything, scientifically speaking.

But in the Land of Dyslexia, for example, we know what the place looks like in winter—what the climate and landscape are like for the undiagnosed and/or untreated people with language learning problems. If we think of these people, for the moment, as the country's flora, the landscape may seem pretty bleak. Yet nature is resilient; closer inspection shows very live buds on most of the plant specimens, despite some scholastic winter-kill. We can hope that a reasonably good summer and some therapeutic horticulture will encourage new growth and permit healthy and flourishing plant-forms, able somehow to accomplish the missions given them by the genetic instruction in their seeds.

Case histories can describe many kinds of plants—those that have been blighted, those that are in process of treatment, and those that have recovered full, or even partial but considerable, health, as well as those that have succumbed. Individual case histories can give full and exhaustive reports of extensive examinations and periods, often long periods, of treatment, with observations of results that may extend over many years of subsequent living. They can be thumbnail sketches of a sentence or a paragraph, or of any length or degree of penetration suitable to the occasion.

Study material can also be collected and presented as series of real-life, real-time instances clustered around an idea. This form might serve the same purpose as a statistical report in which the abstraction from reality is more formal. We need perennially to be reminded that every form of presentation is, in fact, its own kind of abstraction from the reality of experience.

Of course case instances are not proof-positive; they are only as good as the data bases and the clear-headedness, wisdom, and integrity of those who present them. Are these not the constraints science places upon itself in every valid form of investigation in pursuit of truth and upon every presentation of results to those interested?

There is a difference in kind—but there should be no difference in standards of quality—between the survey or manipulation of grouped phenomena and the careful study of unique instances. The investigator takes the greatest care he can to guard against bias or conscious or unconscious self-interest in the collection of data and in the presentation of results. This applies to the most sophisticated of scientific procedures and reporting and also to individual case treatment and history presentation. The former takes pains to build disinterest into the situation, while the latter also makes demands on the professional ethics and integrity of the theoretical or empirical scientists that are, by necessity, more often ideals than full achievements.

This is why we have set up both the impersonal regimens of science and the rigorous personal disciplinary training of medicine and such analogous professions as social work and academic therapy. Both are aspects of truly professional education, with the emphasis placed as it is seen to be appropriate to the demands of human reality. It is, I believe, quite possible, and a hallmark of maturity, to be guided by either mode predominantly or by both within the same person at the same time. This is what it means to reach toward a goal of what Leon Eisenberg has called the fully *"human* nature of the human nature."

There are, in our specific field of the study and treatment of the phenomena of human language, many areas of necessary background or specific knowledge and skill without which we cannot use our disciplinary capacities to the full. There are also special kinds of demands placed upon us by the nature of our specific professional involvement with the field. There are, for instance, the two kinds of attitudes and ways of behaving summed up in the theoretical and the applied approaches.

There are places where phenomena can be studied as grouped—objectively, to give insight into nature and into ways of using knowledge and skills for overarching purposes. Here we need to be guided by the strict canons of the scientific method, as well as we can master them. This is recognized as one of the essential parts of professional education.

The other approach is rooted in our knowledge that every smallest particle in the world, and, in our particular world of functioning, every person in the world is unique, and our belief that in practice it is incumbent upon us to recognize and act upon the recognition of this uniqueness. If we accept this view, then we need to learn how to use our selves as the instruments with which we work responsibly in the interest of the well-being of our patients, clients, students (however we designate them). This takes as sophisticated and committed a course of preparation and lifetime growth as does the discipline generally called "science."

Few of us can achieve maximally in both disciplinary worlds. Most of us do best when we emphasize one mode or the other. However, if we are to deal constructively with the problems of language mastery, whether it be in theory and research or in the person-to-person areas of clinical diagnosis or educational treatment and therapy, we need to understand and believe in both kinds of professional approach. We have to, if we are to work with each other toward our common goal.

If it becomes our task to gather and present findings in which others are interested—or we want them to be interested—we can act in the scientific mode or the clinical mode and tell what we have found in the appropriate language, translated accurately into the intellectual vernacular of those with whom we are trying to communicate, whether it be statistical or medical terminology or informal narrative or "plain English."

If we are physicians or research clinicians dealing with individuals, it is recognized as quite proper for us to demonstrate a finding or a point we need to make by introducing case material concerning a single person or several appropriate persons. On the fully individual level it can be argued that it is inappropriate to think that we can really match one person with another; there are too many variables. (Even monozygotic twins are not truly identical.) If we do attempt to group people with respect to a few variables (age, IQ, etc.) we have always to be conscious of the abstractions that we are making and the truth of the statement that "behind every statistic there is a person, and it is with the persons that we are humanly concerned."

This being the case, those of us who are making clinical studies or engaging in clinical practice should be as free as our physician colleagues to use case material in illustration, providing—and this needs special emphasis—that we do so with appopriate professionalism, that is to say without self-interest and with as little bias as is humanly possible. We should be illustrating reality as best we can, not selling a nostrum.

To help ourselves to achieve such freedom from ego-involvement, incidentally, is the reason for building into our ethos such checks as supervision or consultation or public presentation of papers. In the use of case material we need to hold to the same high standards of objectivity and respect for the persons described, whose assistance we are, in a sense, drafting in the interest of advancing understanding of the needs and services we are trying to further for them and for others to whom we are, essentially, responsible.

And so, when we need to use case material, not only are we justified in doing so but we should feel comfortable about this mode of thinking and presentation. It is only necessary that it be appropriate and carried out in accord with the highest standards which we are capable of achieving.

In this volume there is space for only a few vignettes of students or clients whose detailed histories comprise inches-thick records typical of those in many a colleague's files.

Part V
Interfaces and Reflections

1

Dyslexia and Learning Disabilities:
Their Relationship

Year after year, in discussion after heated discussion, we in our field are divided among ourselves and deflected from our tasks of helping children and older students by the clamor "for definitions," or "against labeling," or by other verbal hassles. One says, "You don't know what you are talking about!" and the other, "I do so, but *you* don't!"

There are at least two ways of avoiding the debilitating and distracting activities that sometimes ensue. One is in friendly, honest seeking for cooperation with our opposite, though not opposing, numbers from related fields; the other is in clarifying our thinking by adding to and putting in order the best we can get of modern knowledge. The first is already being done in increasing measure, as witness the work of the National Joint Committee on Learning Disabilities and other cooperative endeavors including the Task Panel on Learning Failure and Unused Learning Potential of the President's Commission on Mental Health (1977–1978).

But it is difficult, if not impossible, to push off to higher goals from a murky swamp of confusion, however rich it is in tradition and idealism. We need to establish firm ground to stand on and to step from, so it is through the second way, clarifying our own thinking and putting in order the best of modern knowledge, that we can probably do most to accomplish our purpose.

We are often asked not only "What do you mean by dyslexia?" but also, "Are dyslexia and learning disabilities the same?" or "How do you distinguish between them?" The questions vary but point to the same

Reprinted and revised with permission from The Orton Dyslexia Society from *Bulletin of the Orton Society*:43–61 1978.

The reader will have met much of the beginning of this paper in other connections above. The statements are here organized to address the common dyslexia-interface question embedded in the title.

end. The easiest and simplest answer is that of the two umbrellas in Figure 16. The picture may be sufficient, or it may be a temporarily satisfactory answer to say that some children (the umbrella group on the right) have specific lanaguage difficulties; some (the umbrella group on the left) have learning disabilities; and there are some (under both umbrellas) who have both problems and often we do not know which way to send them for help.

Or we might think of an iceberg as a model for either concept. There would be several peaks above the waterline which we could label with various names descriptive of the kinds of learning or language difficulties we observe. They would differ in configuration and prominence and might be marked to call attention to reading or math failure, speech delays or disturbances, abnormal clumsiness, confusion about time or directions, and a tendency to general disorderliness about possessions and "keeping it all together." A prominent pinnacle would refer to "spelling, atrocious!" The learning disabilities iceberg would have some of the same language peaks and some others. As is the nature of icebergs, most of the connecting mass would be under water, out of sight. We could mark it "learning disability," as some people always do, "language learning difficulty," or by some other generalizing term that fits with our conceptions. The major ideas to hold in mind are: first, that there often seems to be something in common among the clustered evidences of the troubles that are freezing out many chil-

Figure 16.   Which umbrella is yours?

dren's capacities to learn as they should; and second, that one can expect an almost infinite variety of patterns in any field of icebergs.

Stages, Tasks, and Difficulties in Human Learning

It looks as though we had better go back to a more fundamental level and think not only about failure or difficulty in learning, but about the nature of that learning itself—the why, what, and how of this basic aspect of life. Then, perhaps, we can do better at alleviating and preventing failure and at freeing each person more nearly to achieve his own best in learning.

The inherent biochemical, neurophysiological, and neuropsychological structures and processes through which learning takes place and is made lasting are the province of laboratory research and theoretical speculation. Their investigation is well-begun but nowhere near its end. Although the findings are always interesting and often of practical value, for our present purposes we may be justified in leaving their rationale mostly to their own experts. Personal observation and experience give empirical evidence that animals and humans *do* learn. Through what course of biological history and individual development can we see this learning take place in the readily observable world? What are some of its problems in present-day reality?

Evolution and Animal Learning

As the species on the evolutionary scale leading toward humankind develop their characteristic forms and functions, the sensory systems most involved in the kinds of learning which interests us here become more important to survival and effectiveness. True, as best we know, they still issue from their fundamental physical and chemical bases.

There are maturational timetables, such as how early the eye can focus on an object—and perhaps how early the mind can imagine the ball hidden under the blanket. Yet the major, though not ultimate, development of human sensory prowess takes place and is of paramount importance very early in childhood. It does not primarily depend upon the language powers soon to come into prominence. Although humans no longer depend on taste and smell as heavily as many other animals do, the senses of vision, hearing, and somesthesis are still vitally important to all animals. (Somesthesis includes touch, awareness of the muscular activity of the vocal apparatus, position in space, movement of body parts, and the like.) Much of what human and other animals do in making use of their sensory equipment is made actual in

the course of maturation, but it is very largely also guided and modified by the teaching of elders. For example, the cat teaches her kittens
to see, pounce upon, toss, kill, and eat a mouse or, in play, a mouse-like
object. Such learning uses forms of communication but not what we
are here defining as language, that is, the use of verbal symbols.

A further step in evolution—actually a quantum leap—
differentiates us humans from our nearest relatives. We are no longer
as sure as we once were that we differ sharply in kind; chimpanzees
have shown some capacity to learn to use symbolic language as we
know it, not merely to communicate on a prelinguisitic level (Gardner
and Gardner 1969; Premack and Premack 1972). Still, it is with the human species that we see clear specialization of some functions in either
the right or left hemispheres of the greatly enlarged, more convoluted
cortex, or "new" brain. For well over a hundred years, it has been recognized by scientists that the control of speech in most people resides
in the left hemisphere. Only since 1936, however, has it been known
(Benton 1965) and, in 1968, unequivocally demonstrated (Geschwind
1972) that this dominance has a correlate in anatomical differences in
the two brain halves. Indeed, it was not until 1969, when Wada reported his study of infant brains (Geschwind 1972), that it became
known with certainty that this difference is already present at birth.

Many of the early insights into language disabilities, however,
based on the extensive understanding of brain functioning, had already been attained by Orton by 1925. Although he did not give it
much emphasis, Orton was ahead of his time in his recognition, even
in that period, that the right hemisphere, like the left, also seemed to
have its specialized and valuable functions. A few people investigated
and talked about this concept in the 1940s and 1950s and Benton (1965)
reviewed their work and his own in a paper that he concluded with:

> However weak its present status may be, the concept of right
> hemisphere dominance should not be dismissed. On the contrary,
> it should be subjected to even more intensive exploration than it
> has had in the past . . . I believe that we shall see some surprising
> developments.

Hemispheric Differentiation

Indeed, we are seeing "some surprising developments." Currently, we are beginning to get a balanced view of the behavioral facts
and of their neurological background as well. It has long been said that
one half of what makes us human is the ability to use language and to
be mentally conscious, while the other half is the ability not only to use
tools but to invent them, build them, and carry out the other activities

of technology and the arts. It seems now that these highly developed and differentiated capacities are based not just in left hemisphere "dominance" for language but rather in hemispheric specialization—two partners, equal yet opposite in many ways. This whole set of ideas enormously increases our understanding. So much has developed in recent years that this revised paper is very different from the way I first wrote it about a decade ago. (See also, 1988 addendum, below.)

Instead of talking only about language development in the late stages of human evolution, it makes sense to think concurrently of a parallel right hemisphere differentiation as having taken place at about the same time as the left hemisphere specialization, leading to spoken language in the one side, with stone or bronze technology, cave paintings, and the like in the other. For the present, however, let us leave the outcome of the right hemisphere's changes and examine more closely the left hemisphere's contribution, as seen in behavior.

Early Cultural Developments

We are surprised to find that an infant of four weeks or less can already discriminate between such basic speech sounds as /p/ and /b/. From there he goes on to develop familiarity with all the sounds of the mother tongue, the language of whatever culture he finds himself in. At first, these sounds mean little to him as true language. He begins to vocalize, to babble at random, and then, more and more, to make the sounds he hears around him. Then comes the time when almost suddenly, as Vygotsky put it in 1934, ". . . thought (which has obviously been going on) becomes verbal and speech becomes rational." The child has become a language user in the true sense. In the normal course, he has made almost the whole evolutionary leap by the time he is about five years old. He can code thought into the words, grammar, syntax, and intonations of his culture; he can understand five or six thousand words in several standard kinds of arrangements; and he can express his own meanings, somewhat less extensively and perfectly than his receptive comprehension, but still with a very high degree of skill. No child is born knowing how to do this but he is born, so to speak, "wired up" to learn it with relative ease from his culture. The complex of language skills has been around for enough eons to have worked its way into the genes as a readiness to learn and needs only—but needs surely—the triggers of culture to influence the natural "mother's-knee" type of teaching and learning of the skills of basic spoken language, the first-order code. Every culture, throughout the world, has its well-developed spoken language, and most of its children master it reasonably well and at about the same ages.

Let us not forget, however, that there is a parallel development going on in the nonverbal, exploratory, acting and "making" aspects of life, and that some of this makes its way into talk while much of it does not. It, too, has become part of the human genetic and cultural heritage.

The next stage of life, in whatever society, sees a growth in the understanding and use of both spoken language and the nonverbal skills as the child takes on the ways of his people and grows into an adolescent and an adult. Whatever their ideological and artistic sophistication, however, many cultures that comprise intelligent and effective peoples have come this far without taking the next cultural steps into literacy and complex technology. That the capacity to take these steps is there is suggested both by experience of Margaret Mead's friends in New Guinea (Mead 1955) who adapted to being catapulted, in only 25 years, from the Stone Age into the Twentieth Century, and by the Chinese peasants who became airplane mechanics in the 1940s (Kirk 1972) and now have (many of them) learned to read. Such transitions are not always successful or smooth, but that this came about seems to be a matter of cultural experience. The capacity, it seems, is inherent.

Both literacy and modern technology take deliberate teaching and conscious, effortful learning. For both, it is a tremendous step, not beyond our capacity, but not yet a built-in result of our genetic make-up. In the history of humankind, systematic written communication beyond the picture-story stage developed only yesterday, as it were, while that most useful of social inventions, the alphabetic-phonetic scheme of writing came into being just before dinner—some 5000 or so years ago. The printing press came on with the after-dinner coffee, only a few hundred years ago, and the computer has just rung the doorbell. Think of what that means to the 6-year-old entering school. He can make it if we teach him well, and he has to make it if he is to survive in the modern world as an independent, healthy, happy person. What is this giant step into the second order symbolization that experience tells us a child can take when supported by favorable circumstances?

The Language Learning Task

As linguists like to put it, the use of words, i.e., arbitrary, spoken sounds in sequences to stand for ideas, is a process of devising and using a code. All human beings use this kind of code. If they have command of the same code, i.e., know the same language, they can communicate ideas from one mind to another. While this is not perfect communication, bound as it is by a single track in a time sequence and, in oral language within audible distance, it is nevertheless a beautifully powerful and efficient tool, one that with the facilitation of physical artifacts has made possible the transmission of culture.

Speech to Writing

What is needed beyond speaking are ways of overcoming the limitations of timing, of time itself, and of space, and that is accomplished by visual-motor routes which bridge the gaps of space-time by using writing systems. (See Rawson 1975.)

It is really a much simpler task to add a writing system to a spoken one than to devise the spoken code in the first place, but for many people it seems to add a major barrier to learning. Why? It could hardly be the level of abstraction or the two-step process, for primitive astronomy and other activities make at least as great cognitive demands. Perhaps it is the necessity for taking the stuff and processes that belong with right hemisphere functioning, transforming them into the orientation and sequencing patterns that belong to the left hemisphere, and then asking the two hemispheres, so different from each other in "temperament," to pull in double harness. This is a neurologically cumbersome kind of activity. The human child, however, seems able to simplify it by transferring the visual processing of verbal symbols—and these only—to the last myelinated, language association, areas of the left cortex (Orton 1925; Masland 1967). The child can be expected to do this at about the age of five or six or seven years, a time of many other maturational changes. According to Bakker (1973), the child up to that age is helped rather than hindered in learning to read by the lack of cerebral dominance for language. It is an advantage later, as Geschwind (1972) has pointed out, to have the whole process being carried on through the cortical surface networks in single brain area, a possibility apparently unique to man.

The Verbal Language to Be Learned

In any case, we are not born ready to read but we mature and learn in childhood. The capacity to manage this neurologically based skill is, perhaps, and just in this connection, truly "the latest (and least finished) development in man." The words are Orton's, as is the concept of "establishing the physiological habit of use" of actions in the brain through appropriate educational exercise. Note that this does not make claims about organic change but only of functional learning, of the kind of which we are capable because of our initial plasticity and adaptability. We are inherently able to achieve this kind of cultural advantage, without waiting for the completion of the evolution of further visible differences in brain structure such as is already evident in the planum temporale of the left hemisphere that subserves language (Geschwind 1972; Galaburda et al. 1978). Physical evolution takes the species countless ages to develop structures but cultural transmission speeds things up. Perhaps it is useful to think of the development of literacy skills as one of the ways in which we have learned to use technology (print in its various forms) and computers—to extend our bodies, our senses, and our basic language capacities, as we do with other cultural inventions. The implication of such an approach seems significant. However we accomplish this remarkable feat, it is man alone who, to high degree, can replace and recall with an arbitrary sign that which is different or absent and who can think by manipulating the resulting symbols.

Learning Disability—a Different Umbrella

Before all else there are the basic physical and social needs which every person, including every child of whatever origin or status, has a right to have met. There can be an overall impoverishment of life and learning; it should go without saying that such needs ought to be attended to (however far we presently are from doing so). This is, at least to begin with, on the level of being, more than specifically of learning, however much the former undergirds the latter. It is important, but not specifically what we are talking about here.

Next, the individual needs keen eyesight, sharp hearing, and good motor control and coordination for learning through the senses as must be done in school and life. Wherever these sensory capacities are inadequate, help of either a remedial or compensatory nature is needed.

But a child may be well-equipped to learn through the senses and yet not learn as he is expected to. Something about the child's learning processes is "disoriented," as it has been aptly put by McCarthy and McCarthy (1969). His disorientation in learning may have to do with perceptual intake, motor ability, activity level, emotional response, or some combination of these and other factors on nonlinguistic or prelinguistic levels. And so "he doesn't learn as he should." This, in my thinking, is properly classified specifically as learning disability at the basic level.

In such a case, the disability may result from the life history or from the organizational structure but is not language-derived, and the child probably needs prelinguistic or nonlinguistic treatment. The child is not able, on his own, to take full advantage of his basic animal heritage and status. Unless he is too severely handicapped, which is rare, we can give him the help he needs if we are clever enough and persistent enough. The abilities he needs are based on traits which are probably of genetic origin, spread among us as described by a normal probability curve, so that inherently he has a range of possible development. He may, of course, have been unfortunate in his environment or his birth, so that his potential has been interfered with. Both of such circumstances may set limits on how far he can go, but those limits allow for growth beyond what society may be providing for him. The shape of the curve may show more individuals at the end representing low functioning because of the inclusion of both inherited and acquired ineptitude.

At a somewhat higher level of expectation, we find interferences which more closely parallel those of linguistic processing, the thinking disorders which we may label "cognitive" rather than sense-based, perceptual, and the like. Some people do poorly on the visuospatial parts of intelligence tests and may fail on tests of mechanics, recognition of faces, or other right-hemisphere-mediated thought processes. Often such difficulties do not cause practical or academic disabilities, and so they are not called disabilities. One says, as many people do, "I'm terrible at remembering faces," or "I never could paint," or it might be "model" or "find my way," or whatever. But these difficulties are not usually considered to be more than relatively mild idiosyncrasies. When they make sufficiently hampering trouble for their victims, however, they may properly be called *higher level learning disabilities*—perhaps a learning disability component of adjustment or developmental difficulties. Some of the social or affective inadequacies of some of our clients may well be in this class. With older boys and girls and with adults it is often difficult to sort out the strands, but I think these are not specifically language-based however much they may be language-entangled. (See Addendum 88, below.)

Specific Language Learning Difficulties
Spoken Language—Dyslexia I

It may well be that a child has no learning difficulties on sensory-motor levels and begins to have trouble only when he encounters language. This may show itself early when he hears but does not seem to understand or when his understanding is not adequate for his age and needs. Complicated sentences or multiple commands may be beyond him although his agemates process them readily. He may be obviously thinking and reasoning well while his speech may be delayed or defective. He may even use spoken language forms precociously although only his mother can translate them into common words (Clarke 1973). This seems to be not just the expectable "infant-jargon-stage" but a more linguistically complex issue. The child may also have difficulties with abstractions like *before* and *after*, perhaps knowing what some of them mean but giving the ideas the wrong labels. Perhaps he stutters, though this may have other causes, or he may have other difficulty with the rhythmic or tonal patterns of his mother tongue (Orton 1928b, 1937). In sum, his ability to perform as expected may be either delayed or distorted or both.

Here we can begin properly to think of *specific language* difficulties

which are not necessarily based on defect or deficiency but on difference in kind of development. I am inclined to think of this as First
Stage Language Difficulty that I sometimes call **Dyslexia I.** If the problems presented by the child's speech patterns are enough in kind or
degree to make trouble for him, we are likely to say he has a specific
language *disability*. Under the circumstances, he is at least temporarily
disabled in meeting the demands of his culture, and he needs help
from people who understand the variations possible in language development. It does not seem to me appropriate to refer to such a child
as *learning-disabled* as we have described that condition. Orton thought
it a more accurate appraisal of people we now call dyslexic to recognize
in them demonstration of the normal, and considerable, variation in
the complex human trait of *language learning facility*. This view seems to
many of us still sound and increasingly supportable.

Such a variation seems to be a familial or genetic trait, not corre-
lated with degrees of intelligence or giftedness or ineptitude in such
other traits as musical talent, athletic ability, or social aptitude. In this
case, we would indeed have a learning problem but it would be associated specifically with a *language* learning need, and it would require
and respond very well to specific and expert teaching of spoken language skills.

One can have a language difficulty without having a learning disability. Conversely, one can have a learning disability and still have fluent language skills. There are some, however, whose basic learning problems send them into the language development periods ill-prepared to
cope with the added complications of dealing with words. These are
children in the middle of Figure 16 (p. 192) under the overlapping umbrellas. Shall we call them *learning-disabled* or *language-disabled*? They
are both, and we find that a learning-disabled child is, as the jargon has
it, "at high risk" of having language learning problems as he gets older.

Whether or not it makes a difference what we call these children,
in our long-run educational approach, most of them need pretty much
the same kind of skilled teaching at the hands of people who know
langauge, its pedagogy, and the nature of learning. One of the components of "teaching the language as it is to the child as he is" is to know
him as he *individually* is. It is the individual behind the label or the statistics who must do the learning. Often, if he is learning-disabled and
then has a next-level language problem, it will take him and his
teachers longer and require harder work as he comes to terms with his
early handicapping condition. This is not to say that he will not come
out as well in the long run as the children who respond more quickly.
One cannot and should not write people off, no matter how unpromis-
ing they seem at first. And one should not necessarily lower academic
sights. So ". . . the impossible takes a little longer!" and sometimes it

is only partially possible, but let us not assume so. Against all predictions, I have seen success happen many times with such young people and the adults they become.

Written Language: Dyslexia II

As with Al (Rawson 1972 and in this volume, pages 27–38), the problem with reading, writing, and spelling is with managing the written (or printed) word.

After the basic language, prereading, period comes the difficult transition to the tasks that underlie literacy, the work of the school years. This is the time when it is the child's job to become competent in the skills that provide the keys to his educational, occupational, and personal future. Without all the three "Rs" (arithmetic here becomes an aspect of language and spelling is included in writing), he will be truly disabled in growing into a modern, literate, technological culture. I need not belabor that point; we know all too well the cost of failure. (See Rawson 1979)

Let us suppose, as often happens, that a child enters school at six with no history of either basic learning or basic language difficulty. He "looks ready" and seems to have everything going for him as a future academic success. And yet he may find himself in trouble as he tries to master the second level code. There just does not seem to be anything else wrong with this child. He simply—or not so simply—cannot seem to learn to read, write, spell, or perhaps compute. His aptitude for mastery of the written skills, while there underneath, does not flower readily. For any given child there may be just a bit of tough going at first, or acquiring the necessary skills may be of intermediate difficulty, to be achieved with some effort. For many a youngster it may seem almost impossible for him to learn and for his teacher to teach him. This is Specific Language Difficulty commonly called dyslexia, or as we might say here **Dyslexia II**.

It is not, I emphasize again so much a permanent disability as one of the normal variations in the human condition. It is a disability only because without our helping him to come to terms with it successfully the youngster *will be* disabled in meeting his otherwise reasonable goals and expectations. But if the right kind of help is forthcoming, the outlook for him is very good indeed. He is not learning-disabled; his general learning ability may be, in fact, of any quality up to very, very good.

A child may have been properly categorized either as basically learning-disabled when he was younger or all right as to learning in general but with a specific ineptitude for mastering spoken language, Dyslexia I. If either (or both) of these conditions has been true and he has had appropriate help in the preschool years, the child will be in better position to take the next steps into literacy than if he had not been helped or had been improperly taught, and so forced to start from "behind scratch."

Still he can do so and come through satisfactorily in the end. It will be harder but not impossible. He will have to learn to manage the challenges of what we have called Dyslexia II. Even if he has done well with the early language skills and is ready in many ways for academic learning, he may have persistent difficulties of other sorts. The words we use—"learning disabilities"; or "the almost inevitable concomitants of dyslexia"; or whether we say he has "a learning disability with a dyslexia component"; or whatever—these words are important to us, but they matter for the learner, who is our primary concern, only as their consideration helps our thinking about him and about what to do for him.

Organization-Formulation-Dyslexia III (1988 Addendum)

Dynamic organization is characteristic of all life and especially salient in human functioning. Inadequacy here can be a learning disability that basically involves organization per se, rather than being specifically rooted in the language function. In its linguistic form, however, it concerns mastery of language at the level of what Henry Head called "symbolic formulation and expression." This we might call **Dyslexia III.**

As the decades have passed and our profession has grown, we have been increasingly faced with advanced language problems of older students and adults. They become of overriding concern in high school and especially in college, graduate school, and adult professions or personal fulfillments that are based on organized language thinking and its *verbal* expression.

Like Piaget's "formal operations" and each of Erikson's psychosocial "crises," this phase of concentration on development of language skills has its precursors in earlier growth in childhood—in effective listening and speaking, in reading comprehension, and in written composition.

It has its later uses in the person's freedom to concentrate on the lecturers' or authors' ideas as he listens or reads, and on the messages he, himself, wishes to convey in writing. In his effectiveness in doing so in high school, college, and adult life the organizational factor in language comes particularly into prominence. It is advantageous to be able to use this factor consciously, or, we might say, metacognitively (knowing about knowing) or metalinguistically (in language about language). It is when linguistic organization is underdeveloped or goes awry to a hampering degree that it fits under my dyslexia rubric as Dyslexia III.

Which Umbrella?

Of course, there can be insufficiencies of organization in all dimensions of life, of varying degrees and at any stage of general development. They may be so inextricably bound up with language as to seem part of it, as might be the case with the children under both umbrellas in Figure 16, above, as they grow older. This, I think, is one source of the confusion that in common parlance leads to the use of *learning disability* as a synonym for *dyslexia,* thus muddying the waters of discourse and practice. The dyslexics under the right hand umbrella are still dyslexic, although often they have become good readers and manage most aspects of their lives from satisfactorily to outstandingly. They are, quite obviously, *not* learning disabled! Unless one knows their history, the dyslexia connection shows itself only in aspects of their use or writing of language. One might say that this is the residual stage of what Denckla (1985) has recently named "dyslexia-pure."

Summary

In summary, we have placed the human person in the evolutionary scheme so that we might best consider his ways of learning. We have talked of the nature of the disorders of learning at the prelinguistic levels and in the nonlinguistic areas of development. We have described his language, specific to his species, in some of its varieties and developmental stages in the race and in the individual. Finally, we have placed in our schema the specific difficulties encountered in the mastery of language skills and suggested, in a general way, appropriate approaches to education, including training, to facilitate or remediate language learning. We have expressed faith, based upon experience, in human capacity to learn language and to teach language skills to all students, and thus to free the learners for further growth. Throughout, we have tried to keep a balance between focus on a special topic and perspective on the whole of the life and the education which prepares for life and enriches living.

2

A Diversity Model for Dyslexia

How shall we look upon the phenomena we group as dyslexia? What is the human significance of this condition? Is it "real"? How can we obey the injunction. "Define your terms"? Before we ask what the word really means, perhaps we should ask what it means to be a word. Where do any words come from and how do they get their meanings? Let us follow the life history of Jimmy's word *d'b'm*, for it is typical of the basic process.

One September, many years ago, when Jimmy had just rounded his first birthday, he was beginning to find, usually to coin, one-word labels for the experiences he was identifying. Oscar's friendly collie made overtures and produced a joyous, "d'b'm!" Then, as the family started on a long car journey Jimmy recognized, named and waved a farewell to, "D'b'm," so the parents knew the boy had a new word. On the trip, every dog, cat, cow, horse, and sheep, and a small host's white mouse, was excitedly identified by the now inclusive common noun as a "d'b'm." As the weeks wore on, all living creatures, every stuffed toy and even a strip of fur ("big, 'ong d'b'm") joined the category. Clearly the experiences were specific but the concept was open-ended, the boundaries loosely defined. Santa brought a teddy-bear, taken to the heart as "I [*my own*] d'b'm!" Gradually specific words, *horse*, etc., re-placed the general term, but "D'b'm" remained for years the proper name of the beloved bear-companion. Then, one night when Jim was eight he said firmly, "Put that bear away. I don't need him anymore, and besides, his name's not D'b'm', either!" Years later, the old friend was retrieved with pleasant memories, and Jim provided each of his children with a d'b'm to love. And so a word was born a label, became a consciousness-filling concept, was refined by definition, made personal and emotionally significant, and moved into the background of consciousness where it was available to memory and for cultural transmission.

Reprinted with permission from John Wiley and Sons Ltd. from *Dyslexia Research and Its Applications to Education* 13–34 1981.

Observation suggests that this is an elemental pattern for the acquisition of interrelated words and concepts, progressing from the unknown and hence nonconscious to recognized globality, to the definition of embedded related specificities, and finally to assimilation into the personal linguistic matrix, out of conscious awareness but available on triggered demand for memory and the mind's creative or personal and social uses. (For a mentally stimulating analysis of this kind of "holographic" provocation of thought through language, see Pribram 1971, p. 370.)

The growth of an abstract concept like "dyslexia" and its symbolic formulation is similar but more complex. Its way into assimilation by both individuals and societies may be rapid and easy or beset with obstacles to understanding and acceptance. First one has many experiences, large and small, personal and distant, significant to one's self and casual, specific and ill-defined. They are not thought of as related. If we bother to explain them, each may be from a world more or less its own. Some have names, like "stubbornness," some do not; some are loosely grouped with others, like "reading and spelling failure," while some are thought of as individual "quirks," like being confused by "turn right" (directional) but not by "make a right turn" (a physical maneuver). Something in our own lives or someone else's puzzling problem, like "Peter's five-year failure to learn to read," may be instrumental in bringing a new term into our awareness and leading us to relate many hitherto unrelated phenomena. A further result may be the taking of a new vocational direction by the individual or the development of something new in the scientific, technological, or therapeutic spheres, with an open-ended future of possibilities.

There are two contrasting tendencies in people's initial reaction to new terms: to accept and go along with them, or to reject and deny them. These start chain reactions in other people, who may want to be "open-minded" but not to "get carried away," to hunt for categorical solutions or to be made uneasy by change, and to react, as a habit, simplistically to the words themselves. Upon reflection, however, one realizes that what is important is not so much what one says as what one means by one's words and what meanings they have to the person who hears them. Just now we are trying to get away from the effects of tying "badness" labels to groups of people either by denying that individuals can be grouped at all or by changing the labels to others that are benign or neutral.

Whatever our motives, neither extreme course will be likely to have a useful outcome. If we refuse to categorize, we may miss the essential point of understanding and helping by becoming sentimentally confused about our students' or clients' needs and our responsibilities, or, on the other hand, by being overwhelmed by the complexities and giving up or applying shotgun remedies. In the second case—the

changing of labels—since there has been no fundamental reorienta-
tion toward the labelled persons, the speaker (who favors them) may
be trying to mollify the hearer's attitudes, while the listener, if he ac-
cepts the new term at all, merely shifts his language while retaining his
old opinions and feelings about the subject and the persons. The new
term soon becomes as objectionable as the old; the change is in the
wrong place—the word rather than the mind.

Dyslexia, like the forty or so terms related to it, has in many places
been involved in such semantic confusions (Rawson 1978). Most definitional arguments avail little to improve life for the learners affected. It is
true that the etymology of this Greek term, dyslexia (initially used by
Berlin in 1887 and discussed by Thompson in 1966, and others), points
to an entity, a syndrome or an area of meaning: *dys* (poor or inadequate) and *lexis* (language, as words, related to speech and to lexicon).
One humane and informed designation we now give to those having
trouble with language is "language different." The problem of the language-different child is not general, for his physical and intellectual
equipment and his maturity are within normal range; his emotional
state and his social and cultural background are unremarkable. The
range of advantageous and disadvantageous factors which make up
each unique dyslexic would not make him stand out among his peers.
Only, and specifically, in his encounters with his own language is his
clearly distinguishable as different. We may properly call him dyslexic.
His history (see Rawson 1972) makes developmental dyslexia appropriate and more than suggests the constitutional nature and familial,
probably genetic, origin of this aspect of his makeup.

He is in trouble with language learning because he is different.
This is obviously true, but what is different about him and from whom
does he differ? Is he unique in these respects or is he part of a group? Is
this a large or a small part of the human race? Do all its members differ
in the same ways and to the same degrees from the rest of humanity
and from each other? Does different mean deficient, damaged, or defective? Always, sometimes, never? Can similar signs point to different
differences? Is it important whether we substitute "language-learning-
different for dyslexic" or for the (by our criteria) nonsynonymous term
learning disabled? What differences will ensue in our attitudes towards
the *subject matter* and the *subject persons*—our understanding and treatment of them? What changes of fundamental attitudes are involved
and, finally, what difference does it all make?

In the first place, when we say a person is different we need to ask
"from whom, and who is saying so?" Is the word used simply descriptively or denotatively, as we recognize that all persons (even, in minor
ways, identical twins) are unique? To this we readily agree, while we
also agree that people can be grouped in terms of certain characteristics
or patterns of characteristics. It is in this sense that many of us have no

semantic discomfort in saying that the problems we name dyslexia are real, and experienced by real people we handily call dyslexic. So considered, especially in our modern, literate world, dyslexia is certainly real. If you doubt it, ask the person who has these characteristics. So dyslexics are different in their makeup and needs from people who pick up language skills without apparent effort or can be taught them relatively easily by teachers who themselves were in most cases facile language learners. For most such teachers and the linguistically successful opinion-framers generally, to be different from themselves is a "deviance from the norm." Such a deviance, if not reprehensible or indicative of inferiority, is at least unfortunate and should be treated remedially by especially effortful and skilful teaching using sound educational principles—and directed by sound school principals!

This is entirely understandable. For instance, fish and cetaceans (whales and dolphins) are equally skilful in getting about and supporting themselves in the sea. One might imagine the tuna, the mackerel, and the perch looking on the minority, whale-like, species as somehow deficient because they must surface periodically to—"what is it they do up there? breathe?" Perhaps with instruction, determination, and practice they could become independent of surfacing and live like "real fish." They are different from fish, all right, and disadvantaged if circumstances require that they stay too long submerged—as any whaler could testify. On the other hand, from the whale-dolphin viewpoint, it is the fish who are different, at a disadvantage above water, and deprived of the joys of breathing air and enjoying activities and experiences that the two-world life makes possible. If either part of the sea population were in charge of the basic or remedial education of the other, different, meaning deviant, could lead not to "correction of an oxygen intake problem" but to ecological disaster. Or we could vary the analogy by thinking of dolphins as less like fish than like men with a constitutional walking disability, or men as like dolphins whose writing is superior but whose swimming is rudimentary. It is enough to note that innate differences do make a difference in how one learns to live in the world.

Early treatment of dyslexia, our interest here, was primarily centered on remedial education of school-age children and was carried on in independent (that is, private) schools or by tutors or therapists working alone or in nonpublic facilities. More recently, there has been increasing concern with young children's development of the listening and speech components of the basic language continuum. Early screening and preventive teaching of vulnerable children is becoming less rare. More public schools have classroom and individual programs than was the case, say, 20 years ago, but the coverage is spotty in both availability and excellence. Federal laws in my country make mandatory the provision of "free public education" for every child in accor-

dance with his needs, but the administrative and pedagogical resources of the schools are not yet anywhere near ready to meet the
law's demands. Still, dyslexia is now specifically designated as one of
the recognized areas requiring the deployment of educational resources. The United States is a large and pluralistic society with a high
degree of autonomy in its educational structures; it is far less easy to
secure near-universality of provisions than it is in smaller, more homogeneous societies.

Since both language and the difficulties of its learning are universal, whatever the differences in specific languages, it is not surprising
to find both understanding and action running parallel courses in several languages and cultures. One group focuses on one "hot spot" in
the field, while others take hold elsewhere, each seeing or relating especially to what he or she has experienced as important, true, or sig-
nificantly troubling, but with much in common. It would, of course, be
surprising if this were not true, man and language being what they
are. And yet, it is taking a long time for these similarities to emerge in
the face of variations in the disciplinary, rather than the national,
modes of thought. The neurologist, the psychologist, the linguist, the
psychiatrist, the educator, and each of the many others who share interest in the problem may or may not be aware of the interrelatedness
of the phenomena and disciplines involved. Despite the variations resulting from their several world views and fields of practice, each has
had to come to grips with the learning of his own language and the
necessity of his country's children to do so. With the widening and
deepening of experience and study, the fundamental unity of the human predicament and its solution must become more apparent. It is
not that the differences, often felt so strongly, are merely semantic, although semantic they truly are in part, nor that there is one true answer and certainly not a simplistic one.

Take, for example, those proverbial blind men and their elephant.
Each man was sure he knew the whole animal, extrapolating from the
part he felt. "It's a rope" (the tail); "No, a moving tree trunk" (the leg);
"A leathery wall" (the side); "A big leaf" (the ear); "A hard, smooth
prong" (the tusk); "You are all wrong! It's a writhing boa constrictor,"
said the sixth man as he was lifted from his feet by the trunk. Each of
us has a part of that ponderous pachyderm to feel, to feed, to groom or
train, and to name in his working model, but if we share our world
views we can talk together better about the whole.

Although I speak most securely about the English language and
its American users and learners, I believe that what is said here applies
to a much broader world.

Certain facts may be accepted as almost axiomatic. Symbolic, verbal language and verbal thinking as major components of cultural interchange and transmission are an almost distinctively human ca-

pability. Spoken languages have been developed in every human society. Language is potential in each new human being, but it is not instinctive; it must be learned and is taught, however informally, by the culture which surrounds the child. Language is phylogenetically late in the development of the race, and ontogenetically perhaps the last characteristic to be established in the growing individual, the specific neural myelinization on which it depends being the last myelinization to occur in the child. Written or graphic language has come about even later in the development of the race and the individual, and literacy is not universal, either on the globe or within those cultures which have written language. In evolution, it seems, the later and the more complicated the function involved, the greater the variation in its degree of perfection, its universality in the species, and the individual facility in its achievement, as for example in the acquisition of language skills. And yet, given appropriate circumstances, the basic potentiality, at least in language, is there to be developed.

There is, and as far as we know always has been, wide individual variation in language learning and use, as there has been in the learning and practice of any other skill. Some of these differences have been the results of history and opportunity; the swineherd, the vintner, the tailor, the sailor, the warrior, and the prince are among the not necessarily language-facile cases in point. Of old, if a person lacked aptitude or opportunity in one field, many others were available. Increasingly, however, the openings in the modern technological world require not only the verbal or visual memory which sufficed for the bard or the steward, but also literacy, so that aptitude for learning the skills of written language has become more and more critical. It is not enough to have spatial, mechanical, practical, or social skills; one must also use the media of language from moderately to maximally well if one is to avoid the failure, frustration, and despair resulting in and from one's unused unusuable potential in almost all spheres of life. It was said as early as 1977 that in the United States already about 85 percent of occupations require some degree of literacy, and the percentage is rising. If someone should say, "Well, he can at least dig ditches," the speaker's next assignment should be a few minutes watching a mechanical backhoe and tamper. The neglected illiterate, be he dyslexic or simply unschooled, is almost sure to be at a crushing disadvantage in any society dependent on tools or machines and the print one needs to cope with them.

An initial question about language almost always concerns the prevalence of its hampering disorders. How many dyslexics are there? The answers vary from country to country to some extent, but much more from respondent to respondent. A range of estimates of incidence from about 3 percent to 25 percent or more suggests that not everyone is talking about the same thing or people or is equally well informed, and perhaps *nobody* knows just what he himself is talking about. Figures at the low end of the estimates are those we expect in the case of a defect or disability, such as mental retardation, hearing loss, epilepsy, and the like, but language learning problems make trouble for more people than that. As a conservative estimate, experienced teachers and large-scale surveys put the fraction of those in major scholastic difficulty at 10 percent to 15 percent in English, Danish, and some other language communities. Numbers seem somewhat lower where sounds and symbols are more simply related as, for instance, in Czech or Spanish. Nobody is sure of these figures, and some place them much higher, especially in certain disadvantaged populations. My own experience suggests that the better we get to know language-based phenomena and the more discriminatingly we observe language behavior, the larger becomes the percentage of those having trouble, with, it seems, almost everybody doing now and then what dyslexics do commonly and with failure-inducing results. With data of this kind, perhaps the preponderance of cases can more acceptably be explained as showing normal constitutional variations in the evolutionarily "unfinished" human race. *The differences are real; make no mistake about that!* When not understood and not properly provided for, they make for serious difficulties which can lead to disabilities, even to disaster. At the "severe" end of the line a clear diagnosis of specific language disability is quite in order, but still allows prognostic optimism. Even when they are not cripplingly severe, the problems may interfere tellingly with enthusiasm for securing full educational, professional, and personal development. Distaste for school, a sense of inadequacy, and early discontinuance of study are common. On the other hand, if appropriately dealt with, the difficulties can be challenges to be surmounted and can undergird the achievement of diversity and its enrichment of our cultures. Masland (1976), discussing this kind of diversity, spoke of, "the potential advantages of being the kind of person who might have difficulty learning to read."

There are, of course, other types of language learning difficulty which look very like the several "syndromes of specific dyslexia" (Klasen 1972; Rawson 1978). They have appeared in the clinic and the literature since the nineteenth century, often inextricably mixed into the general problem population. It may take considerable neurological sophistication to identify true brain damage. Often, too, the treatment is the same as for the extreme dyslexic, though slower progress and less complete alleviation are likely. In known or unknown ways, the "head count" of these people has, as we say, "thickened" or "enriched" the low end of the incidence curve. The patients are there for different reasons but unknowingly help one another. Aphasias of traumatic origin helped Orton and his successors to bring together patterns of language disorders which led to recognizing *developmental* delays and dissonances which he characterized with strong conviction as normal variations of neurophysiological functioning. So, too, with the study of victims of birth injury, endocrine or organic brain malfunction, and other conditions, the insights gained from the pathologically based disorders help to define normal variations. The prognoses may differ, but the treatment plans are often mutually suggestive.

When all is said and done, however, we can allocate each language learner to a part of what we might call the "lexis continuum." At one end are the eulexics, those to whom the mastery of words (*lexis*) comes well (*eu*) and readily. At the other end are the ones whose language is poor or inadequate (*dys*), and learned with difficulty, the dyslexics. On a language learning facility scale those who are specifically dyslexic may be at the low end because of extreme difficulty with one type of language skills, say auditory, visual, kinesthetic, or with intermodal organization. Alternatively, less severe problems in two or several modalities, not in themselves too hampering, may add up to a major, temporarily insurmountable, roadblock. Again, secondary, concurrent difficulties—intellectual, emotional, physical, or environmental—may interact with language learning ineptitudes, each intensifying the others in a baffling entanglement. If the language problem is a significant feature in the complex, we may call the person dyslexic, but whatever the diagnostic judgment, attention to language skills is often the most productive place to start untying the knot which holds him in its grip.

If it is part of a continuum with ill-defined points of limitation, can we think of and treat dyslexia as an entity, a diagnosable condition? Here is Money's (1962) medically phrased statement:

> It is not at all rare in psychological medicine, nor in other branches of medicine, that a disease should have no unique identifying sign, that uniqueness being in the pattern of signs that appear in contiguity. Out of context, each sign might also be encountered in other diseases, or, in different intensities, in the healthy. Specific dyslexia is no exception in this respect. A good example of this is the matter of reversals and translocation of letters. . . . Thus, it appears that the diagnosis of specific dyslexia will continue not to depend on a single tell-tale sign, or signs, but on the clinical appraisal of the whole configuration of symptoms and test findings.

Using this criterion, and after experience with my own hundreds and my colleagues' thousands of patients and students, I feel confident in holding dyslexia to be both real and diagnostically identifiable. The surest and most productive diagnosis is still individual and clinical, but simple identification can often be quick and reliable. One need only ask, "Are his language learning skills, by test or school achievement, disproportionately lower than his apparent intelligence and other

learning, the degree of his physical intactness, his environmental opportunities, and his reasonable aspiration?" Such a degree of disparity
probably calls for therapeutic intervention.

Between the optimum and the rule-of-thumb in diagnostic procedures one makes what compromises one must, with the ideal in
mind but not waiting for perfection at the cost of getting to work helping the student. In general, expert diagnosis facilitates treatment; the
more expert the diagnostician and the teacher the less elaborate need
be the initial testing and the more reliance can be placed on the clinical
judgment of diagnostician and therapist.

With the more severely dyslexic individual, the assessment often
seems unequivocal, unless there is a question of the primacy of some
secondary or concurrent cause of learning disorder or deficiency. But
what of those with less severe problems, those who stand higher on
the language facility scale? How far up the curve shall we draw the line
of diagnostic categorization? When is a difference nameable and when
is it "just diversity"? The answer seems to me to call for the flexibility of
open-ended judgment. As with any other complex and relatively independent trait or phenomenon, most instances lie between the extremes. Unless it is a matter for true dichotomy (one cannot be moderately pregnant, for example!), the distribution tends to be describable
by a bell-shaped curve, perhaps somewhat skewed. Language learning seems to be a case in point.

This is one place (treatment is another) where it seems to me that
viewing dyslexia as a normal, expectable variation in the human condition makes a positive and productive difference. Accordingly, a shift
from a deviance, or even a difference, model to one emphasizing diversity and normal variations seems in order. Orton recommended this in
the 1920s, but it has been hard to keep it in mind as a guiding principle
in the face of the human urge to classification.

Let us say that everyone is *lexic*—a language learner (since he or
she is not born skilled), a language user (by reason of being human),
and part of a society or culture. However gifted, he is still part of that
unfinished species, *Homo sapiens*. He may be a silver-tongued orator
with a phenomenal verbal memory or a fluent reader with generally
perfect spelling and multilingual understanding, but under stress, or
perhaps as a personal idiosyncrasy, he may make some errors characteristic of his equally brilliant dyslexic companions. Is he being, or acting, dyslexic? Or he may have a particular *bête noir*, say a tendency to
frequent speech reversals. Spoonerisms like *cashing the greats* (instead
of *crashing the gates*) or saying *"Segundheit!"* (when his sneezing friend
might expect *"Gesundheit!"*). Perhaps his penmanship is labored, with
legibility rivalling his doctor's prescriptions. Is he, then, "one of those
dyslexics"? When do we call his language by some categorical name? Is
it reprehensible, or pitiable, or a somewhat endearing personal quirk

which may sometimes be a nuisance? Does he need corrective treatment, understanding sympathy, a bit of mirth, polite ignoring, or a touch of self-knowledge which can improve his insight into his blood brotherhood with a true or more dyslexic fellow man? Does he "have it" and is "it" a problem?

Perhaps the answer is that it *is* a problem when it *makes* a problem for *him*, subjectively or practically or both. The 140 IQ medical student who is flunking out because of his spelling and his confusion in taking written tests does not have a problem which may prevent him from becoming the gifted surgeon to which future his other aptitudes point. He may need to have dyslexia explained to him, to his dean, and to his professors, who may then see their way to making adjustments in his examination conditions so they will know they are testing his knowledge of subject matter, not his writing skill and speed. He may find it profitable to take some time out for intensive skill-improvement tutoring.

The driver of a 20-ton trailer truck with the same language aptitude pattern may say he "couldn't care less," though he has to read road and mechanical information and somehow produce adequate logs for his boss. He and the medical student, however, would be relieved to know, whatever they do about it, that this is something real which can be understood and is no reflection on their intelligence, character, stability, or potential as roadmaster or surgeon. If the two men share a failing, this, as well as their mechanical, spatial superiority, is another common characteristic of their brotherhood in valuable human diversity. They are the people whom Masland was referring to in his statement quoted above. They can say, "Some of us are put together that way. Nothing wrong with that! What, if anything, we need to do about it depends on where we're headed." Demonstrably true and good for the ego, it makes a *real* difference when we cast our thinking in these terms.

Using the medical-model parlance, we have said, "The diagnosis is clinical; the treatment is educational," not *cure* but rather a way of learning and living matched to the individual's whole personal configuration, with all its internal variables and its time-and-space singularities. We plan our strategy and tactics, as we say, to "teach the language as it is to the person as he is," and if we do it well it will be effective and lasting. Let us see what this means, what is our base of operations and what is our practice. [See also "Developmental Dyslexia: Educational Treatment and Results" p. 59 and "The Structure of English: The Language to Be Learned," p. 106 Ed.]

First "the language as it is," whichever one it is. Each language, be it oriental or occidental, however it be organized, spoken or written, and so forth, has system and order as part of its nature. A set of constraints is necessary for its use, is known by its users, and is transmitted to their juniors and to others who join their language community. Teachers of any language must, in some usable sense, "know" that language, whether this knowledge be conscious or not. Its transmission may be deliberate or it may be casual—apparent only to a somewhat detached observer, a learning that *happens* as part of the new generation's experiential acquisition of his culture.

The capacity to learn language is part of the inheritance of the human species, but it is the cultural setting which determines the specific language which will be, literally, the mother tongue of each new individual. Those who pass it on to him, whatever their methods of teaching, have made part of themselves the sounds and speech patterns of their language, its grammar and syntax, its vocabulary and semantic forms of expression. If it has a written form, there is also the graphic system to teach and to learn a bit later in childhood, with the interrelationships of the written code to the basic spoken language. To be a competent teacher, one must know the language as it is.

One must also know one's pupil, "the person as he is" of the formula and the ways he can learn best. This depends on his nature as a human being and his constitution and history as an individual.

One of the paradoxes of life is that human beings are all alike and also all different. The structure and functions of the central nervous system provide a constant, generally dependable frame of reference and mode of operation for all of us, a manageable, describable organization. We learn as human beings, not as amoebas, aardvarks, or even apes, much as we have in common with each of them. But individual persons are the resultants of so many and such complex constituents that each is unique. Each combines heriditary traits, inherent developmental patterns, and responses to environmental stimuli, making almost infinite diversity of outcomes inevitable, yet still within the limitations of the species. This diversity is of adaptive and creative value to the person, the culture, and the race. It should be cherished as a resource; hence the value of the "diversity model" for education as a whole and for language learning in particular.

But diversity is most useful if understood and, at least in some respects channelled, not rigidly, but with enough organization to make its creative potential adaptively available. Part of knowing the individual learner as he is, in the light of the understandings of the 1980s, requires consideration of the right and left brain hemisphere cortical functions and their interactions, specifically with respect to the language function and its development.

Samuel T. Orton, following his neurological forebears as far as the knowledge and technology of his time permitted, proposed and validated hypotheses which are still exerting seminal influence. The recent advances in brain science and their applications to education are consonant with these earlier formulations and are important extensions and additions to them.

The nature of the language-dominant (usually the left) hemisphere is being further explored and elaborated. Its way of dealing with life as rational, sequential, linguistic, analytical, and as the controller of verbally mediated consciousness is easily comprehensible because that is the kind of person each of us recognizes himself or herself as being. We tap into, use, and educate these aspects of life through the medium of verbal language.

The language function as centered in the left hemisphere is summarized in Figures 2 and 3; the accompanying text is on pages 62–64.

The positive functional specialization of the other (usually the right) hemisphere was only guessed at in Orton's time but has recently come to the fore. Only in the past twenty years or so (see Benton 1965, and his sources; Sperry 1974; Pribram 1971) has this other hemisphere emerged from its former role as the subordinate, somewhat mysterious, silent partner which was known to have some alternative or residual language ability and suspected of often intruding its activity confusingly into consciousness, especially among dyslexics. With its emergence has come an identifiable home for those abilities which we call spatial, global, synthesizing, and in many ways artistically creative. Still mysterious, and at least presently fundamentally inexplicable, as is all work of the mind, this kind of function is no longer to be vaguely ascribed to inspiration of unknown origin. The right hemisphere provides, if not the fully understood source, at least the primary instrument, as the left hemisphere does for the most part in the area of verbal language.

It has been suggested to me by Edith Gollan (1979) that the apparent recent increase in language learning difficulties may in part be real and explainable in terms of hemispheric differentiation. We, in the dyslexia field, have generally pointed to the increased necessity for literacy in the modern world, to the practice of compulsory academic education of children in many countries, and to the egalitarian ideal of potential upward social mobility for everyone. People both expect and demand more success in education; the public is more aware of the phenomenon of dyslexia; and we are somewhat more ready to believe that where there is a problem a solution can be found. All these are valid observations still, I believe, but Gollan's new component enriches the explanation.

Language learning, she reiterates, requires automatic linear sequencing of symbols which are learned, patterned, and dependent on conscious analysis and ordered structure—a left hemisphere activity par excellence. Such learning was the backbone of a great deal of home and school teaching of the past. In contrast, consider how different is the world of the modern child. He is bombarded by tonality—and atonality—from the air and, especially, by the rapid succession of total experiences of television, often more continuous than sequential, beginning in his prelinguistic infancy. Perhaps he is being right hemisphere stimulated to a high degree and so, unless his left hemisphere aptitudes are strong, he finds their cultivation less comfortable than the spatial, holistic modes. Moreover, he may be more confused by the welter of his experiences and the problem of coordinating them with one another than were his elders in sensorially simpler times. In either case, he may be one who finds the world of words less assimilable and manageable and thus may be more likely to be characterized as dyslexic. It is a challenging idea.

As Whittrock (1978) emphasizes, " . . . the cortical hemispheres overlap greatly. . . . No dichotomy of function does justice to the sophistication and complexity of the human brain." And so we have still not completed the picture, for man as a living system functions as a dynamic whole. To walk, for instance, he needs both legs, and the component parts of each one, working in synchrony. To grow, to think, to act, and to *be,* he needs both of his asymmetrically specialized brain hemispheres to be developed individually and coordinated in their functioning through the instrumentalities of neural networks and action systems and across the corpus callosum. His education as a person should nourish the whole in whatever ways each part requires. Pribram (1971) summarizes the ways man uses language, and hence must learn to use it, in these terms, " . . . as a tool to accomplish his purposes . . . [that is] to express his existence . . . to obtain information from or to achieve control over his environment . . . to explore and achieve control over his World Within" in which service "it becomes thought." Further discussing thought, he says, "My hypothesis is that *all* thought has, in addition to sign and symbol manipulation, a holographic component." Holographic representations, in which the whole is contained in each of its fragments, are, he says, "the catalysts of thought," being the associative mechanisms which perform the cross-correlations available in instantaneous memory and creative recombination of ideas.

As the person develops throughout life, he needs to acquire knowledge, the raw materials of thought, action, and creativity, and to develop skills with which to implement his knowledge. Each is necessary but neither alone is enough for human fulfillment. Leonardo da Vinci worked diligently to learn anatomy, mechanics, and the skills of painting to use in the service of his inspirations and his notebook formulations of theory. Both elements and their mutuality were needed to produce the bihemispheric genius that was Leonardo. In modern education, too, we hear much about the whole child and specifically of late about educating both hemispheres of the brain. We know from the ex-

perience of generations that this whole child emphasis brings rewarding results with all children, whatever their special needs.

Within the population the person we recognize as generally dyslexic or as having marked dyslexic subtraits is often (though not always) gifted in other respects. He may (but may not) be strong in the
use of basic, spoken language and in linguistic thinking. To serve his
other aptitudes in all areas, he needs language *skills* which depend
heavily on the organized sequential memory and processing of linguistic symbols, primarily a left-hemisphere attribute. This need has been
abundantly spelled out by many writers, but no one has yet, I think,
said it better than did Orton in 1937:

> . . . the process of reading is a . . . complex activity requiring the
> physiological integrity and interplay of many brain areas although
> the angular gyrus and its adjacent cortex in the dominant hemi-
> sphere still bear a critical relation to this function.

[The content of the next few pages, here omitted, has been substantially covered in earlier pages in this volume. Ed.]

While structure, system, sequence and order, which come almost
naturally to some people, must be deliberately taught to and purposefully learned by the dyslexic person, each student is unique. Orton
(1937) emphasizes this point:

> We have tried to avoid overstandardization lest the procedure be-
> come too inflexible and be looked upon as a routine method appli-
> cable to all cases of non-readers, which would be clearly unwise in
> view of the wide variation in symptomatology and hence in train-
> ing needs which these children exhibit.

The wealth of detail and the recommendations of empirically
tested procedure in the manuals and guides published for the help of
teachers by Gillingham and Stillman, by June L. Orton, and by others
in the ensuing decades who were facilitators in a structured but not
programmed plan, should be used flexibly by tutors and teachers with
as rich background and as much wisdom as can be found. This is no
task for the unprepared, however well they mean, nor for the person
dependent on authority or tied to the necessity of following a guide-
book ritualistically.

The student will progress faster and more securely if he under-
stands his own nature and the relationship between his makeup and
the way he is being taught. His intelligent participation and immediate
or gradual assumption of responsibility for his own education, including its training aspects, are powerful motivational factors, as are the
recognized achievement of steps towards competence and the formula-

tion of goals which are appropriate and reachable. Goals should not be limited by factors related to dyslexia, but only to degrees of giftedness and opportunity, as is the case with other young people. Of course, the general goal of education for everybody is assumed to be to make the most of given talents and to provide within the culture the greatest degree of liberation for these talents, however far we may fall short of this ideal in practice. Facing the problems of dyslexia often makes both planners and participators in education face the larger issues and their practical interrelationships with the special problems to be solved. To the extent that this occurs, both aims will be forwarded.

That literacy and its achievement have many important individual and cultural values is undeniable. One reads and writes in the service of practical utility and of personal enjoyment and enrichment which accompanies the assimilation of one's culture. Dyslexics share the interests, desires, and capacities of their peers, differing only in the ease and rate with which they acquire language skills. If the ultimate goals are kept in mind while their special needs are being met, their progress and satisfaction will be enhanced. Accordingly, we not only have students reading books appropriate to their ages and interests just as soon as possible, but recommend that students be read to, and where appropriate be exposed to nonprint media, at the levels of their intelligence, practical and scholastic needs, and personal interests. It has been our experience that they will rely on external aids only as long as and to the extent that they need to if they are being appropriately taught. Students want very much to be independent, particularly when they need to prove their competence to themselves and others and come to feel that, indeed, they are. When skills are adequate, comprehension of content and motivation to achievement are limited only by intelligence and experience (a prime reason for keeping the dyslexic student abreast of his peers by reading aloud to him and the like). Motivation usually takes care of itself or responds to the sorts of stimulation effective with everyone else. All this is another reason for viewing dyslexia—a temporary impediment only—as an aspect of acceptable diversity, not of divisive deviance. Imperfections we all have. This is one that is amenable to correction or adequate alleviation.

From the mental health or self-concept point of view, too, the attitudes of all concerned are important. If, for example, we follow the psychosocial development schema of Erik H. Erickson (see page 245), one centers on the psychosocial work of Erickson's Stage IV, appropriate to the school-age child. At this point, if previous stages of growth have taken place appropriately, the child is concerned primarily with the establishment of competence in the acquisition of skill-dependent aspects of culture, many of which are taught and learned in school, and with the reality-based sense of himself as a competent person.

No matter what the emotional problems appear to be and whether they are cause or consequence of learning failures, the education and training necessary to competence and the realization of its achievement cannot be short-circuited. In literate cultures, and to a considerable extent in the technologically influenced nonliterate world, one seldom finds a truly happy or effective person to whom written symbols are literally a closed book from which he is excluded. There are those who claim that everyone has the right *not* to read. No one would quarrel with that, but only with the assumption that a person is free to exercise his right if, in fact, he cannot read. Everyone with even a modicum of intelligence can learn to read; experience tells us this. It is society's responsibility to provide the opportunity for this learning, and also for the development of the ability to write, even if only on a functionally minimum level. If the first steps have been taken, the learner knows that all the rest is within the realm of possibility. For his self-concept, and hence his mental health, he can profitably think of dyslexia as a facet of diversity. In some ways it is a nuisance but perhaps also it is the other side of some of his most valuable attributes— his adaptability and flexibility. It is a part of himself to which he is entitled by nature rather than by our sufferance. He can come to terms with it as a challenge he is capable of meeting successfully and even turning to advantage. Our acceptance of this as a society can influence his outlook as a person.

An encouraging climate of opinion supports an instructional approach such as that here summarized, and those of us who use it do so because it seems best suited to the dyslexics whom we know, that is, to be theoretically and practically sound. The test of the approach, with its careful structure flexibly used, is to be found in the histories of students as they first respond and then, growing older, go on to further schooling and into adult life. With very few exceptions our follow-up contacts and studies find our former students doing satisfactorily, as they would have had they not found language skills initially so difficult to master as to justify our thinking of them as dyslexic. A few studies about them have been published, like Enfield (1976) and Palatini (1976). Others include a longitudinal study of a sampling of graduates of Gow School established some 50 years ago especially for dyslexics, and an intensive scrutiny of the genetic background and current history of the whole population of a more recently established school with the kind of total educational program envisioned by this author as approaching the ideal. These studies are the work of Barton Childs and his group at the Johns Hopkins Hospital Department of Pediatrics in Baltimore (Gottfredson, Finucci, and Childs 1983).

My generation-long study of former students (Rawson 1968) shows that they have all done well, surprisingly enough a degree better than their nondyslexic schoolmates, also studied. They are by no means unusual, except in having been subjected to statistical study, for histories like theirs have been repeated many times over by individuals whom we know and have worked with, some of them far exceeding our initial estimates of their potentialities. There are, alas, uncounted numbers of others, some identified and some not, who have not had the needed help. Some have won through the hard way, often with psychological effects which might have been avoided, but many others have not, swelling the ranks of personal and social casualties. For all our need for more knowledge and refinements of skill, it appears that among us here in North America and elsewhere (e.g. Pavlidis and Miles 1981) we have made a very promising beginning in the past 60 years or so in solving this very troubling problem. Whether or not any of our successful students reach the degree of eminence attained by da Vinci, Einstein, Niels Bohr, Hans Christian Andersen, Auguste Rodin, Woodrow Wilson, Nelson Rockefeller and a long list of others who have struggled with language learning problems, they are contributing to their own productive lives and society's well-being with deserved satisfaction and, it is to be hoped, a comparable sense of self-worth.

People of their kind of constitution, whatever difficulties they may have, are not usually to be thought of as victims of pathology, I believe, but as examples of the diversity that is to be expected in the present state of the evolution of the human species. Placed in a larger context, they are very often recognized as being especially capable of adaptability and of the creative contributions which we all need. The view we take of those among us who function in these ways is that our task is not to treat a defect but to provide the opportunities for optimum development. Such an outcome would, I believe, be fostered by a change of mental set which considers dyslexia an example of diversity, for the ways we view people and the ways we speak of them can make profound differences in the ways we act toward them. We influence both ourselves and others by our use of language in talking about language and in meeting the challenges which it presents to its learners and to those who teach them. The concept of *dyslexia as diversity* can be both liberating and productive.

3

Variations in Language Development and Mastery

"Each of us is like all other human beings; each of us is like some other persons; each of us is not like anyone else in the world." Perhaps this succinct and comprehensive statement by the psychologist, Douglas Heath (1982), makes so clear the point of this paper that we might as well close the book and go home to tea. What can we say that is not already obvious? And yet, what I propose to talk about here is what we are already engaged in every day, that is working with the realities of variations of language development and mastery in people of all ages and circumstances, all levels and varieties of capacity and motivation. This is what has made our professional field what it is and given it a place of central importance in the lives of many of us. If that *is* the case, then it is important to consider the special topic of this paper, to agree in principle, and to see if and how the principle can bring a valuable kind of unity into our own highly desirable diversity and that of the intellectual subject, as well as the human subjects, of our concern.

Those of us who have been part of it are fond of thinking of The Orton Dyslexia Society as a place of confluence in a chaotic maelstrom of variations of many sorts and levels. The variabilities of language and of life are obvious to all of us. It is part of the temper of the field of interest which brings us together that it attracts to itself people who admit variability, tolerate it, even like it mightily as a state of affairs and, in particular, find the variations in which variability is expressed to be of absorbing interest, a stimulating and pleasurable challenge.

Because of occupation, need, or predilection of one sort or another, we focus here on the various aspects of *language*, which is, after all, the concern that draws us together. We note, too, that with all our awareness of variety, we also harbor a desire for unity, for common understanding, purpose, and effort. We cannot find satisfactory answers

Reprinted with permission from The Orton Dyslexia Society from *Annals of Dyslexia* 32:259–273 1982.

in over-simplification—the single cause, the narrow category, the only cure, the Magic Bullet, the following of the One True Way. Life is not like that. Nor are we satisfied with a crazy quilt made up of patches from one aspect of confusion or another, held together primarily by a diffuse tolerance that justifies itself as eclecticism.

Somewhere between those extremes of unrealistic simplicity and unmanageable diffusion we try to develop attitudes toward variability, understanding of variations, and practical behavior toward their various manifestations in ourselves, our clients, and each other. We try, even, to evolve and describe a common philosophy which may contribute to the fruitful management and use of these very variations in human language development and mastery.

From this vantage point one can get a positive view of what we call dyslexia. Many of us believe that we can look upon dyslexia as one complex aspect of a quite common diversity (Rawson 1981) in human language functioning, a view which has consequences in the lives of people. I believe our taking this position makes a real difference in our own world-view, in what we do, and in the effect of our participation in the lives and thinking of other people—clients, colleagues, and public. If this be so, then it is appropriate that we consider together the basis and implications of looking upon dyslexia as normal diversity. We may examine some of the variations in language and their relations to dyslexia.

However he comes by the faculty, man is a language-using, and, in some measure, a symbol-determined, animal. Does the basis for this lie in the chemical, electrical, hormonal, or even the subatomic structure and functioning of his central nervous system? Or is it to the architecture and functioning of man's brain itself or to certain features of its cortex that we must go for the definitive explanations—if, indeed, they are ever to be available to us? In the development of the human race, of man as a species, or in the growth of each new, complex, unique individual, we may assign some responsibility to inheritance or to the timetables of embryology and postnatal development and some to the effects, gross and minute, of the environment at different times on each physically, genetically given individual. Scientists and philosophers can spend entire lives on small parts, or intermediate complexes, or on the whole of the language question, to say nothing of the relations of language to the rest of Man, and to the Universe. Does it boggle *your* mind, too?

Still, in all this complexity, we need not be completely overwhelmed. Our options are not limited to denial or defeat. We have observed that some explanations seem more rational, more pertinent, more interconnected, and have more to offer than do others. Some practices seem more informed or effective. We cannot give up the search for answers when the way seems unclear, the task Gargantuan, the going hard, or when the Opposition scoffs or has the upper hand. Look back: We've come a long way. Look around; there are resources, and there is support. Look ahead; this is the kind of challenge man seems designed to accept and to answer with zest. *Homo sapiens,* at his best, is built to respond to challenge, within the limits of his ability and his hunger for growth and wisdom. In some sense, he does it because he must.

While man in his least responsible mode may be what Loren Eiseley (1963) called "the lethal factor" in the life of the planet, nevertheless, man may still have time to use himself to save himself and play the part he could play in his own unfinished evolution, using his capacity to be conscious of himself, to envision purposes beyond the immediate, to formulate through symbolic thought and to achieve through inventive action. I like to say, and perhaps *have* to believe, and surely have said more often than enough, that when man is built to take this kind of responsibility, this may result, as I believe Jonas Salk puts it, in "the survival of the *wisest.*" For an instance of the apparent innateness and even necessity of man's symbolic capacity, I suggest a look in wonderment at the autobiography of Helen Keller (1902). (See also Lash 1980). Few people are the same after that experience.

Volumes could be written about large philosophical generalizations, but in our present quest we can but mention the pervasiveness of variation and its values for long-time physical evolution as species develop useful attributes, like prehensile tails, or the whole complicated apparatus that makes speech possible. Human cultural evolution is, of course, enormously faster, because it can build cumulatively on the past as man makes intentional use of the variety of the world's resources and his own seemingly endless practical and imaginative gifts, with language playing one major role at almost every turn.

We recognize, too, that *all* is not variation. Within life as a whole, and within its categories, there are limits outside of which individuals or whole species cannot survive or do not breed and reproduce. Sometimes these critical factors are small, a degree or so of temperature in a salamander's brook or in the human bloodstream. Sometimes the band of acceptable variations is comparatively wide, like an omnivorous animal's adaptation to variety in foods, or people's ability to live in deserts or cities, yet always there are limits to which *hubris* must give heed. That man's ingenuity can outrun his capacity to see ahead to *all* its results and so can catapult him into war or ecological disaster is an important part of the story, and often failure is as dependent on language as is success.

Many of the broad but bounded characteristics are species-specific, like verbal symbolic language in man. Other animals have gifts of, say, vision, hearing, smell, and other capacities for awareness beyond our own and may even have greater capacity for symbolic processing than we have hitherto suspected. Chimpanzees can "ape" their human cousins not only in amusing (or exasperating) behavior, but, with long and careful training, in rudimentary linguistic communication using vocabularies of plastic symbols or gestural signs. Cetaceans (whales and dolphins) show high intelligence in practical and social behavior and use vocal language in intra-species communication. Lacking the manual and technological equipment for doing so, they have deposited no historical or cultural archives. We can but wish they could tell us, and we could understand more. There is, however, little doubt of the distinctive nature, range, and quality of human language. The effect that it has had, and continues to have, on man is profound and enormous.

Whatever their relations to animals, and however widely they differ among themselves, it is a striking fact that for human beings verbal language is a universal attribute. Every culture, the world over, has its own form of speech, highly organized in vocabulary and linguistic system. Given even a modicum of intelligence and sensory intactness, every one of its children uses the language of the culture which surrounds him. He uses it humanly, as a symbol system, giving names to objects, events, and actions. Each child uses speech for communication exactly as do his elders, with only the minor variations of individual, and sometimes subcultural, uniqueness. The languages with their internal dialects may present thousands of variations on the universal theme, but the children are genetically set to learn whichever one they hear.

They develop on built-in timetables which vary little from culture to culture, but within each culture they differ everywhere as individuals. They are apparently distributed from precosity to backwardness within a similar range and with roughly the kind of normal probability distribution one finds in measuring any complex trait. Babies everywhere respond with attention and growing understanding to the speech of those around them. They babble and coo at the same ages, first making a wide variety of speech sounds, then narrowing their repertoire to that of their surrounding speech community. When they begin to speak, after perhaps experimenting with a few words of their own coinage, it is in English syllables, Chinese tones, African clicks, or whatever, no matter what their parentage, and it is in the second year of life that most of them achieve this feat, no matter where they live.

While spoken language is universal, seemingly by now in the evolutionary scale a genetically determined capacity, its derived forms, such as literacy, systematized sign language, and so on, seem less directly close to the genetic building blocks. Reading and writing are not so securely built in as is spoken language, which often seems to the casual observer more "triggered" into spontaneous learning than taught. The skills of literacy are by no means universal. They require more deliberate teaching and learning, and yet they, too, have inheritance factors, as the study of biography suggests and the histories of families studded with dyslexics attest. There is, apparently, a usually valid timetable here, too, though with a broader range. John Stuart Mill read at the age of two, but Woodrow Wilson, whose adult writing was also highly sophisticated, was barely becoming literate at eleven, and General George Patton, declaiming epic poetry at length on the eve of battle it is said, could scarcely read at all. The necessary mental wiring can be presumed to be present in almost everybody, for there have been very few who, with sufficient and appropriate tuition and motivation, have entirely failed to master written language skills. You *can* (sometimes) "teach your baby to read," or he *may* never learn, but in the normal course, and this is true the world over, the age from five to seven seems generally the optimum time to begin to "go to school." The ability is there for the cultural leap, as it was for Margaret Mead's (1956) Manus people to move in one generation from the Stone Age to modern competence. For some it comes easily, for others it takes more doing—truly an area of great, yet still normal (nonpathological) variation.

Some years ago, when I was trying to sort out the complexities of language, I made up some models for which I am still finding new uses as I bring new problems to them. There is one you may have seen before, even more than once if you have exposed yourself to my papers. I make no apologies for using it again, for like the old family car, I propose to take it over a new road to a different destination. I think it is still a viable vehicle, good for some more mileage; indeed, we have been traveling in it for some distance already in these pages. (See Figure 2, p. 62 or Appendix)

This diagram started life as a descriptor—"the language as it is" (as in the directive, "Teach the language as it is to the child as he is. That means you have to know what language is all about.") Obviously, as it stands, it is the *literate* person's, or the literate culture's language. For this volume I revised the central box to include Metalinguistic among the thinking processes; consciousness of language as itself a part of thinking has come into more prominent awareness within the past decade.

How can we use this aging schema as a framework for our present exploration?

To work backwards from its surface, if we cut off the boxes on the right—the visible or graphological achievements of reading and writing or printing—we bring into focus how much of the power and richness of language is beyond the grasp, whether or not beyond the awareness, of the preliterate child or culture or of the illiterate person in a literate society. Yet all the cognitive processes shown in the Inner Language box, as well as those there neglected, are available to the nonliterate person and he can use them to achieve a very high level of human functioning. He has the sensory way *in* (of audition) and the motor way *out* (of speech, which he experiences kinesthetically and from which he gets auditory feedback reinforcement). High civilizations, like those of Stonehenge and pre-Homeric Greece, were built on what for us is such an incomplete model; but once we see what is possible, the meaning of the right-hand side of the diagram not only reaches our intellects but goes deep into our spirits as we think of dyslexics and those illiterate for other reasons. They are cut off from so much of their heritage, its sources of power, delight, and fulfillment, and, in the modern world, *they know it*, with regret and perhaps with resentment for their deprivations and feelings of inadequacy. You remember the little boy of Hamelin whose lameness kept him from following the Pied Piper? Said he:

> . . . yet I cannot forget that I am bereft
> Of the wonderful sights that they will see,
> Which the Piper also promised me.

We are reminded poignantly but forcefully of the truth of Arthur Benton's statement (1978) that language, especially written language, is "a cultural product and not a biological characteristic" except as a potentiality. In our century, however, it is an achievement which is every child's birthright.

This, then, is a bird's-eye view, the large-scale map of the language continent of man's world. It can also provide the generalized framework for that survey of each individual's personal geography and history that we need if we are to understand his uniqueness and help him attain full personhood as a symbol user.

Each of the five compartments which we have, for convenience, abstracted from the whole subject of language lends itself to more detailed treatment as a modal dimension at several levels of specificity. One can approach the analysis from the perspective of description, or as an historian of development. In either case as we ask ourselves both, "What does this mean in the life of *Homo sapiens symbolicus*?" (to use Kinget's [1975] classification) and, "How does it help us understand and serve this person before us in his unique life journey?" (defining our own role).

There is room for many talents and specialties in this endeavor, from those of the philosophic and scientific generalist to the areas of the laboratory psychologist or the teacher helping a child with a specific sub-sub-skill. It is, we might say, the essence of maturity as a professional to be able to perform responsibly and skillfully at the workbench level and at the same time to keep one's place in the larger scheme of things and still to be oneself as a person in relation to other people—to maintain a balance of rigorous standards and warm humanity. That especially is Social Work's disciplinary contribution.

What does it mean to listen, to speak, to read, to write, and to communicate with one's fellowman? What part does this linguistic mode have in the way one responds to life with one's whole being? To ask these questions sends us to the treasure trove of that huge library which records the findings of our predecessors and coworkers, and to observation and oral discussion of work in progress but not yet written up and published. Here we need all the wise and organized guidance we can get, from within and without, in finding our way through the mammoth array of valuable knowledge—and the disarray of irrelevancies, false starts, and unfinished business that can all but swamp us.

Perhaps we can learn something from Dan (see Rawson 1968). He is a successfully practicing lawyer, a "graduate dyslexic," [nearing 60 in 1988], who is still a rather slow reader with not too good a memory for recorded details, or so he judges himself. He points for us a useful way as he turns his necessity for compensatory strategy to advantage. "Assuming that the Law is, or should be, rational," he says, "I first reason my way through a case. Then with purpose to guide me, I need to read and remember less and I'm not so overwhelmed as you might expect." (We'll come back to Dan later.)

Where, as we look at any individual, does he stand right now in his language competency? How does he listen, and how well? What about his speech, his reading, his writing, his verbal thinking—in short, his mastery of language as a tool for living? It is frequently useful to him and to us to compare his achievements with those of his peers, and even to estimate his capacity in these respects, just as an indicator of where we are at a given moment. It is much more useful to compare his present status and rate of growth to his present and future purposes. Between being satisfied with a generalized feeling that all is well with this or that and asking for a finely tuned examination of specific needs one requires all the knowledge of resources one can marshall and also selective judgement about the extent and timing of their use. These things we need to know or to know how to reach—though not to detail here—for we want to understand this child or older student as he is now if we are to help him become what he can and wants to be.

It helps immensely with this task to know whatever we can about how man, and this man-child or woman-child, came to be what he or she is. What is the history of the evolving race? We can begin by studying the biological and cultural evidence, as to some extent we have already done. We can ask how and at what point in his history as a species man developed his capacity for symbolic thinking and learned to use spoken language in social living. About this we can only infer from meager evidence and speculation, since, alas, early man left no written records. Of what has happened since the beginning of recording we are more aware, with new evidence coming to light all the time as cultural "finds" illuminate the scene.

This latest development in our evolution has left behind straggling ends of its incompleteness to show up in developmental irregularities and constitutional differences among us. The more we know, or can reasonably surmise, as to the origin of these differences, the more effectively we can relate to them. To learn from history is one measure of wisdom, especially when it leads not only to understanding but to greater compassion and more effective helpfulness.

One good way to satisfy our curiosity about our racial inheritance is to watch a brand-new child, or better a succession of children, starting on the personal course each one must run for himself. The old statement that "ontogeny recapitulates phylogeny," even though it cannot be taken literally to mean that each child goes through every physical stage and experience the race has lived through, does seem to point to profound truth. The infant starts, as presumably did the emerging human race, from the "scratch" marked by his genetic heredity and his circumstances of gestation and birth. He is, in the term given impetus by Lauretta Bender (1975), essentially "plastic— unformed but capable of being formed." He reaches out with all his senses, with his whole self, to his new world, and, with tremendous adaptive capacity, makes of it his own destiny, and to some extent influences its destiny as well.

What is the natural history of a person's language development? What can we expect of *this* person on the road from the initial "buzzing, blooming confusion" to the ordered observations of an Einstein or a Whitehead? How does he get from the birth cry to the flowing periods of the "silver-tongued orator"? How much later and by what route does he progress from picture writing and the alphabet to reading *War and Peace* and writing sonnets? How does he get from infant recognition of speech sounds to full metalinguistic competence (studying and using language about language)? And how do these strands weave together and form part of the fabric of his whole life?

What one knows and keeps learning about all this brings both richness and utility into our association with the Dans and the Nans we watch and work with. We got some idea where Dan was on the language time charts when we first knew him at three, obviously thinking and very much frustrated by his inability to make himself understood. At ten, reading eagerly after systematic multisensory teaching and his own strenuous efforts, he still said, "I wanna new book—one what's recīten!" That day's diary spoke of supper "gests," "paes" on the menu, and the discovery that a word needed for a report was not, as he had always thought and written "apnasfear" but "atmosphere." As an honors student in prep school and university and Case Editor of the Review in law school he worked diligently and so, I am sure, did his mentors. When visited in his mid-thirties, he was already a partner in his law firm, a sought-after speaker in the promotion of social causes, an avid reader of intellectually demanding books, a first-rate husband and father, avocationally a gourmet cook and outdoorsman. His hand-writing, like his athletic skills, was always and naturally superior. It is obvious that he was a deliberate and intelligent user of adaptive linguistic strategies. At any point in his life's course, his position on each of the five language dimensions here considered would have made an interesting, vibrant, composite picture of a generally self-confident dyslexic person, different from all others, but in *that* respect not unique.

We have had much to say in times past about the overt patterns of language performance. There have been volumes written, too, about some aspects of inner language, perception, verbal thinking, and so on. The useful phrase "symbolic formulation and expression" goes back to 1920 and the neurologist Henry Head. Recently more and more of our attention, our conscious thinking, has included an important concept made easier to hold in focus and talk about by having a classifying term with which to express it—metalinguistic. The cognate terms are metalanguage (see Cherry 1957), metalinguistic awareness (Hook and Johnson 1978), and metalinguistic competence. The idea is not new to be sure, although its prominence in our field *in these terms* is. Arthur Benton (1978) has defined metalinguistics succinctly as, "the ability to manipulate language as an object."

Those of us who have worked much with dyslexics have generally found this cognitive mode the approach of choice, and usually also of necessity, especially applicable when the learner's abstract reasoning is adequate or better. Very often the necessity brings in its train some real organizational and intellectual advantages. Dan is a case in point.

We who won our spurs and learned to use them under the influence of Orton and Gillingham knew that life did not begin at five or six, although that was the point at which they and we began to take hold. However, there was much in these other disciplinary worlds with which we did not make real, ongoing connections until relatively recently, when we were spurred on by the directions taken by the speech, hearing, and (increasingly) language people and those interested in early (preschool) education and development. Katrina de Hirsch, Jeannette Jansky, Mary Masland, and the others were patient with us, and still are, although we do not always see eye-to-eye (variations even here.). We all knew these things and yet we did not know as we are now coming to know. Also we did not know how fortunate we

had been in our intellectual launching pad onto the deeper understanding of *variations in language development and mastery.*

(PS 1988: A recent visit with Dan shows him, just as we might have
hoped when he was three, in the prime of a life of happy effectiveness.)

4

Pioneering in Dyslexia
Notes From Over Half a Century

As a pioneer who didn't know she was one, I often think about what it was that I was looking for. As a pioneer who knows now that she has been one, what have I found along the way that might be of significance to 1988 readers?

Because it was part of my mind-set when I first met the dyslexia world, there were two things I was looking for. One was a satisfactory answer to how to educate children—our own and others, especially at the School in Rose Valley (Moylan, PA), and that included Peter, who had brought me to the reading problem. My other quest was the continuing pursuit of the urge to know and to understand—the satisfaction of human curiosity at personal and impersonal levels.

I had come to the issue of children's education first through quite self-conscious planning of my own education—what it was to be about and how, practically, to achieve it—and then, in discussion with my husband and our fellow parents, through the founding and development of the School in Rose Valley in 1929. This led to my helping finance our children's way through the school first by becoming librarian, learning to appreciate children's books and then coming to know each of the school's 30 (then more) children and their reading needs and interests.

Of all of the library's users, Peter, especially, was in difficulty with words. Actually, he had had trouble in his beginning preschool days, but it was later, when the others were learning to read and he was not, that I was the one who was asked to help him. (My first profession had, after all, been social casework, called "the art of helping people out of trouble.") I did what I could in Peter's early grades, but to little lasting effect, except perhaps to maintain a degree of sanity for him and his teachers and schoolmates by keeping him at work elsewhere during reading time.

Adapted from and used with permission from *Learning Disabilities Focus* 3:68–72. Copyright 1988 by the Division of Learning Disabilities.

It was not until Peter was 11 that we heard of Dr. Samuel T. Orton in New York, referred Peter and his parents thither, and learned how to put him on his way to literacy.* The beginnings of his breakthrough, however difficult they were at the time, suggested a similar approach to teaching some younger children. It "worked" with them, too, and led me into a new and challenging occupation embracing the full range of the language function.

However, being by nature an intellectual ferret, or explorer, I could not be satisfied with just obeying doctor's orders. I had to wonder why, and to try in every way to find out. Yet no matter how strongly I was drawn to the "groves of academe," economics and family life insured a balance of practicality. It was to my great good fortune that circumstances started me with a real problem in the life of a real child and kept me working always in a succession of real-life situations, with their almost infinite variations. I think not only in my own life but, for whatever use my work has had in the development of our special field, this dual drive into theory and practice has helped me (and others) to stay on track.

Nevertheless, because this was then largely a new field, I had to be at least a second-echelon pioneer. (Orton and Gillingham were, for me, the prime innovators). I knew of no one near to whom I could "go to school." Wisdom was wherever one could find it; I had to hunt. In many ways this suited my preferred style of learning. I went to New York two or three times to consult the Ortons and Dr. Paul Dozier and to visit schools, including Ethical Culture School, which Anna Gillingham had lately left. I took a 4-day course with Orton's former psychologist, Marion Monroe, leaned on Dr. Dozier for diagnoses and guidance in teaching after he came to Philadelphia, went to lectures and read a lot of neurology that was at first mostly beyond my understanding; and I badgered authors and experts with my ignorance. Especially, I kept on reading.

I talked a reluctant Anna Gillingham into selling me the then new 3rd edition of her and Bessie Stillman's (1936) famous Manual. I hadn't studied with her or the Ortons who alone taught this approach, so, quite realistically, she feared I did not know enough to use the Manual properly. However, I found it a pedagogical life-saver. I had to make up most of my teaching materials with a rubber stamp set, a typewriter, a brush-pen, and such. Fortunately, I soon found that knowing children's real literature better than I knew standard basal readers was far from being a handicap.

With continued thirst for "reasons," I found Dr. Orton's early pa-

*Of course we could not know then that this would lead, in the long, long run, to educational success—prep school, college, a Harvard Ph.D. in chemistry—and a university teaching career.

pers on language (J.L. Orton 1966a) and got his book when it was new (1937). Each work took several readings, then and over the years, but they were worth the struggle. For other study I followed my Swarthmore College training and went, whenever possible, to sources rather than to commentaries—to books and journals, however far they were above my level of understanding. Education, for the pioneer, even the neopioneer in a relatively unknown and unaccepted specialty, has to be *self-* education, but often that is the best kind anyway, if one is sufficiently motivated to pursue it.

Wherever background or tangential courses are available, such a one takes advantage of them, and I did that, too. As soon as the Stanford Revision of the Binet Intelligence Test was available in 1938, I got my minimum (but then adequate) credentials in psychological testing at the University of Pennsylvania—so that I could test our school's children myself instead of taking someone else's word for the nuances underlying the scores. These courses, with old and new credits from the School of Social Work helped toward an MA (1940), as did courses in conventional teaching of reading and arithmetic, curriculum planning, and research methods. I wanted to make sure I didn't become narrow, but could make informed choices. And so I put together such a training medley as I could as a "language re-education teacher." For a beginning it served, but the rounding out of the fuller course has taken the rest of my life—and that is how I think it should be with education, pioneer or not. When, after 60 years, Swarthmore College did award me a doctoral degree it was not in Philosophy but in Humane Letters, which seemed to me more personally satisfying and more appropriate to the subject of my work.

The School in Rose Valley, where I had been introduced to dyslexia, was of a "pioneer" kind in several different ways, not least of which was the opportunities for education it offered to us adults as well as to its children. I was not thinking of myself as a pioneer but as a curious person pursuing an interesting problem and trying to serve some useful purposes, and so I continued work at the School in Rose Valley after our sons moved on. Fortunately I was not only allowed but encouraged to "try all things and hold fast to that which is good," so I investigated all the viewpoints and materials I could—studying the conventional and the innovative and learning to avoid panaceas. Where new plans seemed promising or sometimes where my experience had been limited, I tried things out or persuaded my colleagues to do so. I used "Dick and Jane," "language experience approach to reading," "Fernald for writing," and so on, in regular classes. I helped a teacher and children write a publishable reader (Holmes 1948), planned and taught a rational "new math" curriculum in every grade, promoted, and was engaged in, the IQ and achievement testing program, all while I was testing and teaching the children we now call

dyslexic as we discovered them. A few such children came to us because we were known to "have a program," but most of the children
were from the school's regular enrollment. That the school did its job
for the youngsters is reflected in my follow-up study of many years
later (Rawson 1968).

As this experimental school developed, it was important to balance the spontaneous creativity in its progressive program with consistent attention to the academic skills component these children need to
make up the whole their education should be. So, among these appreciative friends, I became a watchdog for academic standards. I know
now how lucky I was in that opportunity!

Almost every School family spent countless volunteer hours on its
projects, but on school days I was at first there only part-time. As appreciation of poor readers' needs grew, in the '40s, I tried having an
occasional parent-assistant, with mixed results. Novices needed more
structured study and help than I was then able to give, but two of them
did stay for a while after I moved away in 1947. They have contributed
more than they know to many later courses I have given. Pioneering
can be a many-person job.

For a long time I was almost the only "specialist" of my kind in the
area, so I found myself working with more and more private pupils as
well as those in our school. A few people in my own world were helpful; but most were either merely tolerant or actually scornful of my
aberrant ideas, or, more often, shrugged them off. In this field, I was
professionally lonely, I suppose, but I did not have time either to feel
particularly sorry for myself or to think of myself in a more than local
role. I was just having a generally rich and interesting life.

In 1947, after more than 17 years of connection with Rose Valley,
our family moved to Frederick, Maryland. I planned to retire from
teaching to country living, but that resolve did not last long. Almost
immediately I was drafted, and encouraged by my husband, to fill part
of a midyear teaching vacancy in sociology at nearby Hood College,
back in my old field of social work and social research. That is a story for
another time, since this account is about dyslexia. Most of my life in the
later '40s and '50s (my *own* 40s and 50s also) was spent on our home
project, on Hood College, and in community activities, mostly volunteer, that came to me through the sociological door. I wasn't adequately
prepared for any of these activities, unless being accustomed to taking
on whatever life brought was a form of preparation. Years before, I had
discovered that a sort of self-imposed "professional fieldwork student"
frame of mind was a productive way to meet such challenges. It
seemed useful in Frederick too. Perhaps I had stumbled upon one recipe for being a pioneer. "When something new cries out to be done,
try it."

For example, for seven years I spent one day each week as psychologist for the county mental health clinic and did some diagnostic language testing there and at home, recognizing a few dyslexics along the way, and sometimes offering a minimum of help. I was, of course, not surprised to find specific language disability unheard of in the county. The then-Superintendent of Schools said, "Reading problems? Of course not! I know of two—only two—retarded children, even." The town librarian followed up a casual mention of my former job by sending a friend with her obviously "bright language disabled" son. One child led to another, until within a dozen years I had more pupils than available time, and no helpers. The Orton-oriented, individually tailored teaching, when indicated, kept on working in Frederick as it had up North.

At Hood, in a small way, I developed a once-a-week program for girls I thought of as "on the Dean's other List." A few of them turned out to be dyslexic in my terms; the others had other needs served better by counseling and help with study skills than by language re-education. (Naturally, I don't find a dyslexic behind every D or F grade! I just try to recognize one when he or she comes along.)

When the local tutorial supply-demand problem got really out of hand after several years, I pulled out of community volunteer responsibilities and persuaded the college to allow me to set up a year-long advanced-credit evening course to prepare other teachers to do what I was doing with dyslexics. The course's theoretical content, pitched at graduate-school level, was designed for selected interested professionals (psychologists, pediatricians, librarians, etc.), with supervised training included for specializing teachers ("tutors"). I did most of the testing of children and tried to match pupils with appropriate student-teachers—with considerable success, from a "by their fruits ye shall know them" view.

Now, this I knew really was pioneering. There had been good nonacademic courses and training projects elsewhere about which I had learned all I could, but in 1959 Hood's was, as far as I know, the first *college credit* course specifically for the preparation of teachers for dyslexic students (Slingerland's in Seattle followed shortly.) I continued giving the course for four years (until I retired from Hood), and thereafter used it as a model or part-model for other university courses I taught (Claremont, Loyola-Baltimore, University of Virginia, University of Connecticut, etc.) Such courses have now become encouragingly more common, both here and abroad. Still, Hood's had a pioneering flavor that I have relished.

Here I must go back ten years to pick up the Orton threads. In 1948 Dr. Orton died. The Orton Society was formed in 1949, had its first meeting in 1950, and came to my grateful attention in 1951. I joined it forthwith and started going to its annual meetings in New York. There, at last, and at least once a year, I could be with people who talked my preferred language. I envied them their long-established camaraderie and joined in with it as soon as I could. I have enjoyed it ever since. I was soon on a committee, then Vice president (1963), President (1965–1969), and Editor, first of the Bulletin and then for the Society (1965–present). I learned to do jobs (some of them innovative), began writing papers, traveling about North America and Europe, being on commissions, giving lectures, exploring new areas, and lately, being called a "pioneer." There have been meetings, conferences, workshops, world congresses, scientific projects—hard work but also some honors and awards—more I think than I can possibly deserve. Still, it all adds up, in one segment of my life, to some 37 years of very great joy and satisfaction caught up in the development of The Orton Dyslexia Society.

One of the first things I learned through my association with Orton was about the need for research on "treatment" designed and reported in such a way that it might carry weight with scientists and other skeptics. Life with dyslexics whom we had known well had given some of us a lot of experiences, but people were not going to accept our accounts as significant just because we said they were. We had to find language that conveyed meaning to others than ourselves.

That seemed fair enough, so I decided to do what I could about it, on an economic shoestring, with some material I had available. Beginning in 1963, I restudied the childhood records of 56 of the boys I had known at the School in Rose Valley. They were of the full range of language-learning talents. I found them all (26 or more years later), compared the accomplishments of dyslexics and nondyslexics, subjected the results to statistical procedures, and in 1968 Johns Hopkins University Press published the findings (Rawson 1968).

The book's message of reassurance has continued to give hope and courage to dyslexics and their mentors for whom it was written. Now under the imprint of the Educators Publishing Service, it continues to say, "Here is at least one piece of evidence that dyslexics need not fail *because of dyslexia;* they *can* fulfill their innate promise, however high." There are calls for longitudinal studies. I like to think this study, by my good fortune unique, though imperfect, rates a notch on the pioneer stick. (But really to make history, I am working now on a follow-up after still another 20-some years, seeing how the survivors are doing after about 50 years since childhood. I'd rather like to be remembered for this kind of pioneer project!)

Another sort of beginning that you may call pioneering if you'd like has to do with treatment of dyslexia in schools in whose startings I have had a hand. First there was the School in Rose Valley, well recounted by Grace Rotzel (1971). That venture in education, with its dyslexia component, has had widespread effects through many channels. Speaking only for myself, it has been part of every educational enterprise I have engaged in, but especially in the fabric of its direct cultural offspring, Jemicy School, near Baltimore, my especially engrossing "godchild" since 1972. Other schools and agencies, including TRI-Services, Inc., have roots here, but if I start to name the ones I have been privileged to be involved with, I shall become entangled in a network that is a happier source for activity than for exposition.

However, I do feel pleased and proud to be the Margaret Byrd Rawson for whom TRI-Services (Chevy Chase, MD) has named both their Center for Professional Training and their Annual Dyslexia Awards. The former is a continuation and enlargement of the teachers' courses I have taught. The awards are the Rose Valley study's true offspring, with an original Rose Valley boy receiving one of the earliest citations for his continued accomplishment in medicine and research.

That one should have so much honor and immortality while yet alive. How fortunate can one be? One of the joys of such a way of life is that you don't work for the honor and appreciation, but it seems to me quite a justifiable pleasure to revel in them if they come your way unbidden—a special benefit that goes with being a pioneer.

5

The Self-Concept and the Cycle of Growth

Those of us concerned with dyslexia have not, I think, paid enough attention to the role of emotion. This may have been because we were either taking it for granted or over-reacting to the apparently undue emphasis put upon it by many of our fellow laborers in the vineyard, or for both reasons. I am, of course, thinking of the role of the emotions in the language and the language fields. I don't suppose we could find one among our diagnosticians or therapists who would gainsay the importance of emotional factors, but we do sometimes downplay them. We think we see many, many times when a child is really emotionally hung up because he hasn't been able to function well in the communication endeavor as a preschooler or in the school years, rather than the chicken-egg sequence being the other way around, as our psychiatric, social work, and school guidance friends would often have it. We cite as quite convincing evidence cases, known as individuals or in such studies as the Klines' (1975), where beginning with language therapy—rather than psychotherapy—either erased the emotional problem or reduced its anxieties to manageable proportions. Of course there are emotional situations concurrent with, but more or less independent of, school learning which sometimes have to have attention on their own. Always when emotions are involved they are likely to tangle up the situation and make it more difficult to handle; but we try, often deliberately though sometimes just on a kind of unstated, or sixth sense basis, to encourage people to become therapists because they have natural or cultivated personalities and skills which are therapeutic. The therapeutic climate is as much a part of the total educational treatment as are the more language-specific theoretical understandings and the instructional skills.

And yet, there is an area of professional discipline, knowledge, understanding, and skill here that we should be making deliberate use of. We do not rely on a teacher's "feel" for the structure of English,

Reprinted with permission from The Orton Dyslexia Society from *Bulletin of the Orton Society* 24:63–76 1974 and Reprint No. 62.

although we are glad if she has high aptitude there, and we should not be so naive as people sometimes are when they think of psychotherapy or social work as "just common sense, you know, dressed up with some current jargon." Nor should we shrink away from the helping professions because they have a vocabulary different from our own. There is something there that we need, and we'd do well to bring our development in it up to date.

We have heard, and said it ourselves many a time, that one of the most vulnerable spots, and one of the most important ones, in our children and young people is their self-concept. How do they feel about themselves and the fact, of which they are only too aware, of their failure to measure up to their own and other people's expectancies in learning to handle language—speech, reading, writing, spelling, self-expression, and the like? What has been the history of their development in this respect? Is there anything we can learn about the general history of human psychosocial development which will throw light on the difficulties which seem particularly marked, and full of variations, among the ones I call "our" children? And, perhaps, can our experience with the interactions between language learning difficulties of the kind we call dyslexia and the feelings of our children about themselves and their interpersonal relations tell our friends in the "helping professions" anything that may be useful to them? Let us see what the formulations of some people in psychiatry can contribute.

Do our children go through the stages of development outlined by Freud (1949) and his professional descendants? The labels oral, anal, Oedipal, latency, etc., and the terms id, ego, super-ego, libidinal, and the like no longer fill us with fear and loathing as they did many people in my youth, though we may prefer to use other names for similar concepts.

Then there is Adler's (1951) inferiority complex, and his theory that one often finds his greatest interest and, later, expertise, as a compensatory excellence in a field where he had to overcome weakness. There is Dan, of my Rose Valley study, who has become an excellent public speaker and briefwriter in the legal world, by his own deliberate effort, and Tom who followed his interest into a major in American Literature and is teaching English in prep school—both despite severe and undoubted dyslexia in childhood.

Familiarity with the formulations of Jung (1939)—his personality types, and other concepts—has helped us to meet some very different individuals where they are and to go on from there with them. Though it may be a frivolous sample, the persistence with which children throw themselves back 500 years with insistence on the long-a pronunciation of *ea*, in spite of our precautionary measures, almost convinces us that racial memory does not deal only with long-buried myths.

From another line of descent—William James (1962) to William

Glasser (1965), with his "reality therapy," which, despite his protesta-
tions, finds some sanction among the analysts—comes reinforcement
for our here-and-now emphasis.

Of all the writers in the psychiatric-psychology field, though, I believe I have had most help in thinking and practice with students of all
ages from Erik Erikson (1961, 1964a, 1964b, 1968), a neo-Freudian, and
his psychosocial development schema. Whereas Shakespeare's somewhat cynical nonhero, Jaques, in *As You Like It*, outlines a famous but
hardly satisfactory seven ages of man, Erikson does much better by
childhood and by the continuity of life through eight psychosocial
stages. These ring more true to fact and add to both our general insight
into human life and our understanding of the young people we are trying to help. As any good diagnostic study should, this formulation
gives suggestions or prompts creative thinking about how a non-
psychiatrist—a plain teacher or other friend, and especially a tutor or
language therapist—can use the schema to help, without ever pre-
suming to go outside the helper's own defined role. An outline of Erikson's contribution to our understanding is, I think, in order.

According to Erikson, on the basis of what we know of human development there appears to be a kind of developmental ground-plan,
called by scientists epigenetic, for the psychosocial, as well as for the
physical, growth of each individual. At each age-period there is a normally appropriate growth problem, which Erikson calls a psychosocial
crisis, using crisis not in the sense of impending disaster but of a crucial issue which needs to be settled or established before the individual
can satisfactorily go on to the next period. If it *is* properly passed or
resolved, then he is free for the next stage of growth. On this basis,
Erikson divides the Ages of Man into eight, quite unequal in duration,
but, he feels, equivalent in importance.

First, in infancy, roughly the child's first year, before he is able to
walk or talk, is the period of complete dependency, when his elders
must take care of him. If he is grow properly, they must give this care in
such a way that he feels trust in his environment. He is safe, warm,
nourished, comfortable, and especially, loved, and he can count on
this. The ways in which various societies implement this caring and
trustworthiness are different, but if their children are to flourish, it
must be provided. The personal aspect of the nurture is most important, as we have had pointed out in the experiments and experiences in
institutionalized care of infants with the use of mother-substitutes
who made the difference between growth and stultification in babies
who were physically adequately provided for. The Czech film, "Children Without Love," which some of us saw when Dr. Zdeněk Matějcěk
lectured in the U.S.A. in 1968, is a beautiful and moving documen-
tation of this idea. So is "Roots of Happiness," the film about life in

Puerto Rico, and the one about family life in Gainesville, Georgia, of some years ago. We can all, doubtless, think of other instances. It is the spirit, not the standard of living which matters.

If this first stage is normally gone through, the child goes on with a sense that things are going to work out, that he has justification for optimism and basic, persistent, life-long hope, that he can generally expect people and events to be not necessarily easy but possible for him to cope with and he, in turn, can *give* to others. In Erikson's words he feels "I am what I have and give."

If this stage is not properly consumated, the result can be *mis*trust, a constant need for reassurance, insecurity in personal relationships, and a general pessimism about life and the world. Even very poor physical surroundings and hardship, however, need not have this result, as long as the little child feels that there is someone, usually his mother, who really cares for him and whom he can depend on to have his interests at heart. Nor is it, necessarily, too late to make up this stage in the eras after its appropriate time has passed. In Axline's powerfully insightful *Dibs, In Search of Self* (1965) we see the retrieval of the trusting attitude taking place between an initially apparently psychotic child and his psychotherapist. On a less deep level, *we* have an opportunity to provide something of the missing sense of trust with some of our children when we really do care about them individually and let them know it in all our actions toward them—our reliability in meeting them as planned, our support of them, even when we have to be firm, and our genuine caring about their progress toward the overt therapeutic goal of language learning competence. We cannot—must not—attempt to be either psychotherapist (in the deep sense) or parent, although we partake of some of the characteristics of each, but we can help the child or young person to experience *now* what he missed, in whole or in part, in infancy—a sense of basic trust in someone with whom he is involved in a positive relationship.

Erikson's *second* stage, what has elsewhere been called the "runabout period," covers roughly the next year or so of the child's development up to about age three. He learns not only to walk, but to move about with skill and assurance, to become, in Erikson's terms, *autonomous,* able to separate himself from others in a way he knows he can manage, to begin to be a self in his own right—"to be his own man." There is a parallel here in learning to talk when, as Vygotsky (1934) puts it, "thought becomes verbal," "speech becomes rational" and the child is launched as a human language user. Normally he can do this, and is permitted and encouraged to do it within the limits of his developing capacities. He has not as yet developed mature discrimination in matters of "holding on" and "letting go," of doing what he wills to do in the short run, and of willing to do what the facts of life make it necessary or desirable to do in his own long-term interests. He must still have the support of adult protection and firmness to help him know that it is all right for him to go ahead, and that he is not at the mercy of either external forces or his own as yet possibly unmanageable impulses, of which he may be justifiably frightened.

I am reminded here of a very overactive and uninhibited somewhat older Johnny I once taught. His father had withdrawn from the battle, and his mother was unable to cope with him, so he generally did as he pleased, often with disastrous results. He felt me as unduly restrictive at first when I insisted on going on with the lesson instead of letting him "tell stories." One day I gave him free rein. As he told a rambling tale, full of murder and mayhem, he became more and more frenzied until, in a few minutes, he was almost literally "beside himself," writhing on the floor. I picked him up, held him firmly but lovingly, stood him between my knees facing outward, with my arms tightly around him. He gradually subsided, as a sobbing child will do, and I said, "Was it a good idea, Johnny, that story?" With real relief he almost whispered, "No, It wasn't." Several times, after that, I held him, more or less firmly, as we worked. He never seemed to resent it, but rather to welcome help in controlling frightening inner forces, and he did work at the presented tasks, and he did learn to read. I do not know how deep this went, for I have lost touch with him. It was probably not enough, but it was not destructive, and I think it was within the limits of my "job description," what I could do as a protective nurturing adult to be helpful to him in developing a controlled will.

If the child goes through this stage normally, working out his capacity to be independent, he develops "a sense of self-control without loss of self-esteem" and if your philosophy permits it, free will. At least he has the feeling of some freedom of will to say "yes" or "no" and to make choices as to his own behavior. If he does not get through the period satisfactorily, he may emerge into the later years of childhood, and the rest of his life, full of doubt of himself and of the wisdom of his elders. Here the factors of impulsiveness and, especially, compulsiveness come into play. Good in reasonable degrees, such traits may become the masters rather than the servants of the individual's life, and in the end he may become an overly rigid, intolerant character, or a slippery "character disorder" individual, or both, by turns, in a baffling sort of life-style, always apologetic and ashamed of himself, perhaps overcompensating for this by bizarre brashness and "acting out." He cannot stand securely on his own feet and go with assurance where he needs and wants to go. He cannot say, as he should be able to, "I am what I can will freely."

When a child comes to us with some difficulties left over from unsatisfactory resolution of this period, we can be especially helpful in seeing how very much he needs what we aim to help all our children get—the ability to feel free to do what is needed, to know that he can learn what he needs to know, and that the therapist will stand by to help him to do it for himself, not holding onto him in any part of the experience longer than *his* needs (not the therapist's) dictate.

The *third* period of life, which we think of ordinarily as the pre-school years, Erikson designates as the time for the emergence of *initiative,* as the positive outcome of play and imaginative activity, in which the child, now moving freely (and we add, communicating effectively in speech) is able to project himself into various roles. Saying, "I am what I can imagine I will be," he can play at being a daddy (or she a mommy) at being "doctor, lawyer, merchant, chief" . . . particularly chief, or cowboy, or cop. He can play *with,* not just alongside his age-mates, and follow the lead of older child-heroes. He may adore his older brother, who may not reciprocate, just as he, himself, may be resenting his younger siblings. The ideals of parents, whom children at this age hope they may someday be able to be like, are incorporated as conscience and, in Freudian terms, the super-ego and the ego-ideal. Work (which looks to the adult to be play) and games (though not yet formalized) form the beginnings of the drives to aggressive pursuit of goals.

If things fail to go right here, the child may become inhibited, un-able to act on his own, full of guilt feelings for having desired to rival father or mother and cut him or her out, in favor of self. He may become so passively compliant as to seem an "empty" personality. Or the child may overcompensate for his sense of guilt by a vast show of activity, strutting, "bathroom talk," and the other, to adults, obnoxious, characteristics of the "furious fives." It is not just "I'm the king of the castle," then, but especially, "you're the dirty rascal!" And just how dirty, a visit to the kindergarten or the equivalent of its locker-room will tell our shocked adult sensibilities some things we've forgotten, or perhaps some things we never knew. To make sure of his kingly status (of which he is in such guilty doubt) the youngster may not only call names, but also throw "sticks and stones" and physically bully anyone he can, not so much to hurt the other guy (though there is some satis-faction in that), as to show how high he can climb on the corpses of his, often trumped up, enemies. Sometimes, says Erikson, the effects of inadequate surmounting of this crucial episode in the growth cycle may not be apparent until later, but the alert adult can recognize them by their outcomes in social behavior, though the diagnosis from the symptoms is by no means sure-fire.

When a child comes to us in school, or later, with this unsolved difficulty in his background, what can we do? It is rarely possible to get anywhere by just telling him about it in rational or moralistic terms. Certain reality factors, such as, "Do you think that's going to make the other kids like you, or want you around?" or something of the sort, may have some value. Better still, from our position in his life, perhaps he can recognize in us, on a level deeper than words, something he'd like to be like. If so, we can set him free, and encourage him to act positively and effectively, with initiative, in pursuit of his own goals, within the limits of social acceptability and the developing conscience. He can come to do what *he* wants to do, not simply depend on or accede to our specifications, as in, "How many pages do you want me to write?" Then, under circumstances more favorable than before, we shall be making use of his reliving of this era, to set the stage for his effectiveness as a school child and, later, in both technological and social achievement.

In language, specifically, if between three and six he learns that he can get himself across, can talk about present and future so that other people really understand his verbal formulations and their expression, certain large paving stones are thereby laid for future success in the verbal disciplines. If he is older, he may well have to recapitulate this stage at the same time he is working on the others, and if we recognize his needs in this respect we are better able to weave these strands into both formal instruction and bibliotherapy. Who knows how much of the popularity of the *Little House* series of Laura Ingalls Wilder lies in the readers' needs for just such people as Pa and Ma, and for the example of their children's living with them? One does not "point the moral," though it is often wise to talk about the things and people and the events of their lives wherein the "moral" lies buried. Children's living of these experiences vicariously and with delight should take the place of any satisfaction the adult might get from making proclamations in a sermon.

Perhaps this is the place to interject a word of caution, which I remember needing when I was first learning about when to give and when not to give insight in verbal terms. Often, perhaps always, undesirable behavior toward oneself or others is a defense against the laying bare of a very tender vulnerability. The individual *needs* these defenses; they are his Linus blanket against "the slings and arrows of [what seems to him] outrageous fortune." If he is to be rid of the defenses and the rest of the world is to live tolerably with him, two things are needed. He must, perhaps with our help, grow beyond his need for them before he can let the defenses go, or we can sometimes suggest, privately, of course, that he doesn't need to do *that* anymore. For his own protection and that of the rest of the world, he has to understand that, no matter how much we value him as a person (and that's a lot), "his right to strike ends where his neighbor's nose begins"— whether the "nose" be taken literally or whether it means the whole person, including the feelings, the "face," of the other person, adult or child. He can know that between him and ourselves, in the therapeutic teaching relationship, certain expressions of feeling, in words or clay-punching, can be accepted and understood for what they are. If we have our own role and responsibility clearly in mind we can do this, like all our therapy, without becoming "amateur psychiatrists." As in defining a word, we can know better what something *is* by also knowing as much as we can about the things it *is not*. Hence this present excursion into the psychiatric realm.

And now, at long last, we come to the really "crucial crux" or crisis of development from the point of view of the teacher of most language-learning-disabled children. This is Erikson's *Stage 4*, where the desideratum is what he calls "industry" or "skill." He sometimes designates it, as I prefer to, as the establishment of a justified sense of *competence* in the real work of childhood in any culture, the learning of the technological and cognitive skills which are everywhere taught in what we call the grade-school years. This is Freud's "latency period," before the beginning of the storm and stress of adolescence. In literate cultures, this means the period of learning literacy and its concomitants. It is here, particularly, that we are likely to meet the child we often call dyslexic. If the educational institutions his society has set up have not been able to teach him the competencies necessary to a justified *sense* of competence, he may, or should, be on our doorsteps. If we think about this difficulty as primarily rooted in his feelings about himself (which are extremely potent) and deal with them only, or almost exclusively, the best we can hope for is an unrealistic or resigned and unhappy acceptance of his lot. He knows himself as less than fully capable, one to whom many options are closed, and for whom there must be constant and difficult circumlocutions in dealing with a world where signposts are often of critical importance and full citizenship requires use of the printed word as well as of its technological substitutes. No matter how completely *we* accept *him, he* cannot accept *himself* as a fully worthwhile, competent, effective person unless and until he gets at least functional mastery over the verbal and mathematical skills which will permit him to do what he wants to do. His objectives may be simple or highly complex, from riding the bus to work and reading the plant bulletin board for himself to practicing law, medicine, literary research, or teaching, as many dyslexics have succeeded in doing. There is *no substitute* for genuine competence and he needs the help which makes it possible for him to develop it. This competence is the only real solution to the sense of inferiority and all that it leads to in personal and social waste, unhappiness, and often tragedy. If he lives the life of "Garam, the Hunter," and, later "Garam, the Chief," in a nonliterate African culture (Berry 1935), it is the skills of that culture that he must learn; but in modern literate, technological cultures such as our own, somewhere he must get the skills of school. It is in this fourth Eriksonian stage that we have particular responsibility and opportunity. "I am," the child needs to be able to say, "what I can make work."

"The search for identity" is the focus of Erikson's *fifth stage,* and the one on which he has spent the most thought and energy in formulation, diagnosis, and treatment in his distinguished career as the psychiatrist whom legions of young people would call blessed, if that were the idiom of the times. He spells out for this period what the establishment of one's identity means, how it comes about through the eventful and often stormy years of adolescence, and what are the personal and social consequences of the quest, whether successful or unsuccessful. With all the volumes and papers on the subject surrounding us, it is not necessary to go into description of the phenomena of adolescence, a period in its own right and a preparation for full adulthood. The significance of Erikson's discussion, I think, lies particularly in his pointing up the appearance, for positive or negative value, of the results of the successful, unsuccessful, or partially successful passage of the individual through the earlier stages of psychosocial growth, and the foreshadowing in each of them of the likelihood of events and tendencies in the three adult stages to come. How can one achieve a satisfactory and satisfying identity as a worthwhile, whole, and happy person unless he feels justifiably competent in meeting the demands the world seems sure to lay upon him and unless he can go forward with faith and hope, confidence, and initiative built up in early childhood?

If he comes to us as an adolescent, it is doubly challenging, for he not only has more to learn than does the younger pupil if he is to catch up, but we may have also more of what he calls "hang-ups" to help him deal with. We can do this with him, given adequate time and expertise, but we can do it best and most expeditiously if we know not only his cognitive and skill needs but his psychosocial ones. Without going into emotional diagnoses, we need always to behave in such a way as to make it possible for him to trust us, to feel that we are ready and eager to give him freedom to take responsibility for himself all along the line, but ready, too, to help him to take that responsibility, that we want him to exercise and enjoy initiative in handling his difficulties, be they of any sort among the myriad demands life makes, and particularly that our special expertise is at his service in the establishing of genuine, long-lasting, reliable competence in handling the world's demands, especially the academic ones *because* they are a key to his establishment of himself and his mastery and enjoyments of his world.

In the *sixth stage,* which marks the transition from adolescence to full adulthood, the young person establishes his capacity for intimacy, especially with a partner of the opposite sex. He is not now "playing the field," but if he is secure in this stage of his development he can get on easily and securely with persons of both sexes because he is freed of the ambiguities and uncertainties which he has now grown through and out of. "Now," for instance, says the hitherto socially shy and awkward girl, "now that I am engaged to Pete, whom I truly love, I find it so much easier to get along with other fellows as if they were just *people*, not boys I have to worry about as boys. I think I even get along better with my girl friends, too, and with all the other people I know and just meet. It has cleared up life all around!" Perhaps, as is the case with one such girl of my acquaintance, this developed followed a long period of dyslexia, recognized and treated only in college years, and then successful professional education and job experience. She looked very different at this point from the freshman I knew first. I was, I may say, influenced in my part in her education, and reeducation, by Erikson as well as Orton, Gillingham, and the General Semanticist, Wendell Johnson (1946).

The next, *seventh*, stage of adulthood—the years of maturity—is characterized by Erikson as the period of "generativity." This includes the bearing and rearing of children, best accomplished if the first six stages have been met and lived through to successful outcomes. But this is by no means all of the concept of "generativity," for it includes successful professional performance and growth, both as a learner, an executive, and a teacher of one's juniors; as a "helping person" in one of the helping professions, such as teaching or social work, psychology, medicine or nursing, or hairdressing, or domestic service. A prime example, of course, is homemaking and motherhood as a profession. The generation of things and ideas are part of it, too, and all the aspects of what Erikson calls "care for one's products." One need not be married nor the biological parent of children to deal most creatively with the period of "generativity"—and the avoidance of "stagnation," which Erikson designates as its opposite and of which any of us can all too easily supply examples.

Here, too, the influence of all the preceding periods is felt, often in most complicated and distress-producing ways. There comes to mind as one of many examples the charming, chic, socially adept mother of one of our pupils. Her husband was a man of professional competence and in a position of considerable responsibility and authority, especially in the lives of young men in government service. He was an understanding father, and was especially helpful with one of our teenagers who was in deep trouble. He was, as far as we could tell, also a loving and supportive husband. But his wife could not re•d at all, and he was unable to convince her that she could confide this in one of us and perhaps get some help for the problem with which her son was learning to cope through his language therapist's teaching. She found it necessary to engage in all manner of subterfuges, which she did with great skill, in order to hide from the world a situation which she could not but feel as a deep disgrace and source of shame. As an adult, it was her right to choose this path, and not ours to violate her husband's confidence by approaching her on the subject, but she stays in our memory as a concern about how much her path was costing her in effort and fear and anxiety.

There is one more stage, which more and more of us are experiencing as life-expectancy grows; that of the latter end of life, "for which the first was made"—if we are lucky. In the folklore of geriatrics there is the statement that whatever a person is, up to old age, he or she will be even more that way as an oldster. Erikson's contrast here is between "integrity" and "despair"—as seen in the "wise elder" (whom we'd all like to be if we can make it), still active and full of life and verve to his dying day, and on the other hand, the park-bench-warmer, who with nothing to do is doing it discontentedly, if not bitterly. I think of an octogenerian of my acquaintance who worked certain repetitive kinds of puzzles because, he said, "It helps to pass the time." In contrast was the great lady of 94, a polio heroine from childhood (heroine because, very largely, of her mother's wise management). She was unmarried, beloved by many nieces and nephews of three generations, many children whom she had expertly and lovingly taught, friends and relatives of her own and younger generations. Despite her inadequate left hand, she played the piano, in her last years from her wheelchair, and she followed the baseball world enthusiastically on radio and television. Her last words, from inside the oxygen tent, were, "How's the ball game going?"

"How's the ball game going, Erik Erikson?" With your help, perhaps we can help it go better for our students, patients, clients, and children, especially if we give thought to our very primary responsibility for making it go well for ourselves, as those who, to the best of our ability, are givers (phase one); the masters, as far as it is given to man, of our own souls and behaviors; actively taking initiative; continually increasing our own competence in our affairs and so our sense of self worth; trusting our own continuously growing feeling of identity; warm, understanding, and at ease in our relations with others; giving to the world what has been given to us and as much as we can manage; and approaching the end of our years with a sense of integrity and the hope and faith in life with which, if we were fortunate, we began. Thus we may bring the life cycle fully around the circle, with a satisfying self-concept supporting us all the way, from infancy to all we can know of immortality.

Appendix

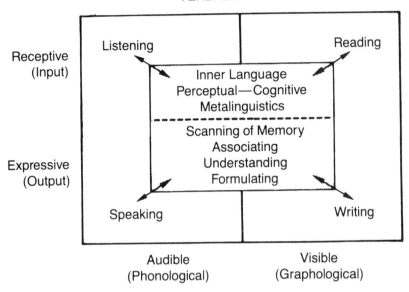

Figure 2. *Analysis of verbal language. (After Rawson 1968.)*

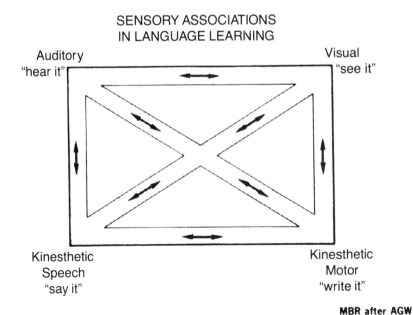

MBR after AGW

Figure 3. *Sensory associations in language learning. (After A.G. Wolff 1970.)*

Bibliography of Rawson Works

Published Works

[bulleted titles appear in this volume. ED.]

1922. Future Statesmen: The Political Ambitions of College Students. *National Municipal Review.* 11(10):313–316 (Oct 1922).

1961. Learning Language. *Parent's Bulletin.* The School in Rose Valley.

1966. After a Generation's Time: A Follow-up Study of Fifty-six Boys. *Bulletin of the Orton Society.* 16:24–37.

1966. *A Bibliography on the Nature, Recognition and Treatment of Language Difficulties.* The Orton Society.

●1966. Prognosis in Dyslexia. *Academic Therapy* 1(3).

1968. *Developmental Language Disability: Adult Accomplishments of Dyslexic Boys.* Baltimore: Johns Hopkins Press.

1968. What's Wrong is My Words. *Hood Alumnae Magazine* 63(3): 4–7.

1969. Dyslexia and Social Work. *Bulletin of the Orton Society* 19: 80–81.

1969. The Forgotten Child of 1969. *Bulletin of the Orton Society* 19:121–123.

1969. Harry Wilson and the Stratostreak. *Bulletin of the Orton Society.* 19:141–144.

1969. Teaching Children With Language Disabilities in Small Groups. National Advisory Committee on Dyslexia and Related Disorders Monograph No. 11. Bethesda, MD. NINDS, HEW. Also published 1971 in *Journal of Learning Disabilities* 4(1):17–25.

1970. I Can Think, But What's Wrong is My Words. *Medical Insight* 2(12):20–39.

●1970. The Structure of English: The language to be learned. *Bulletin of the Orton Society* 20:103–123.

1971. Let's Get Down to Essentials: What are we trying to do in language teaching? *Journal of Learning Disabilities* 4(4):48–49.

1971. Let's Shoot for Eulexia not Hyperlexia. *Journal of Special Education.* 5(3):247–252.

1971. Perspectives of Specific Language Disability Part One: Past. *Bulletin of the Orton Society.* 21:22–34.

●1972. Language Learning Differences in Plain English. *Academic Therapy.* 7(4):411–419.

1972. Response to The 1971 Samuel T. Orton Award. *Bulletin of the Orton Society.* 22:5–6.

1973. Semantics 1973– Diagnostic Categories: Their use and misuse. *Bulletin of the Orton Society.* 23:140–145.

Jeff—A Case Study. *Bulletin of the Orton Society.* 23:182–186.

1974. *A Bibliography on the Nature, Recognition and Treatment of Language Difficulties.* Baltimore: The Orton Society, Inc.

●1974. The Self-Concept and the Cycle of Growth. *Bulletin of the Orton Society.* 24:63–77.

●1975. Developmental Dyslexia: Educational treatment and results. *In* M. Rawson and D. Duane (eds.). *Reading, Perception and Language.* Baltimore: York Press, 231–258.

1975. "I Am Me!" with "Louise Baker." *Bulletin of the Orton Society* 25:185–199.

1977. Dyslexics as Adults: The possibilities and the challenge. *Bulletin of the Orton Society.* 27:193–197.

●1978. Dyslexia and Learning Disabilities: Their relationship. *Bulletin of the Orton Society.* 28:43–61.

●1979. Beyond the Alphabet: From competent reader to avid reader. *Bulletin of the Orton Society.* 29:191–204.

●1979. The Social Implications of Dyslexia. *In* R. Richardson and M. Monsour (eds.) *Dilemmas of Dyslexia.* Proceedings of a conference at the University of Virginia.

●1981. A Diversity Model for Dyslexia. *In* G. Pavlidis and T. Miles (eds.). *Dyslexia Research And Its Applications To Education.* Chichester: John Wiley and Sons.

1982. Louise Baker and the Leonardo Syndrome. *Annals of Dyslexia* 32:289–305.

●1982. Variations in Language Development and Mastery *Annals of Dyslexia.* 32:259–273.

●1985. The Bright Future. *Annals of Dyslexia.* 35:13–20.

1986. Developmental Stages and Patterns of Growth of Dyslexic Persons. *In* G. Pavlidis and D. Fisher (eds.). *Dyslexia: Its neuropsychology and treatment.* Chichester, England: John Wiley and Sons.

●1986. The Many Faces of Dyslexia. *Annals of Dyslexia.* 36:179–191.

●1987. The Nature of the Dyslexic Learner. *In Intimacy with Language: A Forgotten Basic in Teacher Education.* Baltimore: The Orton Dyslexia Society.

●1987. The Orton Trail 1896–1986. *Annals of Dyslexia* 37:36–48.

●1988. Pioneering in Dyslexia: Notes from over half a century *Learning Disabilities Focus*. 3:2. (in press 5/11/88).

●1991. Linquistics and Dyslexia in Language Acquisition. *In* D.J. Napoli and J.A. Kegl (eds.). *Bridge Between Psychology and Linguistics: A Swarthmore Festschrift for Lila Gleitman.* Hillsdale, NJ: Lawrence Erlbaum Associates.

●1992. Dyslexia: The Pot of Gold. *In* W. Ellis, (ed.). *Their World.* New York: The National Center for Learning Disabilities.

Unpublished Papers Included in *Many Faces of Dyslexia*

1972. The Jemicy School: A Philosophy. Prepared for The Jemicy School.

1973. The Dyslexic College Student and the Arts. Paper given at Consortium of the Union of Independent Colleges of Art, during the Annual Conference of the Orton Society in Baltimore, MD, Nov. 1973.

1974. The Meanings of "Reading". Excerpted from paper: Dyslexia: What It Is and What It Is Not, given at a Conference of the International Reading Association, New Orleans, LA, 5/2/74.

1976. "Fish." for Alice Koontz's class at Johns Hopkins University. 8/20/76.

1981. Some Thoughts for Graduating Students. First presented at Commencement, Linden Hill School, Northfield, MA. 6/13/81.

1982. Guidelines for Teaching. Excerpted from *What is Dyslexia?* Prepared for the Board of Directors, Orton Dyslexia Society.

1983. Decoding and Comprehension.

1983. Education: Its essence.

1984. Education and Dyslexia: A comprehensive view. New York Branch, Orton Dyslexia Society. Conference paper presented 3/24/84.

1985. Orton the Educator.

1986. The Boswell Function.

1986. Case Histories as Evidence in Dyslexia.

1988. Invent the Wheel—At Least Once.

1992. In Preparation. *Fifty Year Follow-up of Developmental Language Disability: Adult Accomplishments of Dyslexic Bays.*

References

Adler, A. 1951. *The Practice and Theory of Individual Psychology.* Humanities Press.

Anderson, C. W. and Main, H. G. 1973. *A Workbook of Resource Words.* Minneapolis: R. S. Denison and Co.

Angell, M. 1976. We weep not only for ourselves. Letter to editor. *The Washington Post.* August 30.

Annett, M. 1981. The right shift theory of handedness and developmental language problems. *Bulletin of the Orton Society* 31:103–121.

Annett, M. and Kilshaw, D. 1984. Lateral preferences and skill in dyslexics: implications of the right shift theory. *Journal of Child Psychology and Psychiatry* 25(3):357–377.

Ansara, A. 1969. Maturational readiness for school tasks. *Bulletin of the Orton Society* 19: 51–59.

———. 1973. The language therapist as a basic mathematics tutor for adolescents. *Bulletin of the Orton Society* 23:119–139.

———. 1972. Language therapy to salvage the college potential of dyslexic adolescent. *Bulletin of the Orton Society* 22:123–139.

Arthur, C. 1934. *Tutoring as Therapy.* New York: Commonwealth Fund

Atzesberger, M. 1974. Excerpts from a study for Rhineland-Pfalz Education Office, West Germany. (Courtesy of E. Klasen, Munich.)

Axline, V. M. 1965. *Dibs: In Search of Self.* Boston: Houghton Mifflin.

Bakker, D. J. 1973. Hemispheric specialization and stages in the learning-to-read process. *Bulletin of the Orton Society* 22:15–27.

Bakker, D. J., Satz, P. 1970. *Specific Reading Disability: Advances in theory and method.* Rotterdam: Rotterdam University Press.

Bannatyne, A. 1973. *Reading: An auditory vocal process.* San Rafael, California: Academic Therapy Press.

Bender, L. 1958. Problems in conceptualization and communication in children with developmental alexia. *In* Hoch and Zubin (eds.). *Psychopathology of Communication.* New York: Grune and Stratton.

———. 1975. A fifty-year review of dyslexia. *Bulletin of the Orton Society* 25:5–23.

Benton, A. L. 1965. The problem of cerebral dominance. *Canadian Psychologist* 6A:4.

———. 1978. Some conclusions about dyslexia. *In* A. L. Benton and D. Pearl (eds.). *Dyslexia: An appraisal of current knowledge.* New York: Oxford University Press.

Berlin, R. 1887. *Eine besondere Art von Wortblindheit (Dyslexie).* Weisbaden: Verlag von. S. F. Bergmann.

Berry, E. c. 1935. *Garam the Hunter; Garam the Chief.*

Blom, G. and Jones, A. 1970. Bases of classification of reading disorders. *In* E. Calkins (ed.). *Reading Forum* Monograph 11. Bethesda: NINDS, NIH.

Bloomfield, L. and Barnhart, C. L. 1961. *Let's Read: A linguistic approach.* Detroit: Wayne State University Press.

Born, M. 1978. *My Life: Recollections of a Nobel Laureate.* New York: Taylor and Francis.

Bowen, C. C. 1972. *Angling for Words.* San Rafael, California: Academic Therapy Press.

Bowen, C. D. 1970. *Family Portrait.* Boston: Little Brown and Company.

Brotten, M., Richardson, S., and Mangel, C. 1973. *Something's Wrong with My Child*. New York: Harcourt Brace Jovanovich.

Chall, J. 1967. *Learning to Read: The great debate*. New York: McGraw-Hill Book Company.

Charnow D. 1987. Samuel T. Orton, MD: New York City Physician, 1928–1948. Presentation at the 38th Annual Conference of the Orton Dyslexia Society, San Francisco, CA.

Cherry, C. 1957. *On Human Communication*. Cambridge, MA: MIT Press.

Childs, S. B. (ed.) 1968. *Education and Specific Language Disability: The papers of Anna Gillingham*. Towson, MD: The Orton Society.

Childs, S. and Childs, R. deS. 1963. *Sound Spelling*. Cambridge, MA: Educators Publishing Service.

_____. 1973a. *The Childs Spelling System: The rules* (revised). Cambridge, MA: Educators Publishers Service.

_____. 1973b. *Sound Phonics*. Cambridge, MA: Educators Publishing Service.

Clarke, L. 1973. *Can't Read, Can't Write, Can't Talk Too Good Either: How to recognize and overcome dyslexia in your child*. New York: Walker and Company.

Cox, A. R. 1974. *Structures and Techniques: Remedial language training for use with Alphabetic Phonics*. Cambridge, MA: Educators Publishing Service.

Critchley, McD. 1970. *The Dyslexic Child*. Springfield, IL: Charles C. Thomas.

Cronin, E. M. n.d. *Raskob Letter Box and Teachers Manual*. Oakland, CA: College of the Holy Name.

de Hirsch, K. 1970. Preschool intervention. *In* E. Calkins (ed.). *Reading Forum Monograph 11*. Bethesda: NINDS, NIH.

Denckla, M. B. 1985. Issues of overlap and heterogeneity in dyslexia. *In* D. B. Gray and J. F. Kavanagh (eds.). *Biobehavioral Measure of Dyslexia*. Parkton, MD: York Press.

Dewey, J. 1944. *Education and Democracy*. New York: The Free Press.

Doehring, D. 1968, 1973. *Patterns of Impairment in Specific Reading Disability: A Neuropsychological investigation*. Montreal: McGill University Press.

Downing, J. 1973. *Comparative Reading: Cross-national studies of behavior and process in reading and writing*. New York: Macmillan Company.

Duane, D. D. and Rawson, M. B. (eds.). 1975. *Reading, Perception and Language*. Baltimore: York Press. Towson, MD: The Orton Society.

Durbrow, H. C. 1968, 1973. *Learning to Write*. Cambridge, MA: Educators Publishing Service.

East, C. 1969. A study of the effectiveness of specific language disability techniques on reading ability of potentially retarded readers. *Bulletin of the Orton Society* 19: 95–99.

Eisley, L. 1983. Man: The lethal factor. *American Scientist* 51–83.

Enfield, M. L. 1976. An Alternate Classroom Approach to Meeting Special Learning Needs of Children with Reading Problems. Doctoral dissertation: The University of Minnesota.

Erikson, E. H. 1961. Roots of virtue. *In* J. Huxley (ed.). *The Humanities Frame*. New York: Harper and Bros.

_____. 1964a. *Childhood and Society*. New York: W. W. Norton.

_____. 1964b. *Insight and Responsibility*. New York: W. W. Norton.

_____. 1968. *Identity: Youth and crisis*. New York: W. W. Norton.

Evans, M. M. 1982. *Dyslexia: An annotated bibliography*. Westport, CT: Greenwood Press.

Freud, S. 1949. *An Outline of Psychoanalysis*. New York: W. W. Norton.

Gag, W. 1928. *Millions of Cats*. New York: Coward, McCann.

Galaburda, A. 1983. Developmental dyslexia: Current anatomical research. *Annals of Dyslexia* 33:29–40.

_____. 1985. Developmental dyslexia: A review of biological interactions. *Annals of Dyslexia* 35:21–33.

———. 1986. Human studies on the anatomy of dyslexia. Paper delivered at the Thirty-Sixth Annual Conference of The Orton Dyslexia Society: Chicago.

Galaburda, A. and Kemper, T. 1979. Cytoarchitectonic abnormalities in developmental dyslexia: A case study. *Annals of Neurology* 6:94–100.

Galaburda, A. M., LeMay, M., Kemper, T. L., and Geschwind, N. 1978. Right-left asymmetries in the brain. *Science* 199:852–856.

Gardner, R. A. and Gardner, B. T. 1969. Teaching sign language to a chimpanzee. *Science* 165:664–672.

Geiger, H. 1970. Archetype of speech. *Manus* 23:15.

Geschwind, N. 1962. The anatomy of acquired disorders of reading. *In* J. Money (ed.). *Reading Disability: Progress and research needs in dyslexia.* Baltimore: The Johns Hopkins Press.

———. 1972. Anatomical evolution of the human brain. *Bulletin of the Orton Society* 22: 7–13.

———. 1982a. Comments made on the occasion of the dedication of the Samuel Torrey Orton Library, College of Physicians and Surgeons, Columbia University. *Annals of Dyslexia* 32:9–11.

———. 1982b. Why Orton was right. *Annals of Dyslexia* 32:13–30.

———. 1983. Biological associations of left-handedness. *Annals of Dyslexia* 33:29–40.

———. 1984. Personal communication.

Geschwind, N. and Galaburda, A. (eds.). *Cerebral Dominance: The biological foundations.* Cambridge: Harvard University Press.

Geschwind, N. and Levitsky, W. 1968. Human brain: Left-right assymetries in temporal speech regions. *Science* 161:186–187.

Gillingham, A. 1968. *Education and Specific Language Disability: The Papers of Anna Gillingham.* Towson, MD: The Orton Society.

Gillingham, A. and Stillman, B. 1956, 1960. *Remedial Training for Children with Specific Disability in Reading, Spelling and Penmanship.* Cambridge, MA: Educators Publishing Service.

Gillingham, A., Stillman, B., and Childs, S. B. 1966, 1970, 1971. *Phonics Proficiency Scales.* Cambridge, MA: Educators Publishing Service.

Glasser, W. 1965. *Reality Therapy.* New York: Harper and Row.

Gollan, E. B. 1979. Personal communication.

Gottfredson, L. S., Finucci, J. M., and Childs, B. 1983. The adult occupational success of dyslexic boys: A large-scale long-term follow-up Report 334 Center for Organization of Schools. The Johns Hopkins University.

Gough, P. B. 1972. One second of reading. *In* J. F. Kavanaugh and I. G. Mattingly (eds.). *Language by Ear and by Eye.* Cambridge, MA: MIT Press.

Hagin, R. 1973. Models of intervention with learning disabilities: Ephemeral and otherwise. *School Psychology Monograph* 1:1–24.

Halacy, D. S. 1970. *Man and Memory.* New York: Harper and Row.

Hall, E. T. 1974. *Learning the English Language: Skillbooks I and II and Teachers' Manuals.* Cambridge, MA: Educators Publishing Service.

Hathaway, E. T. 1973. *The Teaching Box.* Cambridge, MA: Educators Publishing Service.

Hayakawa, S., Hamilian, L., and Wagner, G. 1964. *Language in Thought and Action.* New York: Harcourt Brace Javanovich.

Head, H. 1920. Aphasia: An historical review. *Brain* 43:390–450.

———. 1926. *Aphasia and Kindred Disorders of Speech.* New York: Macmillan.

Heath, D. 1982. How are Friends to rise to the future? *Friends Journal* 28:16–21.

Herjanic, B. M. and Penick, E. C. 1972. Adult outcomes of disabled readers. *Journal of Special Education* 6(4):397–410.

Hermann, K. 1959. *Reading Disability: A medical study of word blindness and related handicaps.* Translated by P. C. Aungle. Springfield, IL: Charles C Thomas.

Hinshelwood, J. 1895. A case of dyslexia: A peculiar form of word-blindness. *Lancet* 2: 1451–1454.

_____. 1917. *Congenital Word Blindness*. London: Lewis.

Holmes, E. 1948. *Henny and Jenny Penny.* Moylan, PA: The School in Rose Valley.

Hook, P. E. and Johnson, D. J. 1978. Metalinguistic awareness and reading strategies. *Bulletin of the Orton Society* 28:62–78.

Howard, N. 1974. Personal communication.

Hunt, J. McV. 1965. Traditional personality theory in the light of recent evidence. *American Scientist* 3:1.

Irvine, P. 1969. Pioneers in Special Education: Samuel T. Orton. *Journal of Special Education* 3(4):317.

James, W. 1962. *Psychology: Briefer course.* New York: Macmillan.

Jansky, J. J. and de Hirsch, K. 1972. *Preventing Reading Failure.* New York: Harper and Row.

Johnson, D. 1968. The language continuum *Bulletin of the Orton Society* 18:1–11.

Johnson, D. and Myklebust, H. 1967. *Learning Disabilities: Educational principles and practices.* New York: Grune and Stratton.

Johnson, W. 1946. *People in Quandries.* New York: Harper Brothers.

Jones, F. E. 1978. Robin's story. *Bulletin of the Orton Society* 28:175–180.

Jordan, D. R. 1972. *Dyslexia in the Classroom.* Columbus, OH: Charles E. Merrill Publishing Company.

Jung, C. G. 1939. *The Integration of the Personality.* New York: Farrar and Rinehart.

Keller, H. 1902, 1961. *The Story of My Life.* New York: Dell Publishing Company.

Kerr, J. 1896. School hygiene in its mental, moral and physical aspects. *Royal Statistical Society* 60:613–680.

Kinget, G. M. 1975. *On Being Human.* New York: Harcourt Brace Jovanovich.

Kirk, I. T. W. 1972. Personal communication.

Kirk, S. A. and Kirk, W. D. 1971. *Psycholinguistic Learning Disabilities: Diagnosis and remediation.* Urbana, IL: University of Illinois Press.

Klasen, E. 1972. *The Syndrome of Specific Dyslexia.* Baltimore: University Park Press.

Kline, C. L. and Kline, L. 1975. Follow-up study of 216 dyslexic children from a group of 750 children evaluated in the past four years. *Bulletin of the Orton Society* 25:127–144.

Kline, C. L., Kline, C. L., Ashbrenner, M. et al. 1968. The treatment of dyslexia in a community mental health center. *Journal of Learning Disabilities* 1(8):456–466.

Kolson, C. and Kaluger, G. 1970. *Clinical Aspects of Remedial Reading.* Springfield, IL: Charles C Thomas.

Korzybski, A. 1933. *Science and Sanity: An introduction to non-Aristolean systems and general semantics.* Lancaster, PA: Science Press Printing Company.

Kowarik, O. 1972. Excerpts from a study of educational treatment of 356 reading disabled children in Vienna, Austria, with follow-up 1962–1972. Personal communication, E. Klasen, Munich, Germany.

Lash, J. 1980. *Helen and Teacher: The story of Helen Keller and Anne Sullivan Macy.* New York: Delacorte Press/Seymour Lawrence.

Lee, L. L. 1974. *Developmental Sentence Analysis: A grammatical assessment procedure for speech and language clinicians.* Evanston, IL: Northwestern University Press.

Leong, C. K. 1972. An oblique glance at reading disability. *Bulletin of the Orton Society* 22:69–79.

Ley, D. and Metteer, R. 1974. The mainstream approach for the SLD child: A public school model. *Bulletin of the Orton Society* 24:130–134.

Lytle, V. 1985. Edison, Rockefeller, Rodin, and the reading problem. *NEA Today.* October 10–11.

Markkiewicz, J. and Zakrezewska, B. 1973. Dual remedial training of dyslexic children in Poland. *Bulletin of the Orton Society* 23:39–51.

Masland, R. L. 1967. Brain mechanisms underlying the language function. *Bulletin of the Orton Society* 17:1–31.

_____. 1976. The advantage of being dyslexic. *Bulletin of the Orton Society* 26:10–18.

_____. n.d. Etiological variants in dyslexia. Personal communication.

Matejcek, Z. 1971. Dyslexia: Diagnosis and treatment. *Bulletin of the Orton Society* 21: 53–63.

McCarthy, J. J. and McCarthy, J. F. 1969. *Learning Disabilities*. Boston: Allyn and Bacon.

McClelland, J. 1973. Shadow and substance of specific language disability: A longitudinal study. *Bulletin of the Orton Society* 23:160–181.

Mead, M. (ed.). 1955. *Cultural Patterns and Technical Change*. New York: New American Library, Mentor Book.

Miles, T. R. 1970. *On Helping the Dyslexic Child*. New York: Barnes and Nobles.

Money, J. (ed.) 1962. *Reading Disability: Progress and research needs in dyslexia*. Baltimore: The Johns Hopkins Press.

_____. 1966. *The Disabled Reader: Education of the dyslexic child*. Baltimore: The Johns Hopkins Press.

Monroe, M. 1932. *Children Who Cannot Read*. Chicago: University of Chicago Press.

Morgan, W. P. 1896. A case of congenital word-blindness. *British Medical Journal* 2:1378.

Oliphant, G. 1972. Auditory perception and reading disability. *Bulletin of the Orton Society* 22:27–40.

Orton, J. L. 1964. *A Guide to Teaching Phonics*. Cambridge, MA: Educators Publishing Service.

_____. (ed.). 1966a. Word-blindness in School Children and Other Papers on Strephosymbolia (Specific Language Disability-Dyslexia) 1925–1946. by S. T. Orton, M.D. Monograph No. 2. Baltimore: The Orton Society.

_____. 1966b. The Orton-Gillingham Approach. *In* J. Money (ed.). *The Disabled Reader: Education of the dyslexic child*. Baltimore: The Johns Hopkins Press.

_____. 1975. Samuel T. Orton, M.D. Who was he? *Bulletin of the Orton Society* 25:145–155.

Orton, S. T. 1925. "Word-blindness" in school children. *Archives of Neurology and Psychiatry* Also in J. L. Orton 1966a. 14:581–216.

_____. 1928a. Foreword to Methods for Diagnosis and Treatment of Cases of Reading Disability, by Marion Monroe. *Genetic Psychology Monographs* 6:4–5.

_____. 1928b. A physiological theory on reading disability and stuttering in children. *New England Journal of Medicine* 199:1046–1052.

_____. 1937. *Reading, Writing and Speech Problems in Children*. New York: W. W. Norton.

_____. 1946. Some disorders in the language development of children. *Proceedings of Child Research Clinic Conference of the Woods School*.

_____. 1966. *Word-blindness in school children and other papers on strephosymbolia (Specific Language Disabilities) 1925–1946*. J. L. Orton (ed.). Baltimore: The Orton Society.

Owen, F. 1973. *Educationally Handicapped Progress Report*. Palo Alto, CA. Unified School District.

Palatini, L. 1976. Informal Study of Early Intervention Aspects of Learning Disability Program. Cambridge, MA: Public School Bureau of Public Services.

Pavlidis, G. Th. and Miles, T. 1981. *Dyslexia Research and Its Applications to Education*. London: John Wiley and Sons, Ltd.

Penfield, W. and Roberts, F. 1959. *Speech and Brain Mechanisms*. Princeton: Princeton University Press.

Piaget, J. 1928, 1959. *The Language and Thought of the Child*. London: Routledge and Kegan Paul.

Pollack, C. and Brandon, A. 1982. Odyssey of a "mirrored" personality. *Annals of Dyslexia* 32:275–288.

Pollack, C. and Lane P. 1970. *The Hip Readers*. Brooklyn: Book-Lab.

Premack, A. J. and Premack, D. 1972. Teaching language to an ape. *Scientific American* 227(4):92–99, 128.

Pribram, K. H. 1971. *Languages of the Brain: Experimental paradoxes and principles in neuro-physiology.* Englewood Cliffs, NJ: Prentice-Hall.

Ramos, P. (ed.). 1978. *Delinquent Youth and Learning Difficulties.* San Rafael, CA: Academic Therapy Publications.

Rawson, M. 1968, 1978. *Developmental Language Disability: Adult Accomplishments of Dyslexic Boys.* Baltimore: Johns Hopkins University Press. Cambridge, MA: Educators Publishing Service.

Rawson, M. B. 1970a. The structure of English: The language to be learned. *Bulletin of the Orton Society* 20:103–123.

——. 1970b. Teaching children with language disabilities in small groups. *In* E. Clakins (ed.). *Reading Forum Monograph 11* Bethesda: NINDS, NIH.

——. 1971. Perspectives of specific language disability. I. The past-what has been learned. *Bulletin of the Orton Society* 21:22–34.

——. 1972. Language learning differences in plain English. Academic Therapy 7(4): 411–419.

——. 1973. Semantics—diagnostic categories, their use and misuse. *Bulletin of the Orton Society* 23:140–145.

——. 1974. Semantics—what is S.L.D.? *Bulletin of the Orton Society* 24:1.

——. 1975. Developmental dyslexia: Educational treatment and results. *In* D. D. Duane and M. B. Rawson (eds.). *Reading, Perception, and Language.* Baltimore: York Press.

——. 1977. Dyslexics as adults: The possibilities and the challenge. *Bulletin of the Orton Society*

——. 1978. Dyslexia and learning disabilities: Their relationship. *Bulletin of the Orton Society* 28:43–61.

——. 1979. Social implications of dyslexia. *In* R. B. Richardson and M. Monsour (eds.). *Dilemmas of Dyslexia.* Proceedings of a conference held in October 1979 at the University of Virginia.

——. 1981. A diversity model for dyslexia. *In* G. Th. Pavlidis and T. T. Miles (eds.). Dyslexia Research and its Applications to Education, pp. 13–34. London and New York: John Wiley and Sons.

——. 1982. Louise Baker and the Leonardo syndrome. *Annals of Dyslexia* 32:289–304.

——. 1983. "Why Orton was right"; the 14th reason: his educational strategy and tactics. Unpublished letter.

——. 1987. The Orton Trail 1896–1986. *Annals of Dyslexia* 37:36–48.

Robinson, M. H. 1969. "Kenneth Johnson": A progress report on a search for literacy. *Bulletin of the Orton Society* 19:134–140.

Rochmes, B. D. 1976. Robert Angell: What went wrong? Letter to the editor. *Washington Post* August 23.

Rome, P. D. and Osman, J. S. 1972. *Language Tool Kit.* Cambridge, MA: Educators Publishing Service.

Roswell, F. and Natchez, G. 1971. *Reading Disability: Diagnosis and treatment.* New York: Basic Books.

Rotzel, G. 1971. *The School in Rose Valley: A parent venture in education.* Baltimore: The Johns Hopkins Press.

Ruchles, M. 1973. *Guidelines to Educations of Nonreaders.* Brooklyn: Book-Lab.

Sarton, G. 1931, 1956. *History of Science and the New Humanism.* New York: George Braziller Inc.

Saunders, R. E. 1962. Dyslexia: Its phenomenology. *In* J. Money (ed.). *Reading Disability: Progress and research needs in dyslexia.* Baltimore: The Johns Hopkins Press.

——. 1971. Perspectives of language disability. II. The present—where do we stand? *Bulletin of the Orton Society* 21:35–44.

Saunders, R. E. and Malin, D. H. 1970. Parents as tutorial participants: An experiment. *Bulletin of the Orton Society* 20:99–101.

————. 1971. Dyslexia, Prevention and Remediation: A classroom approach. Film.

Saunders, R. E., Gialas, A., and Hofler, D. B. 1969. *Lines to Writing, Reading and Spelling.* Cambridge, MA: Educators Publishing Service.

Schiffman, G. 1972. Dyslexia as an educational phenomenon: Its recognition and treatment. *In* J. Money (ed.). *Reading Disability: Progress and research needs in dyslexia.* Baltimore: The Johns Hopkins Press.

Silberberg, N. and Silberberg, M. 1971. Hyperplexia: the other end of the continuum. *Journal of Special Education* 5:3.

Silver, A. and Hagin, R. 1964. Specific reading disability: Follow-up studies. *American Journal of Orthopsychiatry* 34:95–102.

————. 1972. Profile of a first grade: A basis for preventive psychiatryry. *Journal of the American Academy of Child Psychiatry* 11:645–674.

Simpson, B. 1985. Cross-cultural study of dyslexia: Preliminary report. Unpublished.

Simpson, E. 1979. *Reversals: A personal account of victory over dyslexia.* Boston: Houghton Mifflin.

Slingerland, B. H. 1971. *A Multisensory Approach to Language Arts for Specific Language Disability Children.* Cambridge, MA: Educators Publishing Service.

Smelt, E. D. 1972. *How to Speak, Spell and Read: A new way to learn English.* South Melbourne, Australia: Melbourne YMCA.

Spalding, R. B. and Spalding, W. F. 1972. *The Writing Road to Reading.* New York: William Morrow and Company.

Sperry, R. W. 1974. Lateral specialization in the surgically separated hemispheres. *In* F. O. Schwartz and F. G. Worden (eds.). *The Neurosciences: Third Study Program.* Cambridge, MA: MIT Press.

Spier, P. 1980. *PEOPLE.* Garden City, NY: Doubleday.

Strong, L. R. 1973. Language disability in the Hispano-American child. *Bulletin of the Orton Society* 23:30–38.

Stuart, M. F. 1963. *Neurophysiological Insights into Teaching.* Palo Alto, CA: Pacific Books.

Symmes, J. S. 1972. Deficit models, spatial visualization, and reading disability. *Bulletin of the Orton Society* 22:54–68.

Symmes, J. S. and Rapoport, J. L. 1972. Unexpected reading failure. *American Journal of Orthopsychiatry* 42(1):82–91.

Thompson, L. J. 1964. Did Lee Harvey Oswald have a specific learning disability? *Bulletin of the Orton Society* 14:89–90.

————. 1966. *Reading Disability: Developmental dyslexia.* Springfield, IL: Charles C Thomas.

————. 1969. Language disabilities in men of eminence. *Bulletin of the Orton Society* 19:113–118.

Tower, D. M. 1973. A kindergarten screening index to predict reading failure. *Bulletin of the Orton Society* 23:90–105.

Traub, N. 1973. *Recipe for Reading.* Cambridge, MA: Educators Publishing Service.

Vail, P. 1977. *Bulletin of the Orton Society*

Vygotsky, L. S. 1934. *Thought and Language.* Translated by E. Hanfman and G. Vakar (1962). Cambridge, MA: MIT Press.

Wada, J. 1969. Presentation at the 9th International Congress of Neurology. New York.

Walker, L. and Cole, E. 1965. Familial patterns of expression of specific reading disability in a population sample: Part I—Prevalence, distribution, and persistence. *Bulletin of the Orton Society* 15:

Warner, W. 1949. *Social Class in America.* New York: Harper.

Weaver, P. 1978. Comprehension, recall, and dyslexia: A proposal for the application of a schema theory. *Bulletin of the Orton Society* 28:92–113.

What is Dyslexia? 1982. Baltimore: The Orton Dyslexia Society.

White, S. H. 1970. Some general outlines of the matrix of developmental changes between five and seven years. *Bulletin of the Orton Society* 20:41–57.

Whittrock, M. 1978. Education and the cognitive processes of the brain. *In* J. S. Chall and A. F. Mirsky (eds.). *Education and the Brain.* National Society for the Study of Education. Chicago: University of Chicago Press.

Vail, P. 1978. Limerance, language and literature: An essay. *Bulletin of the Orton Society* 28:79–91.

Index

Academic achievement of dyslexics. *See also* Education
diagnosis of dyslexia and, 40–41; diversity model for dyslexia and, 219–20; IQ differences and similar, 163–64; Jemicy graduation speech (story of successful dyslexics) and, 172–76; matched pairs study (dyslexic/nondyslexic students) and, 164–67; native ability and, 180–81; Rose Valley study hypothesis and, 154, 161–62;
higher education achievement and, 158–60;
vocational achievement, 160–61
Adler, A., 239
Adolescence (development stage), 246
Adulthood (development stage), 246–48
Age, dyslexia and, 6, 7
Alphabet, 33
English and, 108–109, 110
Alphabetic-phonetic aspects of language, 66–68
Anderson, C. W., 71
Angina, 14, 15
Animal learning, 193
Ansara, Alice, 71
Antisocial behavior, 45–46
Aphasic patients, 88
Arbuthnot, Mary Hill, 103
Are You There, God? It's Me, Margaret, 100
Autonomous (run-about) period (development stage), 241–43
Axline, V. M., 241

Bakker, D. J., 197
Bannatyne, A., 71
Barbour, R. H., 98
Behavioral disorders, 45, 48
Bellvue Hospital, 45
Bender, Lauretta, 45, 66, 228

Benton, Arthur, 87, 226, 229
Bequest of Wings (Duff), 103
Bibliotherapy, 100
Binder, Arnold, 93
Binder, Virginia, 93
Bond, Earl D., 146
"Books and Children" (Tower), 103
Books, choosing (for children), 100–104
Born, Max, 147–48
Bowen, C. C., 71
Brain, 51
cerebral hemisphere research and, 179; dyslexia analysis and, 18–19, 24–25; Hinshelwood and, 137; neurobiological structure and function of, 6; neurologic research and, 10–11, 15, 16; neurosciences and, 85, 87–89; Orton and, 10, 11, 128–29, 194
Bronner, Augusta, 139
Bulletin of the Orton Society, 47, 76, 146

Case histories
educational procedures and, 60; as evidence of dyslexia, 184–87; language learning differences analysis and, 27–29
Case records (Dr. Orton's), 125–26, 131, 141
Cerebral dominance theory, 129
Cerebral hemispheres
diversity model for dyslexia and, 215–17; dyslexia and, 11, 15, 19, 24; education analysis and, 87, 89; learning stages and, 195; Orton and, 128–29; reading and, 102; research and, 179
Charlotte's Web (White), 104
Charnow, D., 125–26, 131
Children and Books (Arbuthnot), 103
Children and Their Literature (Georgian), 103
"Children without Love" (film), 240
Childs, Barton, 219